Working Hard, Working Poor

WORKING HARD, WORKING POOR

A Global Journey

Gary S. Fields

OXFORD
UNIVERSITY PRESS

OXFORD
UNIVERSITY PRESS

Oxford University Press, Inc., publishes works that further
Oxford University's objective of excellence
in research, scholarship, and education.

Oxford New York
Auckland Cape Town Dar es Salaam Hong Kong Karachi
Kuala Lumpur Madrid Melbourne Mexico City Nairobi
New Delhi Shanghai Taipei Toronto

With offices in
Argentina Austria Brazil Chile Czech Republic France Greece
Guatemala Hungary Italy Japan Poland Portugal Singapore
South Korea Switzerland Thailand Turkey Ukraine Vietnam

Published by Oxford University Press, Inc.
198 Madison Avenue, New York, New York 10016
www.oup.com

Oxford is a registered trademark of Oxford University Press

Library of Congress Cataloging-in-Publication Data
Fields, Gary S.
  Working hard, working poor : a global journey / Gary S. Fields.
       p. cm.
  Includes bibliographical references and index.
  ISBN 978-0-19-979464-5 (cloth : alk. paper)
  1. Working poor—Developing countries.   2. Labor market—Developing countries.   I. Title.
HC59.72.P6F54 2011
331.5'4091724—dc23
                        2011016742

9 8 7 6 5 4 3 2 1

Printed in the United States of America
on acid-free paper

For Vivian,
My constant companion on this journey and my best friend

CONTENTS

ACKNOWLEDGMENTS

Work on this book was supported by Cornell University—in particular, by Dean Harry Katz of the ILR School (previously known as the School of Industrial and Labor Relations), University Provost Biddy Martin, and the Program on Globalization and the Workplace funded by David and Abby Joseph Cohen. To have had so much time freed up, allowing me to learn and read, travel and write, was a marvelous gift for which I am most grateful.

During the 2009–10 academic year, I was fortunate to have been able to work on the book at Koç University in Istanbul, Turkey; the Centre for Development Studies in Trivandrum, India; and the Paris School of Economics in Paris, France. I am very appreciative of the hospitality shown by these three great institutions and the opportunity to get to know three special countries better.

I thank countless students and friends for probing discussions while this work was in preparation. You were my target audience, and I thought of many of you often as I decided what topics I wanted to address and how to try to make my points.

I never would have been in this field had it not been for Professor George Johnson of the University of Michigan who urged me as an undergraduate student to go on for a Ph.D. in economics and who invited me as a graduate student to accompany him to Kenya. George died as this book was being completed, leaving us way before his time. His legacy and extraordinary influence live on though his students, grand-students, and great-grand-students.

And finally, to those workers in Africa, Latin America, and Asia who shared their life stories and sometimes their homes with me, I would say that writing this book is the best way I know to make others aware of the lives you lead and the struggles you are facing. It is my fervent hope that by the time my children and grandchildren have completed their work lives, the kind of poverty you are experiencing will have been eradicated once and for all.

PART ONE

How the Poorer Half Works

CHAPTER 1
A Life's Journey

A VISIT TO HIGH-TECH CHINA

It is Christmas Day 2008. Three thousand workers are busily building Thinkpad computers at a Lenovo factory in Shenzhen, China. The factory is spotless, as are the people themselves. The color of their uniforms indicates their responsibilities: light blue for assembly line workers, darker blue for team leaders, green for factory cleaners, and so on. In white lab coats with black pinstripes designating visitors, the manufacturing manager, his assistant, and I follow the assembly line around, starting with workers collecting the various parts needed for each particular computer (a process called "kitting") to assembly to testing through software installation through further testing to packaging and finally to shipping.

These young men and women, all between the ages of eighteen and twenty-three, work extremely fast. At kitting, a bin with parts used by all Thinkpads arrives, a worker scans the order form indicating which specific additional parts are needed, and within five seconds the parts have been added to the bin. About ten seconds later, another computer arrives and the task is repeated. The entire assembly line crew stand at their stations for two hours working nonstop, to be followed by a fifteen-minute break during which they can sit on stools, go to the toilet, or socialize. Three more cycles follow until the nine-hour work day is completed.

Following the plant tour, I am taken to the dormitory where many of these workers live. Leading me are the labor supplier who recruits workers for the factory and two recent university graduates employed in entry-level positions in Lenovo's human resource function. Groups of young men live on the fourth floor of the concrete dormitory building, young women on the fifth floor. (It is strictly prohibited for men to enter the women's rooms or women the men's rooms.) Each dormitory room is long and narrow with two-story bunk beds placed adjacent to one another on each side. The first room I see sleeps sixteen young women in a space that is said to be fifty square meters—500 square feet—but looks smaller than that to me. Other rooms sleep ten, twelve, or fourteen workers. At the end of each room are two coldwater taps and a single toilet as well as some small windows. The room could be cross-ventilated by propping open the door opposite the windows, but this is manifestly unsafe as it would invite theft of the residents' meager possessions.

My hosts and I then have the opportunity to sit down with the workers for a discussion. Dressed in blue jeans, T-shirts, and sneakers—quite like the more casual outfits worn by young Americans who attend my university lectures—the workers tell us their stories. They regard their work as demanding but also desirable. Nearly all have migrated from other provinces of China. What attracted them to this work, they told us, was the prospect of steady employment, enabling them to earn more than they could have at home. One could have been a secretary at home, she says, but she has a desire for a better life and hopes to be promoted. Another dropped out of school and came to work in the factory because her family needs the income. Another says she left school because she was not a good student. A young man tells us he left his rural village because all the other guys at home had already left before him.

These workers are paid 5.7 Chinese yuan per hour which, at the prevailing exchange rate, is about US$0.80 per hour or $7.20 per nine-hour day. Each resident is charged an amount equal to 15% of his or her pay for dormitory rent. Much of the rest of their salary goes for food. Many send money home to their families.

It is helpful to put these workers' earnings in perspective. Compared to the U.S. minimum wage, which now is $7.25 *per hour*, the Chinese workers are paid very little. But compared to Indian workers, the pay is very good: Kalavati, whom we will meet in Chapter 3, and hundreds of millions of others like her in India can earn no more than one U.S. dollar *per day*.

Like half the world's workers, the ones at Lenovo are working hard, and they are working poor.[1]

GETTING TO TODAY

For me, the story of this book began with a phone call in 1970. My Ph.D. advisor was going to spend a year in Africa as a visiting professor and asked if my wife and I wanted to go along We accepted and arrived in Nairobi, Kenya, a few months later.

This trip produced a dramatic change in me. After spending a few weeks in Africa, I realized that the issues facing people there were far more urgent than the ones I had been examining for my thesis back home. I started then to work on employment and poverty in the developing world. It has been my life's work.

I had never experienced mass poverty before, whether in terms of income, health, education, or standard of living. What I saw was some of the millions of Kenyans who eked out a living from day to day. One of them was Joseph Waweru who, with his family, farmed a plot of land in the beautiful Kikuyu highlands (see Figure 1.1). An exchange of visits to one another's homes highlighted the enormous differences in our standards of living and, incidentally, in our food tastes. (Vivian and I did not find a meal of six hard-boiled eggs and a slice of white bread to be a treat, nor did the Wawerus appreciate Vivian's delicious (to me) spaghetti with meat sauce and garlic bread.)

Later, when I looked at figures from the United Nations and the World Bank, I realized the enormity of the world's poverty problem. According to the initial figures, which have since been updated a number of times and

Figure 1.1
Joseph Waweru and family, Kenya.

are presented below, around 1980, 1.3 billion of the world's people lived on less than one U.S. dollar per person per day (adjusted for differences in purchasing power between their countries and ours) and another 1.7 billion lived on one to two U.S. dollars per person per day.[2, 3]

In both the professional and the policy work being carried out in the field of economic development at that time, much was being done about some important topics—chief among them, economic growth, international trade, and agricultural development—but little attention was being given to labor markets. As a labor economist-in-training, I found the possibility of working on employment and poverty issues in the developing world to be first an opportunity that later became a strong interest and for the last decades a passion and a calling. I have been privileged to teach and do research on these issues, mostly at Cornell University, and to have been able to engage actively and continuously in the policy world through the World Bank, the regional development banks, the International Labor Organization, and other governmental agencies and institutions.[4]

Even now, labor markets and employment receive relatively little attention in the literature on combating global poverty. In 2000, the 189 countries of the United Nations adopted eight millennium development goals: eradicating extreme poverty and hunger; achieving universal primary education; promoting gender equality and empowering women; reducing child mortality; improving maternal health; combating HIV/AIDS, malaria, and other diseases; ensuring environmental sustainability; and developing a global partnership for development. Employment is not one of the eight, though it is a means to many of them. There also is a large literature on poverty traps—that is, any self-reinforcing mechanism causing poverty to persist—and policies to overcome them.[5] Excellent books on ending world poverty can be found, including those by Amartya Sen, Jeffrey Sachs, Stephen Smith, Paul Collier, Abhijit Banerjee and Esther Duflo, Dean Karlan and Jacob Appel, and the staff of the World Bank.[6] These books go into depth on many important aspects of economic development but do not focus on wage employment and self-employment, work and nonwork. *Working Hard, Working Poor* starts where these others leave off.

The lack of attention to the labor market is unfortunate for two reasons. First, most of the world's poor are poor because they work hard but their work does not bring in enough income for them to be able to escape poverty. Second, experience around the world has shown that hundreds of millions of poor household have escaped poverty through increased labor earnings. Two broad means of raising labor earnings—pursuing new crop- and/or livestock-related strategies on the farm and engaging in petty trade, small businesses, or casual or temporary employment within the informal sector in a city—accounted for 78% of all escapes from poverty in Kenya, 70% in India, 69% in Peru, and 54% in Uganda.[7] Access to regular wage employment has proven to be the most secure route out of poverty in India, Chile, sub-Saharan Africa, and Vietnam.[8]

According to the latest figures, today an estimated 3.1 billion people still live in absolute poverty, using an international poverty line of US$2.50 in purchasing power parity terms (abbreviated PPP$).[9] Given that the world population is 6.5 billion people, the absolutely poor comprise almost half the world's people—ten times the population of the United States or six times the population of Europe. Essentially all those living below PPP$2.50 live in the low- and middle-income countries of Asia, Latin America, and Africa, and none of them in what are traditionally called the "developed economies" of North America, Europe, and selected parts of Asia and Oceania.

This book is about how the poor live and work and what actions the world community could take to improve poor people's earning opportunities as a central component of a multifaceted program aimed at ending the scourge of absolute economic misery.

PUTTING OURSELVES IN THEIR SHOES

Suppose you are one of these more than 3 billion poor people. You are trying to do the best you can for yourself and your family. If you are lucky, you can afford to live in a one-room shack without electricity, running water, or sanitation. If not, you and your family live on the street; you become what in India are called "pavement dwellers" (Figure 1.2). You try to earn enough to be able to put very basic food on the table two or three times a day. Leisure is of little value to you—you want work and the money that comes with it so that you can buy the things you and your family need.

You consider working for a daily wage. The best available jobs in your community pay your country's equivalent of one or at most a few U.S. dollars per day. On a good day, you can get work; on a bad day, there is no work to be had. The country in which you live is too poor to have established an unemployment insurance system. Assistance from family members is sometimes available, but the amounts they are able to give are minimal because they are as poor as you are. (See Figures 1.3 and 1.4 for inadequate housing.)

You consider farming. Your parents and those before them were farmers, you grew up on a farm and worked there as a child, and so you too are knowledgeable about farming. You have no land because the family land

Figure 1.2
Pavement dwellers, India.

Figure 1.3
Homes of migrant construction workers, India.

Figure 1.4
Homes of migrant construction workers, India.

was inherited by your older brother. You try to find an unused plot of land that you could cultivate, enabling you to earn a subsistence livelihood. However, the great majority of others around you are landless as well, and so no land is unused.

You consider setting up your own business. This would be difficult because the authorities extort bribes and hassle street vendors and craftspeople who don't have licenses, confiscating their merchandise, arresting them, throwing them into jail, and making them pay impossibly heavy fines. Because you are so poor, you cannot build up enough working capital to stock a small shop adequately and meet day-to-day expenses.

You consider moving to a faraway city where jobs are more plentiful and the pay is better. However, many others like you wish to do the same, so that each time a job vacancy arises, tens, hundreds, or even thousands of other workers try to get the same job that you would be trying for.

You even consider moving to a distant country in which people like you earn more in a day than you could earn at home in a month. Sadly for you, the rich countries try hard to control their borders and keep people like you out. Some people you know have drowned or suffocated trying to make their way to other countries. Others saved for years to pay a fee to a "helper," only to have their money stolen and be left penniless. And of those who made it, many face an enormous debt to those who paid their way, working in what is essentially indentured servitude until the debt can be repaid.

So what do you do? You make the best of a bad situation, eke out an existence, and do all that you can to increase your earnings. You work hard, but you still work poor.

And what should we do? Blame you for your poverty, because if only you tried even harder, you wouldn't be in poverty in the first place? Ignore your poverty, because you are one of "them" and not one of "us"? Exploit your poverty, pitting you against others who are as desperate for jobs as you are?

The premise of this book is that none of these is the answer. The reason is because help can come from many sources including home country governments, the private sector, and the international community.

Companies and workers each have their own interests. While private sector firms do not necessarily need the workers of any given developing country, the workers in each poor country desperately need the private sector. There are those who see anything that benefits one side as hurting the other. I believe the opposite: that win-win solutions are possible from which both sides benefit. But to create the opportunity for such solutions, each side must understand what the other wants and accept its legitimacy.

As for the international community, I firmly believe that we citizens of the richer countries of the world, in addition to helping our own people, have a moral obligation to help the less fortunate global citizens earn their way out of poverty. Since 1970, the United States and many other countries have pledged repeatedly in the United Nations and other bodies to contribute 0.7% of our Gross Domestic Product to help improve the lives of people in the poorest countries of the world. But what the developed countries have delivered—0.19% in the case of the United States, 0.45% overall—falls woefully short of what we have promised. It is time to deliver on those promises.

Those of us who are policy makers, businesspeople, and researchers know a great deal about how the world's poor work and what has improved conditions for them, at least in broad outline. (One qualifier: without careful investigation, we cannot tell you what specifically should or should not be done to deal with a particular problem in a particular country any more than a medical doctor could prescribe a specific remedy without carefully examining an individual patient.) We know how the poor have managed to invest in improving their own self-employment earning opportunities.

We know what it takes for the private sector to want to set up operations in a developing country, thereby creating jobs and paying the taxes that can be used to build roads and schools and fund social programs. We know how poor-country governments can stimulate economic growth and make that growth more inclusive of the poor. And we know how the development banks, the rich-country governments, and other development organizations can help poor-country governments and other organizations do what they lack the means to do on their own: create more good jobs, improve earnings levels in the poorer jobs, and enhance the skills and productivity of their working people.

This book shares those lessons with you.

CHAPTER 2
A Problem of Enormous Proportions

THE MAGNITUDE OF WORLD POVERTY AND
THE IMPORTANCE OF WORK

The latest figures show that more than 3 billion people in the world—nearly half of humanity and more than half of the developing world's population—are poor in income terms.[1] Of these, 1.4 billion consume less than US$1.25 of goods and services per person per day. Another 1.7 billion consume between $1.25 and $2.50 per person per day. Here and throughout this book, incomes and expenditures are converted to US dollars adjusted for what money will buy in different countries and at different times and are called purchasing power parity dollars, or PPP$. Likewise, the global income-poverty figures presented in this book are all PPP-adjusted.

Poverty is multidimensional; in addition to income, it includes health, education, and standard of living dimensions. In 2010, the United Nations began publishing a Multidimensional Poverty Index (MPI) that weights ten indicators: child mortality, nutrition, years of schooling, child school enrollment, electricity, drinking water, sanitation, flooring, cooking fuel, and assets.[2] As important as these other indicators are, they are not the focus of this book; income poverty is.

The poor are geographically concentrated. Using the $1.25 line, the latest data show that half the world's poor are concentrated in just two countries: India (456 million) and China (208 million). Another fourth of the world's poor are in sub-Saharan Africa (391 million). The remaining fourth are in the rest of South Asia excluding India (140 million), the rest of East Asia excluding China (108 million), Latin America and the Caribbean (46 million), Eastern Europe and Central Asia (17 million), and the Middle East and North Africa (11 million).

The world has made significant progress in reducing the number who are poor: despite the addition of 2 billion people to the world's population since 1981, the number in poverty in the world has fallen by more than half a billion people using a poverty line of $1.25 per person per day. All the progress in reducing the absolute numbers in poverty has been made in just one country, China. Through the 1980s and 1990s, the numbers of poor were rising in sub-Saharan Africa, Latin America, Eastern Europe, Central Asia, and South Asia. Happily, the poverty headcount fell in most regions of the world during the first half-decade of the 2000s. Since the sharp increase in world food prices between 2006 and 2008 and the Great Recession of 2008–09, during which world gross domestic product fell by 2.2%, poverty is thought to have risen significantly, but hard data are not yet available.[3] Overall, the percentage of the world's people in poverty, known in the literature as the "poverty head-count ratio," has fallen dramatically for all poverty lines used—for example, using the $1.25 poverty line, from 51.8% of the developing world population in 1981 to 25.2% in 2005.[4]

The world community has declared such severe poverty to be unacceptable. All the nations of the world have pledged themselves to the United Nations' Millennium Development Goals, foremost among which is cutting poverty in half by the year 2015.[5]

How is halving poverty to be done? Much has been written about how poor people *live*.[6] In this book, I approach their poverty from the point of view of how poor people *work*.[7] To what extent do they work? How much do they earn for the work they do? What will their earnings buy? What can be done to increase the number of good jobs in the economies in which they live? What happens to those who are excluded from getting jobs in the better parts of the economy because of the lack of such jobs for all who want them and are capable of doing them? How can earning opportunities be improved for those who have no choice but to work in the relatively poor parts of their economies?

In Chapter 3, you will learn the stories of four poor people whom I have been privileged to know, whose photos appear on the cover of this book. Angela makes fireworks in Oaxaca, Mexico. Kalavati hand-rolls cigarettes in Ahmedabad, India. Masibisi makes handicrafts in a village outside Durban, South Africa. Wang is a farmer in Yunnan Province, China.

A mistaken idea, one that I had before working on poverty in the developing world, is that the poor are poor because they are unemployed. This is wrong. Rather, as will be detailed in Chapter 4, for the most part, the poor are in the labor market; they are working, they work long hours, and they want *more* work. Unemployment rates are often very low in the poorest countries. The low earnings of the poor are not their fault.[8]

Central to understanding work is the idea of a labor market. As used throughout this book, the "labor market" is the place where labor services are bought and sold. Some people work in paid employment, whereby they sell their labor services to employers and in exchange are paid a wage or a salary. Others—and the poorer the country, the larger the proportion of workers in this category—are self-employed, selling their labor services to themselves. Different kinds of labor markets are discussed in detail in Chapter 5.

There are both economic and policy reasons for focusing on work and labor markets.

The *economic* reason is the crucial importance of labor earnings. National economic accounts show that the incomes received from labor (that is, the amount earned from wage and salaried employment and self-employment) are greater than the incomes received from all other sources combined. As a result, most of the inequality of total income found within a country is due to the inequality of labor earnings.[9] As for the poor, their main asset, often their only asset, is their labor.

Some people are well-to-do either because they are large landlords and receive substantial rental income, because they live in wealthy families and so receive substantial transfers from other family members, or because at some point they had large sums to invest and invested well and so receive substantial capital income. However, most people receive little or no income from sources other than labor market earnings, from either wage-employment or self-employment. It is not that the typical well-educated professional has so much more income from capital or land than the typical tenant farmer—neither has much income from any source other than his or her labor. What primarily differentiates their economic positions is how much they earn for the work they do.

There are two main *policy* reasons for focusing on work and labor markets. One is that poor people themselves believe that to get ahead, income from wages or salaries and from self-employment activities are most important, above family and kin, education and skill acquisition, migration, saving, and relief aid and donations.[10] Another is that the world community may be more sympathetic to the plight of the world's poor if they know that the poor are working hard, working poor, and doing all they can do earn their way out of poverty. Consider the alternatives.

FIVE WAYS OUT OF POVERTY

One way out of poverty is public transfers. Ours is a world of nation-states, and so our first inclination may be to think that "our" people's needs deserve the overwhelming share of resources compared with "their" people's needs. National governments can and do provide assistance to their people, even in poor countries. However, the countries in which the great majority of poor people live are so poor that their governments lack the means to provide generalized public assistance, and foreign assistance is far too meager and too badly targeted to make up the difference.[11]

Another way out of poverty is private transfers. Indeed, one of the poor people we will meet in Chapter 3, farmer Wang, has family abroad who send him enough money to make an important impact on his standard of living.[12] Most poor people, though, are not so fortunate; if they receive any money or goods at all from others, these transfers are very modest in amount because nearly all the people the poor know are themselves poor.

A third way out of poverty is to migrate from poorer regions to richer regions within a country. The Lenovo workers introduced in Chapter 1 are among the many millions of Chinese workers who have left the interior for coastal cities, where they can earn more in a month than they could have earned in a year if they had stayed home.[13]

A fourth way out of poverty is to migrate from poor countries to rich ones. What enabled nearly all of us Americans to be Americans is that we ourselves or our people before us were allowed to enter the United States from overseas—in my case, my mother and her family from Russia, my father's parents from Poland. When they immigrated, they passed through New York harbor and saw the Statue of Liberty with its immortal words "Give me your tired, your poor, your huddled masses yearning to breathe free."[14] But for decades, the door has been closed to all but a relatively small number of those who would like to follow. Consequently, even for the poor who want to migrate—and for reasons of family, community, language, and cost, there are good reasons not to want to—migration is out, because countries like ours admit only a limited number of would-be immigrants and do what they can to keep others out.[15,16]

There are, however, significant numbers of temporary migrants. During a sabbatical stay in South India in 2009–10, my wife and I saw a great many luxurious houses that had been built with money sent home by workers who lived or had lived in the Persian Gulf or in the United States. One of these workers, Yesu Dhas, had gone to the Middle East and become a skilled woodworker (Figure 2.1). He saved up enough money during his four years overseas to build a fine new house for his family (Figure 2.2). We met the family of another Indian worker who was still in the Gulf but had sent enough money home that his family could live in beautiful new surroundings (Figures 2.3 and 2.4).

Figure 2.1
Yesu Dhas, India.

Figure 2.2
The Dhas home, India.

Figure 2.3
Outside the house of a migrant worker's family, India.

Figure 2.4
Inside the house of a migrant worker's family, India.

It is virtually certain that the nation-state will continue to be the dominant form of global organization, that poor nations will get little assistance from richer nations, that private transfers will make a significant difference for only a minority of the poor, and that the option of migrating from poor nations to richer ones will be closed off to the great majority of the poor. This leaves earning their way out of poverty the only remaining option.

HELPING THE POOR EARN THEIR WAY OUT OF POVERTY

"Helping the poor earn their way out of poverty" could become a rallying cry for public policy and development assistance. I say this for four reasons.

First, global poverty is simply not well understood. For years, the single most popular lecture I have given at Cornell University has been the one in which I explain what it means to be a poor worker in a poor country. (I always time this lecture for Thanksgiving week.) Many of our students do not know how the world's poor work and live. (I didn't at their age, either.) Many others do have an understanding of poverty in the world but no sense of how many poor there are. These students are stunned to learn that there are ten times as many *poor people* in the world as there are *people* in the United States. It is precisely to provide such information about global poverty that this book is being written.

Second, earning their way out of poverty is consistent with the public's preference for work, not handouts.[17] "Social solidarity" and "social exclusion" are powerful ideas in Europe, but they are all but absent in the American lexicon. (In Europe, though, distinctions between "us" and "them"—Germans versus Turks, "true French" versus "guests," and so on—are widespread.)

Third, and linked to the preceding point, it is likely that rich-country taxpayers would be willing to contribute more to help people in other countries if the recipients are working but earning an amount that is deemed unacceptably low. Many countries including the United States, Britain, Canada, Ireland, New Zealand, Austria, Belgium, Denmark, Finland, France, and the Netherlands have an earned income tax credit (EITC). The EITC is a negative income tax, in that low earners get additional money from the government when they work and only if they work. The EITC in the United States is the nation's largest single anti-poverty program, mainly because U.S. taxpayers seem willing to help those who are working but not those who are not. An international EITC could perhaps become a politically acceptable way of raising money to help the poor abroad. Given the high unemployment rates now prevailing in the richer countries, this is probably not a good time to push for an international EITC supported by individual country development agencies such as the U.S. Agency for International Development (USAID), the UK Department for International Development (DFID), or AusAid, Australia's overseas aid program. On the other hand, maybe the World Bank and the regional development banks could start considering such a program as part of their ongoing anti-poverty efforts.

And fourth, even though the United States is a nation of immigrants, public opinion in this country is overwhelmingly against opening our nation's borders to citizens from other places.[18] Helping workers in other nations earn more where they are could be a way of preventing them from entering the United States, legally or otherwise. So even those among us who feel no moral obligation toward people in other countries because of what our help will do for *them* may be willing to assist them in raising their earnings because of what our help will do for *us*.[19]

"BUT WE HAVE TENS OF MILLIONS OF POOR PEOPLE IN THIS COUNTRY"

When I talk about global poverty, I am often asked, "Why do you care so much about poverty elsewhere when we have so much poverty in this country?" This is a legitimate question deserving of a serious answer.

The latest official figures enumerate 43.6 million poor people in the United States.[20] So indeed we do have tens of millions of poor people in this country. Yet what many of my friends and students do not know is how we define poverty in the United States and how it compares with the $1.25 and $2.50 poverty lines presented earlier in this chapter. In the United States, a family is classified as poor if its income falls below the official poverty line. When the official poverty line for the United States was set in 1962, the U.S. Department of Agriculture estimated that the cost of an "economy diet plan"—"for temporary and emergency use when funds are low"—was US$0.70 per person per day. Budget studies showed that poor people spent about one-third of their income on food and two-thirds on housing, clothing, health care, and all other items. Thus, for a family of four, the annual poverty line in 1962 came to $3,165. Since 1962, the poverty line has been adjusted for inflation and only for inflation, so that the 2010 poverty line—$21,756 for a family of two adults and two children—will buy the same amount of goods now that $3,165 would have bought in 1962. Based on this constant real poverty line, the percentage of Americans in poverty was 21% in 1962; it was between 11% and 13% throughout the 1970s; it was 12.5% in 2007 before the Great Recession; it is 14.3% today.

Throughout the United States, local groups publish their estimates of "living wages." In my community, Leni Hochman is the chief operations officer of the organization responsible for monitoring living wages, the Alternatives Federal Credit Union. She says, "It is economic justice that a worker be paid a living wage and have access to affordable health care and be treated with dignity." The Ithaca living wage study calculates that the cost for *one person* to live adequately for one year is $23,104 (based on 2008 data)—more than what the U.S. poverty line was in that same year for *a family of four*. The standard for what a single person "needs" in our area includes $628 per month for rent on a one-bedroom apartment including utilities, $100 per month for recreation, and $56 per month for local telephone, thirty minutes of long distance, and internet access.[21]

It is a serious matter to be poor in the United States. Yet it is a more serious matter to be poor by international standards.

The international poverty line of $1.25 per person per day for a four-person household amounts to $1,825 per year for a family of four. The poverty line in the United States is twelve times that figure. The United States uses an absolute poverty line, defined relative to U.S. living standards (and similarly, India uses a different absolute poverty line, defined relative to Indian living standards). And remember that the international poverty lines are expressed in purchasing power parity dollars that have already been adjusted for what money will buy in different countries. Virtually nobody in the United States would be below the $1.25 line or even the $2.50 line that is used internationally. Essentially all of the world's absolutely poor people live in the developing countries.

Not only that, but the U.S. poor have access to an array of social benefits that simply are not available to the typical citizen in a poor country. Large federal government programs, often run in conjunction with the states, provide benefits in the areas of education, health, safety, public works, and public welfare. Among the programs for the poor are these:[22]

- Earned income tax credit: As already noted, the earned income tax credit is a negative income tax that supplements the labor market earnings of low-earning families. For every dollar earned from an employer, a low-earner can receive as much as an additional 45 cents from the government in EITC.

- Unemployment insurance: When a worker in the United States becomes unemployed through a layoff or business failure, he or she becomes eligible for unemployment benefits. The amount varies depending on the individual's previous work history and also the state in which he or she lives. The benefits continue for as long as ninety-nine weeks. Unfortunately, now that the unemployment rate is stuck at around the 9% level, some workers are unable to find any kind of work, even after ninety-nine weeks.[23]

- Cash grants: In 1997, the Temporary Assistance to Needy Families (TANF) program replaced Aid to Families with Dependent Children (AFDC), commonly called "welfare."[24] Under federal law, a person may receive TANF benefits for a maximum of sixty months in his or her lifetime (with exceptions). According to the most recent data available at the time of this writing, there were four million TANF recipients (out of a U.S. population of three hundred million). The maximum benefits for a TANF family are around $500/month, the specific amount varying from state to state.

- Supplemental Nutrition Assistance Program (SNAP): Formerly called Food Stamps, SNAP helps low-income families afford nutritious foods. Individuals who qualify for the program receive money on an electronic card that is accepted by most grocery stores. More than thirty-five million Americans receive SNAP benefits, a record high.[25]

- Supplemental Security Income: The U.S. government's old-age income security program ("state pension" in British English) is called Social Security. The vast majority of elderly Americans are eligible for Social Security. For those elderly whose incomes would be below a stipulated amount, Supplemental Security Income is provided. The combined Social Security-SSI minimum is $623 per month nationwide, but individual states may use their own funds to increase this amount, and many of them do.

- Medicaid: Medicaid provides assistance to low-income individuals who either cannot afford the cost of health insurance or cannot afford the cost of their medical bills. It is funded jointly by the federal government and the states. To qualify, an individual must be in one of the following categories: children, pregnant women, parents of eligible children, and people with disabilities. Medicaid is either/or: a person either receives Medicaid benefits or does not. The fact that millions of poor receive valuable health insurance benefits while tens of millions of working people do not has provoked a major debate about how to extend health care coverage to all Americans.

- Government housing: Under Section 8(o) of the U.S. Housing Act of 1937, the federal government provides cash to supplement the ability of the poor to secure rental housing in the private market. In addition, local governments build public housing in which the poor may live. In the community where I live, the Ithaca Housing Authority makes affordable housing available to a substantial segment of the low-income population through the Section 8 and public housing programs.[26]

- Regularized private community assistance: In Ithaca, Loaves and Fishes of Tompkins County, an organization supported by area churches and congregations, offers free meals daily to any and all who show up regardless of their faith, belief, or circumstances. It depends on volunteers from the local community as well as donations from the community and local businesses.[27]

Of course, not all is well for the poor in the United States. It never was, and in the recent recession, conditions have gotten much worse. Hardships and insecurities abound, exacerbated by unemployment, wage cuts, and the fraying of the social safety net.[28] My point is that despite the economic downturn and the many severe problems the poor in the United States face, they are able to achieve much better material standards of living than the average person in the world can experience.

As an illustration of differences in standards of living in different parts of the world, the *Economist* magazine ran an informative article with the evocative title "The Mountain Man and the Surgeon."[29] The mountain man is Mr. Enos Banks. Mr. Banks, now in his sixties and living in eastern Kentucky, had to stop working twenty-five years ago because of a heart condition. Mr. Banks receives cash assistance of $521 a month from the government. If he were willing to sell his truck, he could also draw food stamps, but he is unwilling to do that.

Mr. Banks has an ex-wife (who lives in the trailer next door) and three sons, all of whom also receive public assistance. Mr. Banks says that he and his wife split up because they could collect more benefits separately than they could if they lived together. The Bankses are very much aware of how rich people live because they see it all the time on television. A typical poor household in the United States has two televisions, cable or satellite reception, and a VCR or DVD player.

The surgeon, meanwhile, is Dr. Mbwebwe Kabamba, who heads the emergency department at the main public hospital in Kinshasa, the capital of the Democratic Republic of Congo. His salary at the hospital is $250 a month, but he raises his income to $600 or $700 by operating on private patients after hours. Dr. Kabamba supports an extended family of twelve persons in his four-bedroom house. They fetch water in jars. The electricity comes on about twice a week. Air-conditioning is an unaffordable luxury, reserved for VIPs in Congo, of which Dr. Kabamba is not one.

I will leave the final word on this to a television commentator who would be funny were his ignorance not so pathetic. Speaking on the *Daily Show* with Jon Stewart, this commentator said, "Poor people in this country [the United States] have to live on welfare and food stamps and get no help from the government." In my humble opinion, those who do not know that welfare and food stamps are government programs should not talk about them on international television.

CHAPTER 3
Four Workers' Stories

A WAGE WORKER'S STORY: THE LIFE OF KALAVATI (COVER PHOTO)

I first met Kalavati in Ahmedabad, India in 2004 (Figure 3.1). (To protect the privacy of all the workers discussed in this chapter, only their first names are used.) She is a tiny woman who at the time was forty-five years old. She lived with her husband, three (and later four) of her five sons, a daughter-in-law, and two grandchildren.

Kalavati's life has been marked by great personal pain. She was orphaned at age three, married at age nine, and taken far away from her home in south India (Solapur) to Ahmedabad in the north at age thirteen. She has suffered an abusive husband, harsh in-laws, death of a daughter-in-law, and sons who have caused much trouble because of gambling, drinking, and divorce. Following the death of her daughter-in-law, she also has responsibility for two grandchildren, who live with her.

My colleague from Boston and I lived for a time with Kalavati and her family. When I say that we stayed on the ground with them, I mean it literally: the house had absolutely no furniture apart from a wardrobe where clothes and their few valuables were kept. Yet these are relatively fortunate poor people. The family lives in a cement house with a main room, kitchen, and loft. The house has electricity, running water, and an indoor toilet. The house is in quite good shape, much better than those of many other city dwellers doing comparable work in other poorly paid occupations.

I was struck during our stay by the sense of community on her street. The more I took pictures and talked to neighbors, the more people came out of their houses to be a part of things. They invited me into their homes, asked for their pictures to be taken, and offered tea and in one

Figure 3.1
Kalavati, India.

case, sweets. Though these people are poor financially, they have a very rich community.

Kalavati's family derives all of its money from labor earnings. Her husband long ago worked for the Cannon textile mills when they were still making bath towels in India. Sixteen years earlier, the mill shut down, moving to a place where labor was even cheaper, and her husband lost his job. For fifteen years, he did not work. Then finally, he got a job where he works at night. He does not tell Kalavati where he works or how much he earns, nor does he contribute his earnings to the day-to-day expenses. (He does contribute to interest payments to the local money lender, though.)

As for Kalavati, her job is to roll bidis. Bidis are a kind of poor person's cigarette. The bidi rollers purchase their raw materials—leaves, tobacco, and thread—from a contractor. The threads are used to tie each rolled bidi and to tie twenty-five rolled bidis into a bundle which will then be packaged and sold in the market.

There are three major brands of bidis, corresponding to each of three employers. Each employer is supplied by contractors, and each contractor has a sole-source arrangement with an individual bidi roller. Specifically, the color of the thread used to tie the bidis indicates which contractor will buy the product from the bidi rollers and which company will sell the final product. Distinguishing the products in this way also prevents individual rollers like Kalavati from seeking out higher prices from competitors. The industrial structure is thus characterized by three major brands (economists call such a structure a "triopoly") with multiple contractors servicing each bidi brand and thousands of individual home producers servicing each contractor.

The people who roll bidis—about 150,000 of them, nearly all women—are among the poorest workers in India. These women work at home and are paid on a strict piece-rate basis. A skilled bidi roller working at the maximum possible efficiency requires about eleven hours to roll a thousand bidis. These eleven hours of work are in addition to the household work—cooking, cleaning, shopping, and so on—that the women must perform each day.

Bidi rollers are very skilled at what they do. During their long hours, they often gather together in one woman's home so they can work and socialize at the same time. Because they sit in a fixed position for hours at a time and move very infrequently, many have bad backs and other physical ailments. There is no sign that their productivity is hampered by poor nutrition, shirking, or any of the other mechanisms by which efficiency wages might operate.[1] However, their productivity is clearly hampered by their other home responsibilities.

At the time I visited Kalavati, the going piece rate was Rs. 36 (thirty-six rupees) per thousand bidis, or US$0.80. Given that it takes eleven hours to roll a thousand bidis, these women earned about US$0.07 per hour.

On the other hand, one package of twenty-five bidis sells in the market for Rs. 4.60—that is, Rs. 180 per thousand, or 500% of what the bidi roller is paid. The cost of the leaves and tobacco is minimal. The markup is therefore substantial.

Earnings at the level of Rs. 36 per day would be just enough to enable a worker with two dependents to reach the Indian poverty line of Rs. 12 per person per day. To get an idea of what Rs. 36 would buy, we accompanied Kalavati to the market. The great majority of Hindus in that part of India are vegetarians, as are Kalavati and her family. To buy just the vegetables for the evening meal cost considerably more than Rs. 36. Still needed were the rice, lentils, and cooking oil with which to prepare the rice and dal which are part of every meal.

Fortunately for Kalavati and the other bidi rollers, they have been organized and represented collectively by SEWA, the Self-Employed Women's Association of India, which now has one million members. SEWA has already brought these women substantial benefits: higher piece rates, individual savings accounts, a SEWA bank, and a SEWA clinic, as well as the dignity that comes from belonging to a recognized trade union. SEWA's successes in achieving such benefits are a testament to the tenacity and negotiating skills of the organization, particularly two labor lawyers, Manali Shah and Shalini Trivedi.

At the time of our first visit to Ahmedabad, negotiations to establish an industry-wide Provident Fund were just being concluded. (In Britain and its former colonies, Provident Funds are a means of combining workers' and employers' contributions to create individual savings accounts for workers which provide for retirement, help during ill health, and can be accessed for other contingencies.) At the same time, minimum piece rates were being established for the similar thousands of women working as kite makers and incense stick rollers. They too sell their products to contractors on a piece-rate basis. Both sets of negotiations—for the Provident Fund and for the minimum piece rates—were successful, so for Manali and Shalini and the women of SEWA, it was a day of victories.

Alas, the victories were short-lived. Soon afterward, the contractor to whom Kalavati sold her bidis cut back on her purchases to just two days' worth (2,000 bidis) per week.[2] There was no way that Kalavati could make do with less than half her previous level of earnings. After carefully assessing the alternatives, she bought first one secondhand sewing machine and then another one so that she and other family members could take in fabric and sew scarves and handkerchiefs. For a time, the family managed in this way.

Then the next disaster hit: one of Kalavati's sons and his wife had a disagreement which led to a bad divorce. In order to pay the legal fees and make a settlement to the wife, the family had to sell their sewing machines. They returned to rolling bidis for a living.

On my last visit to Kalavati, there was good news and bad news. The good news is that the piece rate for bidis had been negotiated up from Rs. 36 per thousand to Rs. 50, and Kalavati and her household could get as much bidi work as they want. They also started a sewing operation in their home, using industrial-quality sewing machines that my wife and I bought for them (Figure 3.2). After expenses, they were earning twice as much per day as they could have from bidi rolling. On the other hand, although their earnings allow them to pay the rent, put food on the table (which I say metaphorically, because there was no table), and meet other necessities, they never know when these earnings will end. Even when they do have money coming in, their earnings are so low that they live from hand to mouth. As one example, they are compelled to pay high prices for their

Figure 3.2
Kalavati, India.

daily staples such as rice and lentils because they lack the means to buy these items in bulk at lower unit prices. Kalavati and her family continue to live a life of financial peril.

But more distressing are the personal difficulties that continue to plague her life. The problems facing her because of family members—alcoholism, divorce, gambling, perpetual indebtedness, and low-quality education— continue to impose an at-times unbearable burden on her. Because of these problems, the family owes Rs. 20,000 to a local money-lender. The money-lender visits them each month to collect Rs. 2,000 interest on their loan. Almost surely, they will never be able to repay the principal.

Kalavati's words are more eloquent than anything I could say, so I will simply report them:

> "I'm tired of my life. I struggle, struggle, struggle in my working life and my personal life."
> "I have to be strong. I have to earn. Otherwise, everything will fall to pieces."
> "My daughter is happy. One son is good."
> "With courage, I can maintain this life. I cannot lose my courage."
> "Somehow, we have to manage."

A SELF-EMPLOYED WOMAN'S STORY: THE LIFE
OF MASIBISI (COVER PHOTO)

In 2007 and again in 2011, two colleagues and I lived for a time with a South African Zulu family. At the time of our first visit, the family consisted of our host lady Masibisi, her husband, twenty-two-year-old son, fifteen-year-old daughter, and nine-year-old son. They live outside the city of Durban, South Africa, in the beautiful Thousand Hills area, which Alan Paton immortalized in his great novel *Cry, the Beloved Country* (Figure 3.3).

Masibisi is a woman of exceptional strength. She knows what has to be done to meet her family's economic and nurturing needs. She is the one who organizes all of the tasks in the home that are required when people are poor, performing most of them herself. In addition, to earn cash, she does beadwork and makes shields out of leather to sell to tourists. Beadwork is a craft she learned from her mother. Shield-making is a skill her husband learned from his father and taught her and their eldest son. For the last year, her husband had worked six days a week as a gardener for a white family near Durban. ("White" was an important part of their narrative, and so I mention it here.) Normally, the husband stayed at the employer's house from Monday morning through Saturday afternoon, spending Sundays at home.

Figure 3.3
Masibisi's village, South Africa.

All three children were nominally in school. The older son had been out of school for five years for health reasons but was then finishing high school at a private school in Durban; the fees there were 5,000 rand per year (about US$700), a very large sum given the family's means. The daughter was in grade ten at a government school, where the fees were 650 rand (about US$100) per year. The youngest son went to the local school when it was open. Sadly, the teacher had not shown up for the preceding two months, and a substitute had been available only sporadically, so most of the time he had no choice but to stay home.

All of this work and nurturing results in a home in which the important material needs (including food, clothing, shelter, and school fees) are met, in which everybody contributes cheerfully and without being asked, and in which there is an exceptional level of interpersonal comfort.

The family home is actually a compound. The main building is a rondavel (a round house built in the traditional Zulu style) where the husband and wife sleep and the family has its meals and watches television. It is furnished with two wardrobes, two beds, and a table and chairs. The older son has his own small, square single room, where he sleeps and keeps his books and other possessions. Then there is an L-shaped room which houses the kitchen (electric stove; refrigerator; shelf for pots, pans, and dishes), a sink for washing, and a tiny bedroom for the daughter. A covered workspace houses the workshop for the family's shield-making activity and the men's mechanical work. A larger main rondavel is under construction. Finally, they have an outdoor kitchen sink with running water for dishwashing, and a latrine. Each room has electricity. An ancient non-functioning Audi graces the "lawn."

The family lives well for a poor family, both by South African standards and by the standards of the poor in other countries. In the last five years, the government has installed electricity, running water, and state-of-the-art latrines in their compound and throughout their village. (As an aside, because the latrines have two separate compartments, one for urine and another for fecal matter, they have virtually no odor.) Earlier on this trip, my wife and I had spent time in a village where these services had not yet been provided, and so we were able to observe firsthand what a difference they made when the villagers did not have to spend hours a day fetching water and firewood. The husband rides a motorcycle to and from his place of work—a rarity in this village and in South Africa generally.

One afternoon, five of us took a walk to the village shop. The trip was about ten minutes by foot downhill to the shop and about fifteen minutes back up. The day was hot, and so I treated everyone to ice creams. They cost a lot by local standards: five rand, which is about seventy U.S. cents—the amount earned by a South African minimum wage worker in one hour. Though Masibisi and her family didn't say so, ice cream appeared to be a rare luxury for them. I was touched to see that when we weren't looking, Masibisi gave most of her ice cream away to her nine-year-old son.

This family had done several things to try to earn their way out of poverty. The husband had secured a steady though by no means well-paying job. As long as the job continues, for which they have no assurance, they have a steady income. The older son was scheduled to complete school soon. Besides his education, he is very good with his hands and very personable as well, so to the extent that jobs are available, he will be a good candidate for one.

As for Masibisi herself, she has tried and continues to try to improve her and her family's situation. Durban is a large city along a lovely strip of Indian Ocean coast, so naturally the area attracts a great many tourists. For four years, Masibisi had rented a beachfront stall from a woman with a permit, where she sold her handicraft items to tourists. The journey from home to work took about an hour and a half and cost as much as a comparable journey would in the United States, where incomes are very much higher. On a good day, she would earn enough to be able to return home in the evening. On a bad day, she stayed in the city, paying five rand for a place to sleep on a concrete floor in a parking garage and shower in the morning. But then a government inspector appeared at her stall and told her that she could no longer operate with a permit not in her name, that no permit would be issued in her name, and that she would have to leave. She had no choice but to return home and sell the beads and shields when she received orders.

Masibisi was also starting a new activity, a day care center for the neighborhood children. Land was allocated to her by the local chief, and a permanent building was under construction. Her ambition was to earn a higher and steadier income than she could through handicrafts alone.

When my colleague and I met up with Masibisi and her family again in 2011, a few pleasant surprises awaited us: Masibisi herself was visibly more self-assured than when we saw her last. Her personal growth and development were heart-warming to see.

The family is living better than before. Their incomes have grown, their savings are higher, and they have no debt—this despite the addition of two grandchildren to the family (more mouths to feed) but also because of the grandchildren (one additional child's allowance now coming into the household for the one grandchild who lives there).

Contrary to what is widely assumed, wage employment turned out not to be better than self-employment for this family. Four years earlier, the husband had been working as a gardener for a white family. (It was he who brought up "white," reflecting the salience of race in every aspect of South African life.) We learned on this home stay that he had been earning 1,000 rand *a month*, from which he paid 400 in transport. The family calculated that they could make more money if he left his gardening job to work full time in the family craft enterprise. Indeed, we learned that after expenses he could earn as much as 400 rand *a day* making Zulu shields. This illustrates another point: The family had reoptimized within self-employment. Masibisi now spends most of her time making shields rather than doing beadwork, as she had done previously.

The family was doing well because of a skill that previously had been underutilized: the husband's ability to make beautiful shields (Figure 3.4), which skill he had learned from his father and had passed on to his wife and eldest son. In previous work, I had noted the duality within self-employment, recognizing the coexistence of unskilled and skilled segments. The skilled segment, I wrote, consisted of people who had acquired human capital and financial capital in the formal sector, then set up their own self-employment enterprises. But now I will also write about people who acquired human and financial capital in the *informal* sector and then engage in skilled, hard-to-enter self-employment activities.

Figure 3.4
Shield-making, South Africa.

For Masibisi and her family, earning their way out of poverty has not been easy. Besides the difficulties facing poor people everywhere, poor South Africans face their own particular challenges emanating from their nation's history of apartheid and the country's pervasive unemployment.[3,4] I will have more to say about the fight against South African poverty in later chapters.

A FARMER'S STORY: THE LIFE OF WANG (COVER PHOTO)

Wang and his family are farmers in Yunnan Province, China (see Figure 3.5). They are working hard, working poor, and trying to earn their way out of poverty. Though they are not consuming any luxury items, they have enough money to buy the things they need. A decade ago, the Wang young adults could not go to high school because the family needed their labor and could not afford the school fees. The next generation of Wangs should be able to pay for schooling and other needs without hardship.

The Wangs have farmed on their present location for centuries— although nobody knows for exactly how long, there are ancestral gravesites on a nearby hill that go back five generations. As the only son (his siblings are sisters), Wang inherited the right to farm this particular land. His sole son has inherited the right to farm the land after him.

Figure 3.5
Wang and son-in-law, China.

In today's China, land cannot be owned. What the Wang family holds is a ninety-nine-year renewable lease, so this is land that they can call their own (Figure 3.6). They have the rights to more land than most other families because when the Communists allocated land rights, they did so on the basis of the number of family members at the time. The Wang family then numbered twelve, including aunts and uncles in residence, so they got a larger allocation of land than most other families did.

The current Wang family consists of Mr. Wang, his wife, two of their three children, and Wang's mother. One of his daughters has married and moved far away. Wang's son was married the year before, and he and his wife were expecting their first child the last time I last saw them. They live in a room adjacent to Wang's. The other daughter is single and also living with them.

The fact that the Wangs have three children is itself an interesting story. China has had a strict population control policy for decades. Since the Wangs belong to a minority group called the Naxi, they were permitted to have two children. (For the majority Han Chinese, only one child was permitted.) When the Wangs' third child was born, they were fined such a large amount of money that they had to sell most of their farm animals (the equity they had built up over the years) and start building their reserves afresh.

Figure 3.6
Some of the Wang family land, China.

The family compound consists of two main buildings. The older building is the traditional family home/barn/shed. The people live in one part, the animals in another. The farm implements are stored in another section. The Wang grandmother still lives there, her bed in one corner of a room with dried meat hanging from the rafters, chickens and other small animals wandering in and out, and the apparatus of farm life strewn about (Figure 3.7). She lives there because that is where she came when she married into the family decades ago, where she lived with her husband until his death, and where she remains most comfortable. The rest of the family lives in a modern wooden house consisting of several bedrooms, a kitchen with wood stove, a living room where the television and refrigerator are, and (the latest luxury) a shower room. The toilet is still an outhouse hidden behind a low mud brick wall.

A thin wiry man in his fifties, Wang appears the model of physical fitness. He works long days in the fields along with his wife, son, and one daughter. The wife has the responsibility for marketing the produce, which sometimes is sold to a middleman and sometimes sold directly to customers at the village market. She is said to be a smart person and an astute businesswoman.

Figure 3.7
Grandma Wang's house, China.

As with farmers everywhere, Wang's work is seasonal. During the slack season, he and his son supplement their income by making stone decorative pillars from a home-based workshop. The daughter contributes to the family income by waitressing in town in addition to working in the fields.

What is enabling the Wang family to earn their way out of poverty? One factor is the general prosperity of China. For decades, China has experienced real per capita income growth averaging 9% per year, and poverty in China has therefore dropped at a rate unprecedented in world history. As the Chinese people acquire more purchasing power, they buy more of everything, including the farm products grown by the Wang family. Indeed, the prices the Wangs receive in the market were twice as high at the time of our visit as they had been just one year earlier. A second factor in the Wangs' particular case is that the married daughter and her husband (shown in Figure 3.5) have been able to send the family money, which they used to build a new water system so they can pump water from their well. And a third factor is the boom caused by the growth of tourism in the nearby city where the unmarried daughter recently found employment.

These three factors in the Wangs' case are similar to those facing farmers throughout the developing world, raising several questions: What can be done to enable Wang and farmers like him to receive higher prices for their products? What would enable them to increase the productivity of their farms so they could increase the quantity of produce they supply to the market? To what extent can they supplement or even replace their farm incomes through off-farm employment? These issues will be examined in detail in Chapter 10.

In addition, there are some larger questions about how others similar to the Wangs have prospered. Wang has a relative who was able to save up enough money to buy a used van (purchased for the equivalent of US$4,000), which he uses to transport local people along an established route. If they could save enough, one of the Wangs might be able to do the same.

What else might the Wangs do to improve their economic position? Another peasant farmer who lives only a short way from Wang learned enough English to be able to guide tourists through the countryside. As a guide, she can earn up to ten times as much in a day as she can earn from farming. She finds it advantageous to leave the land on any given day and hire others to cultivate it in her stead. Wang's married daughter could do the same, but because she lives far away with her husband and their children, she is not available for such work. Perhaps the daughter who remains at home will learn enough English so that one day she will be able to do something similar.

Life for the Wang family remains difficult. But in recognizing these difficulties, we should not overlook the very considerable progress they have made in recent years. China's economic development has reached far inland, and people like the Wangs are much better off for it.

A SMALL BUSINESSWOMAN'S STORY: THE LIFE OF ANGELA (COVER PHOTO)

The host family with whom we stayed in Oaxaca, Mexico, in 2009 was a large one. Angela, our host lady, is the forty-two-year-old matriarch. The family consists of a twenty-four-year-old son (married with one child), a twenty-four-year-old daughter (also married with one child), a fifteen-year-old son, an eight-year-old son, and two orphaned nephews.

They are a strikingly close lot. They share a roof, a common cooking pot, child care responsibilities, and much of their income. More important, though, they share a profound love on a daily basis.

The hosts' lives are hard but not the hardest. Together, they have a solidly built house, enough food to eat, schools for their children, and a rich community network. On the other hand, they suffer many deprivations: never enough money, inadequate health care, incessant economic insecurity, and constant indebtedness. As a result, they are too well-off for some government programs—most important, Oportunidades, which provides cash grants to families that get pre- and post-natal check-ups and whose children attend and progress in school—yet too poor to be secure and comfortable.

Angela earns her living manufacturing fireworks, a trade she learned from her mother. Their workshop is a separate building up the side of a mountain on the outskirts of town. They built the workshop so that in the event of an explosion, their homes and their families would remain safe. Angela's mother has constructed a shrine to her patron saint, the Virgin of Guadalupe, outside her home. The mother tells us that the Virgin performs miracles; the miracle, she says, is that no explosion has yet occurred (Figures 3.8 and 3.9).

We asked the family members about their hopes and dreams. The answers were heart-rending.

For Angela, it is all about her children and grandchildren, not herself. Because she had a bad childhood and young adulthood, she is trying and succeeding in giving the young adults and the children in her family a good upbringing. Her hopes are to earn more in making fireworks and in a new business she is trying to launch (laundering). Her dream would be to buy land and seeds and start a plant nursery, but she lacks the money to do so. She pictures herself operating several related businesses: producing

Figure 3.8
Angela's mother with fireworks, Mexico.

Figure 3.9
Shrine to the Virgin of Guadalupe, Mexico.

fireworks, growing flowers, and making decorations for weddings and other celebrations.

For the daughter, the hope is to make her mother's dream grow in Mexico and not have to return to the United States. The daughter had emigrated (illegally) to California and worked for two years cleaning motel rooms, walking an hour and a half to and from work each day in order to be able to save the bus fare and remit as much money as possible to the family. While there, she met her husband and had a baby. She now goes door-to-door selling clothing. Her dream is to go to nursing school, but she is not able to afford it.

For the daughter-in-law, the dream is to become a psychologist, working in the mornings in a school and seeing private patients in the afternoons. She started to pursue her dream, but had to discontinue the effort because she could not pay the tuition.

What prevents these women from attaining their hopes and dreams is the inability to finance them. Angela's situation typifies the problem. She has borrowed money from a for-profit lending organization called Compartamos. Here is how it works in her case. She and eighteen other women formed a group and together borrowed 288,976 pesos, of which Angela's share was 22,004. (The exchange rate was thirteen Mexican pesos to one U.S. dollar.) She was obligated to pay 1,570 pesos each week for sixteen weeks beginning one week after the loan began—a total of 3,130 pesos in interest. Not only that, but in the event that one of the borrowers in the group could not pay, Angela and the others were obligated to pay what the others owed. The interest rate amounts to some 90% per year.

Angela sees a clear profit opportunity. If the interest rate were not so high, she would borrow money to buy in bulk the powders for making fireworks. If she bought twice the quantity that she now buys, she would get a 25% discount per kilo on the whole order—in other words, the second lot would cost only 50% of what the first lot cost. To the extent that she used the powder herself, her costs would be lower and therefore her profit margin would be higher. But in addition, she reckons that she could sell powder to other fireworks makers at a price between what they (and she) now pay and what she could buy it for if she got a quantity discount, earning money in this way as well. But because she is credit-constrained, this pathway out of poverty is not an option for her.

For me and the others in our group, the experience of living with Angela and her family brought out three feelings. One was a genuine affection for this loving family which had opened their home to privileged foreigners. (Gringos, we were, in their view—even the guest from India.) The second was a sense of empathy for the struggles they are facing as they try to get by day-to-day and improve their lives. And the third was a sense of anger that their dreams are being dashed by their inability to get credit at reasonable rates. We will return to the topic of credit in Chapter 10.

SIMILARITIES AND DIFFERENCES IN THEIR STORIES

Kalavati, Masibisi, Wang, and Angela live on different continents, are of different races, and work in very different occupations. Yet despite these differences, the similarities between them are many.

They are by no means the poorest people in the world. No bloated bellies, runny eyes, orange hair, or other manifestations of severe deprivation were evident. They did not have dread diseases such as AIDS, leprosy, or tuberculosis. Yet each has a seriously limited range of options. Their incomes are always low and uncertain. They have little scope for saving and therefore limited possibilities for investment. In short, they live on the margin, always insecure and vulnerable.

For each there is an apparent constraint, which, if overcome, would result in an immediate improvement in their economic well-being and a reduction in their poverty. These constraints differ among them: a higher piece rate; being permitted to sell directly to tourists; higher farm productivity; access to credit at a reasonable interest rate.

Each family also has something within their frame of reference that would make an even bigger difference, given the type of work they do: expanding the range of family activities from bidi rolling to garment sewing; moving from making handicrafts to operating a government-assisted child care center; switching from hand cultivation to mechanized cultivation; and transforming a fireworks business into a celebration business.

And then there are also more remote improvements, still within their frame of reference, that could make a very big difference. People like them who work in offices and factories often earn many times more than they do. Kalavati's husband used to work in a textile mill and still could if a job like that opened up. Masibisi's older son, the one who is very good with his hands, could earn a huge amount more if he could do construction and repair work in the town where I live rather than where he lives. Wang has a relative who was able to save up enough money to buy a used van, which he uses to transport local people along an established route. If only they could save enough, Wang or his son or daughter might be able to do the same. Angela's daughter who cleaned hotel rooms in California could also clean rooms in Oaxaca if only one of the tourist hotels would hire her.

Are these people capable of performing jobs like those? Absolutely. Will they ever get jobs like those? Probably not. Why? One reason is that they are too poor to make the needed investments. Another is that there are too many others like them, so only a small fraction of those seeking improved opportunities are actually able to get hired for them.

Here then are the questions. How typical are these four stories? How do other people in the world's poorer half work? What can be done to enable Kalavati and other wage workers like her to earn higher wages for their labor? What can be done to enable Masibisi, Angela, and other self-employed people like them to earn more from their small business activities? What can be done to enable Wang and farmers like him to earn more from their farming? And what can and should be done to enable these people or others like them to change entirely what they are doing, moving from low-earning to higher-earning activities?

The rest of this book tries to answer these questions.

CHAPTER 4

How the Poor Are Working

The people we met in Chapter 3—Kalavati, Masibisi, Wang, and Angela—are working, working hard, yet earning very little for the work they do.[1] How can we understand their situations? This and the next chapter present an analysis of the employment and unemployment outcomes facing them and people like them. As you will see, despite high-sounding pronouncements such as Article 23 of the United Nations' Universal Declaration of Human Rights, for billions of working persons around the world, the rights "to work, to free choice of employment, to just and favourable conditions of work . . . to protection against unemployment . . . and to just and favourable remuneration" are unattainable; they are not rights at all.[2]

THE POOR WANT TO WORK IN GOOD JOBS

In May 2009, under the auspices of the UN's International Labor Organization (ILO), the leaders of many of the world's countries reached agreement on a Global Jobs Pact to combat the ill effects of the global economic crisis. In the words of Cristina Fernández de Kirchner, president of Argentina:

> When you listen to people saying that 50 million jobs have been lost this year, it is not enough just to agree how dreadful it is. It is not just the figure that is important: it is the losses and destruction that have been caused to individuals and to families. It means 50 million people who are living on their wits and nothing else. These are the people we have to think about when we hear people talking pure economics or statistics.[3]

Work to gain a livelihood is a nearly universal aspiration among the poor. Money and the things that money can buy are mentioned repeatedly as reasons for working. A poor elderly man in Thompson Pen, Jamaica, says, "Work makes all the difference in the world. . . . My wife, at 78, is still working. My dream is a little work to make ends meet." In Russia, the poor stress their desire for jobs that pay regular wages, reflecting their desire for productive work to provide an adequate and secure livelihood. In Bedsa, Egypt, another man says, "Lack of work worries me. My children are hungry and I tell them the rice is cooking, until they fall asleep from hunger."[4]

Like everybody else, the poor want to work in jobs that are steady and secure, pay well, offer benefits, meet labor standards, offer social protections, and so on. The problem in the developing world is that not enough good jobs are available for all who want them and who could do them. Figure 4.1 shows an Ethiopian construction site. The work is much more labor-intensive than is the case in the richer countries. And yet, employment opportunities are insufficient in number. Figure 4.2 shows a group of would-be workers outside a marble factory in Ethiopia seeking a day's work. Some aspects of good jobs and bad jobs are detailed later in this chapter.

Figure 4.1
Labor-intensive construction site, Ethiopia.

Figure 4.2
Unemployed seeking work, Ethiopia.

THE UNEMPLOYMENT RATE FAILS TO CAPTURE
LABOR MARKET DISTRESS

Because the unemployment rate in developing countries is lower than it is in developed countries, the unemployment rate often does not reflect the labor market adequately. Economists and other labor market analysts use the terms "employment" and "unemployment" in quite specific ways that do not necessarily accord with their everyday usage. These terms are pre-scribed by the ILO, which is the specialized agency of the United Nations with responsibility for workplace issues around the world; they will be used throughout this book. They include the following:

- labor force (or synonymously, economically active population): Those people in the economy who either are working or who are actively look-ing for work—that is, those who are either employed or unemployed, as defined below.
- Employed: Any worker in paid employment (regardless of the number of hours), plus unpaid workers in a family business who worked fifteen or more hours in the preceding week, plus persons temporarily laid off, ill, on vacation, or on strike.

- Unemployed: Persons of working age (in many countries, age sixteen or older, but age fourteen or even age twelve in many developing countries) who were not employed last week but who are actively looking for work, plus persons who are not temporarily laid off, on vacation, or on strike.
- Out of the labor force (or synonymously, economically inactive population): Those who were not employed last week and who were not actively looking for work, including the young, the old, the disabled, those who voluntarily were not seeking work, and those who were so discouraged by poor job prospects that they stopped looking.
- Unemployment rate: The employed as a percentage of the labor force.

For those who are not working at all and are therefore classified as unemployed, economists typically distinguish four categories:

- Deficient demand unemployment: This is the type of unemployment that arises because the economy does not generate a sufficient number of jobs for all who are seeking work. Often in the sectors of developing economies where earnings levels are high and working conditions good, the demand for labor is much smaller than the available supply.
- Structural unemployment: This is the type of unemployment that arises because of a mismatch between the types of jobs employers are trying to fill and the types of workers available. One type of structural unemployment arises when employers need skilled workers but only unskilled workers are available. Another arises when skilled workers are available but not in the geographic area where they are needed.
- Frictional unemployment: This is the type of unemployment that arises because workers don't know where jobs are available. An employer may post a job vacancy, but it may take time for workers to learn that that particular employer is hiring and to discover the terms and conditions of employment. Relative to deficient demand unemployment, frictional unemployment is believed to be of modest importance in developing countries.
- Seasonal unemployment: Especially in agricultural economies, demand for labor is very high during the planting and harvesting seasons and slack the rest of the year. Some economists regard seasonal unemployment as a particular kind of deficient demand unemployment rather than its own category.

According to statistics published by the ILO in 2011, the world unemployment rate was 6.2%. The developed economies and the European Union had above-average unemployment rates, 8.4%, while unemployment rates were below average in East Asia (4.4%) and South Asia (also 4.4%).[5] The median unemployment rate among twenty-four developed economies was more than one percentage point higher than among seventeen developing economies.[6]

The reason that unemployment rates are lower in developing countries than in richer countries is that few in the developing world can afford to spend an entire week doing no work at all, which is necessary to be counted as unemployed by the ILO definition.[7] Typically, would-be workers in a developing country live with family members or fellow migrants and for a short time are unemployed while searching full-time for jobs. Soon, however, the hosts expect the guests to contribute money or services in return for lodging. If they have not found a paid job in a reasonable time, they will have to create their own earning opportunities, whereupon they will be counted as employed.

Those who can afford to remain unemployed for longer periods of time are primarily well-educated individuals or young people in well-to-do families.[8] This view, termed "the luxury unemployment hypothesis," receives support from a variety of sources. One is the observation that unemployment rates in countries such as India and Brazil are lowest for the *least* educated people, not the better-educated ones. Another is the observation that in Africa, urban unemployment is found predominantly among those who belong to relatively high-income families. And in many countries of the world, unemployment is concentrated among the young, who frequently are dependents living in households in which other family members are employed, enabling them to rely on family support while searching for a job.[9]

The unemployment rates observed in the developing world—ranging from 4.4% in East Asia to 10.5% in North Africa—should *not* be interpreted to mean that 95.6% or 89.5% of the labor force are fully and gainfully employed. Many of the employed would like to work more hours in a week than employers want to hire them for. Many others have limited weeks of work, especially during the slack seasons in agriculture. Many of those who work full-time for a full-year still earn so little that they are poor by the standards of their country or in terms of an internationally comparable poverty line. Taken together, those who work less than full-time in a day or less than a full number of days in a week or who earn less than a low earnings line are sometimes called "underemployed" or "disguised unemployed." But because these terms are not defined consistently, I prefer to stick to the international definitions of employment and unemployment.

This means that the unemployment rate is a flawed measure of distress in the labor market. Recognizing these deficiencies, the ILO has proposed a broader range of measures to better reflect developing countries' labor market conditions, giving equal weight to the unemployment rate, employment-to-population ratio, average earnings, percentage of working poor, government expenditures for social security, the number of key ILO conventions not ratified by the country, the percentage of children economically active, and the gender gap in labor force participation.[10] To my mind, the most important of these additional indicators is how much people earn when they work, to which we now turn.

EARNINGS LEVELS ARE VERY LOW

Wage surveys show that for a wage worker in a typical unskilled occupation, daily wages in many countries of Asia, Latin America, and Africa are no more than one to two U.S. dollars per day. Laborers earn $145 a month in central China, $104 a month in Vietnam, and $87 a month in India.[11] In Sri Lanka, the hourly compensation cost in manufacturing is half a U.S. dollar per day.[12] It costs an employer 26% of what it does in the United States to hire a manufacturing worker for a day in Argentina, 23% in Brazil, 13% in Mexico, and 4% in the Philippines.[13]

The ILO defines a "working poor household" as one in which at least one member is working but the household lives on less than $2 per person per day. The working poor constitute 39% of total employment in the world.[14] The rates of working poor range from about 15% of total employment in Central and Southeast Europe and the Commonwealth of Independent States (former Soviet republics) to more than 80% in South Asia and sub-Saharan Africa. (By this definition, the developed economies of Western Europe and North America have no working poor at all.) Thus, even by this very modest $2 a day standard, in the low-income regions of the world, the working poor constitute a majority of the poor.

Work hours in the developing world are long. In countries with the highest percentage of workers working more than 48 hours a week, Peru topped the list at 50.9% of workers, the Republic of Korea at 49.5%, Thailand at 46.7%, and Pakistan at 44.4%. By contrast, in developed countries, where working hours are typically shorter, the United Kingdom stood at 25.7%, Israel at 25.5%, Australia at 20.4%, Switzerland at 19.2%, and the United States at 18.1%.[15] What makes workers in the developing world poor is how little they earn per hour, not how many hours they work.

On a recent trip to South Africa, one man who looked to be in his forties told my colleague and me that both he and his wife were unemployed. They had no children nor any elderly person in their home, and so presumably they received no transfer income at all from the government. When we asked how they got by, he told us bit by bit about several activities. He is a bishop in his church, which has two hundred congregants. Some of them contribute to the work of the church. He is also a traditional healer. Sometimes, when a cure is successful, those who can afford to give him money. His wife does beadwork, which she sells in the African Arts Centre in the city. Yet, despite these various activities and modest sources of income, he insisted that they are unemployed. When we asked him what it means to be employed, he was crystal clear: "You are employed when you have a steady job that pays you every Friday."

A worker who has a steady job that pays the same amount every Friday has certainty about receiving an income, even if it is low. The great majority of the working poor not only have the problem of low incomes when they work, but they are also uncertain of whether they will have work the next day and, if they do, how much that work will yield. The poor have good days and bad days, great days and terrible days.

The ILO reports:[16] "The informal economy comprises half to three-quarters of all non-agricultural employment in developing countries. . . . Some of the characteristic features of informal employment are lack of protection in the event of non-payment of wages, compulsory overtime or extra shifts, lay-offs without notice or compensation, unsafe working conditions and the absence of social benefits such as pensions, sick pay and health insurance." Virtually all agricultural employment is also informal. One recent study tells us that "informal is normal," including more than 90% of nonagricultural and agricultural employment in the developing countries.[17] The informal economy has been written about widely.[18]

The poor face a "triple whammy": low incomes when they are working, irregular and unpredictable income flows, and a lack of suitable financial tools. Knowing that today's income might not be there tomorrow, even those who earn only a dollar a day do not live hand to mouth—they manage their money, as discussed in *Portfolios of the Poor*.[19]

WOMEN ARE DISADVANTAGED IN DEVELOPING
COUNTRY LABOR MARKETS

Writing about India, one analyst has conveyed the general situation of women workers as follows:[20]

> Women work longer and harder than men, and their wage work is what is available when the tasks are done. They face discrimination in every conceivable respect. Over two-thirds of women have no money returns from their work, though the proportion of wage workers among those working is higher than it is for men. Female labour is heavily concentrated in rural sites, in agricultural work, on casual contracts and at wages bordering on starvation. Women's wages are practically everywhere lower than those of men, irrespective of the tightening effect of male migration or of the development of male jobs in the non-farm economy. In agriculture in the 1990s, women's wages were on average 71 per cent those of men. In non-farm work, women are likely to be concentrated in the lowest grades and stages, on piece rate rather than time rate, and with earnings much lower than men.

What is true of India is true throughout the developing world: women's labor market outcomes are less favorable in a variety of ways.[21] Women are less likely to be working in the paid labor force and more likely to be segregated into low-paying occupations. They are more likely to suffer from labor market discrimination; less likely to have access to inputs such as land, credit, capital, and technology; more likely to be low earners if in self-employment; less likely to own land; and less likely to have secure land tenure rights. Women are no more likely than men to be rejected for loans or be subject to higher interest rates charged by lenders, but they are less likely to apply for loans in the first place. Female workers are more likely to be engaged in informal employment than are male workers, women are concentrated in the more precarious types of informal work, and the earnings levels in these types of employment are insufficient on their own to raise households out of poverty. Women in the labor market have many of the same needs that men do, but they have special needs besides.

Women also have special demands placed on them. Throughout the developing world, fetching water is women's work. This task can take hours every day. One photo shows a Kenyan woman carrying a full water drum on her back while simultaneously weaving a Kikuyu basket. Another shows Indian women carrying full water jars at the crack of dawn. Another task reserved for women is fetching firewood. The loads are huge, far heavier than anything I could carry (Figures 4.3, 4.4, 4.5).

Figure 4.3
Woman at work, Kenya.

Figure 4.4
Women fetching water, India.

Figure 4.5
Woman carrying firewood, Ethiopia.

THE COMPOSITION OF EMPLOYMENT IS DIFFERENT
IN DEVELOPING COUNTRIES

As compared with the developed countries, in the developing countries,

1. *A smaller percentage of people work in offices and factories such as those found in countries like mine.* We see a lot in the media about the information and communication technology (ICT) centers in cities such as Bangalore and Hyderabad in India and the garment and electronics industries in Shenzhen, Dongguan, Huizhou, and Zhongshan in coastal China. What should be understood is that these types of workplaces are the exceptions in the developing world, not the rule. Only one million of India's labor force of nearly half a billion people work in ICT. More typical workplaces are the fields, the streets, and people's homes. Indeed, of the workers we met in Chapter 3, Kalavati and Masibisi work at home, Wang in the fields next to his home, and Angela in a specially constructed workshop up the side of a mountain from her home.

2. *A greater percentage of people work in agriculture.* Of the world's workers, 35% worldwide are to be found in agriculture. Agriculture's share of total employment is 44% in Southeast Asia and the Pacific, 49% in South Asia, and 66% in sub-Saharan Africa. The share is 55% in India and 45% in China. By contrast, in the developed economies and European Union, only 4% of employment is in agriculture.[22] Throughout the developing world—and in particular in low-income countries such as India, Indonesia, the Philippines, Thailand, and Vietnam and in most of sub-Saharan Africa—the concentration of employment in agriculture is problematic because wages in agriculture are lower even than the wages in these same countries' manufacturing sector.[23]
3. *Self-employment, own-account work, and unpaid family work are more prevalent and paid employment is less prevalent.* (The ILO defines an own-account worker as someone who is engaged in self-employment but has no employees.) [24] Figure 4.6 shows a mini-shopkeeper in Ethiopia. His shop could have been no larger than five feet by five feet—that is, one and half meters on a side.

The poorer the country, the larger the share of people who earn their livelihoods in self-employment, own-account work, or unpaid family

Figure 4.6
Mini-shopkeeper, Ethiopia.

work: more than 80% of women and about 70% of men in South Asia and sub-Saharan Africa, more than 50% of men and women in East and Southeast Asia, and more than 30% of men and women in the Middle East and North Africa and in Latin America and the Caribbean.[25] Turning it around, wage and salaried employment is 13% of total employment in Ghana, less than 10% in Zambia, and less than 5% in Burkina Faso.[26] The ILO combines own-account workers and unpaid family workers into a group they call "vulnerable employment." Vulnerable employment accounts for 51% of the world's employment, with rates of vulnerable employment ranging from 10% in the developed economies and the European Union to 32% in Latin America and the Middle East to 77% in South Asia and sub-Saharan Africa.[27] The reason that the rate of vulnerable employment is so much higher in the developing countries is the insufficient number of opportunities in wage and salaried employment relative to the number who would like such jobs.

Putting these pieces together for the case of Senegal, 59.3% of those employed are in agriculture, 30.0% are in nonagricultural non-wage employment, and 10.6% are in paid employment.[28] In India, of those employed, 15.3% are regular wage and salaried workers, 28.1% are casual wage and salaried workers, 32.3% are employers and own-account self-employed, and 23.8% are unpaid family workers.[29] The details differ but the overall picture is similar in all but the richest countries of the developing world: work in agriculture and in self-employment predominate.

MOST WORKERS WORK IN THE PRIVATE SECTOR

Nine out of ten workers in the developing world are to be found in the private sector.[30] In Latin America, 90% of the labor force is employed in the private sector (including both paid employment and self-employment), just 10% in the public sector. Kenya's private sector comprises 84% of registered employment and presumably all unregistered employment. In Ghana, the public sector is 6% of total employment. In China, 30% of formal sector employment in urban areas is in the public sector, which includes government and public institutions, state-owned enterprises, and collective-owned enterprises, and 28% of rural employment is in township and village enterprises. Government is a dominant employer in the formal sector, accounting for a two-thirds share in India, for example, but in the developing world most employment is not formal.

MOST WORKERS DO NOT RECEIVE JOB-RELATED SOCIAL PROTECTIONS

Protective labor legislation is on the books of every country of the world, even the very poorest. These laws typically provide for job security, minimum wages, overtime pay, maximum hours, health and safety regulations, health insurance, unemployment benefits or severance payments, and/or old-age pensions. To receive them, however, workers must be registered with the government. But registering can be quite costly in time and money, so most workers and firms in the developing world do not register, and therefore the workers lack these protections.[31]

In Asia, only 20% of the unemployed and underemployed have access to labor market programs. The relative few who enjoy such benefits are often said to constitute a "labor aristocracy." It has also been said that in rural Bangladesh, "the 'labor aristocracy' is composed of those who have *a* job."[32]

In Mexico, 40% of workers are formal in the sense that they are in wage and salaried jobs where they are supposed to be registered and are registered with the Mexican Social Security Institute (Spanish acronym: IMSS). Then there is another 20% who are informal illegally in the sense that although they are working in wage and salaried jobs and are supposed to be registered with IMSS, they or their employers have chosen not to register, again for reason of monetary or time cost. The remaining 40% are self-employed persons and workers on commission who are not supposed to register with IMSS and do not. The formal workers in Mexico enjoy a variety of benefits including job protections, housing, health insurance, life insurance, workers' compensation, unemployment insurance, old-age pensions and others; the informal workers do not.[33] In Mexico, as in other Latin American countries, informal sector workers earn only about half of what formal sector workers do.[34]

In India, which is a much poorer country than Mexico, the lack of job-related social protections is even greater.[35] There, 86% of all workers are engaged in informal employment in the informal sector and another 7% in informal employment in the formal sector. Figures 4.7–4.10 show some of these workers: two bicycle rickshaw drivers, a construction crew, and an itinerant clothes ironer.

In a 2009 report, the Indian National Commission for Enterprises in the Unorganised Sector issued a detailed report calling for three pillars of a social floor which is now lacking in India: universal minimum social security, a national minimum wage, and minimum conditions of work. Such protections remain an unrealized dream for the vast majority of workers in India at present.

Figure 4.7
Bicycle rickshaw driver, India.

Figure 4.8
Bicycle rickshaw driver, India.

Figure 4.9
Construction crew, India.

Figure 4.10
Itinerant clothes ironer, India.

The ILO estimates that only one in five people in the world have adequate social security coverage. A variety of efforts, some headed by the ILO, are under way to remedy this situation.[36]

WAGE EMPLOYMENT VERSUS SELF-EMPLOYMENT

Typically, the better jobs are in wage employment, not self-employment. But within wage employment, regular wage jobs are better than casual wage jobs. In India, while self-employed households make up 34.5% of all urban households, they are 38.7% of poor urban households. Similarly, in Pakistan, the self-employed are estimated to be about 18.2% of the urban population, but this group accounts for 21.4% of the urban poor.[37] A study of thirteen developing countries concludes that what differentiates the middle class from the poor is who they are working for and on what terms: those who have a regular, well-paying, salaried job are much more likely to be middle class than those in self-employment.[38] In Bangladesh, nonfarm workers earn about twice what farm workers do, and salaried wage workers earn about twice what casual wage workers do.[39] In seven West African capital cities, employees in the private sector and informal sector employers have about the same earnings, but informal sector employees earn about 40% less and informal own-account workers earn about 50% less.[40]

Because wages and working conditions typically are better in wage jobs than in self-employment, "everybody" in developing countries wants a wage job. In India's Tata Steel Company, low-skilled workers earn more than they could elsewhere, have company-provided medical care, good-quality housing, drinkable tap water, and good schools for their children. These workers also benefit from job security and other measures provided under India's Industrial Disputes Act, explained later in this chapter. For these reasons, many of Tata's employees come from families that have worked there for generations.[41]

The Tata Steel Company jobs exemplify what is called regular employment. In regular employment, workers are hired for unlimited duration, often with a written wage contract. Such employment contrasts with what is called casual employment, in which workers are hired to perform a particular task; when the task is completed, the job ends. National data for rural India show that regular wage workers earn three times per day what casual wage workers do, with the self-employed earning an intermediate amount. Consequently, Indian workers seek wage jobs in the formal sector, but if they cannot get them, they tend to prefer self-employment.[42]

The problem faced by the poor is that not enough regular wage employment is available for all who would like such jobs and are capable of performing them. Consequently, in most countries, the poor respond to insufficient wage employment opportunities by creating their own self-employment opportunities.

In 2002, the University of Cape Town in South Africa posted an advertisement for gardeners and cleaners. Thirty-nine *thousand* persons applied. As it turned out, the university wanted to hire only twenty new staff, which they did.[43]

In Chapter 3, you met Angela, the Mexican fireworks maker. Mari, her adult daughter, had spent two years in the United States, earning her living by cleaning rooms at a Motel 6 in California. When she returned to Mexico, she tried to obtain a job at a number of the local hotels including the one where our conference was held. Each time she tried, Mari was told "no." After a while, she gave up and turned to her own small business going door-to-door selling whatever clothing or other items she could.

In nearly all of the developing world, when wage jobs are not available, the poor respond by creating their own, often very small, businesses.[44] The year I lived in Kenya, I came to know a number of such people. One was a man who bought packs of cigarettes twenty at a time and sold them one cigarette at a time at a higher price to people who were too poor to buy a whole pack at once. Another was an old woman who sold newspapers at the entrance to the university; not only did I buy the paper from her whenever I could, but I was treated to a commentary about the news itself, which gave me a kind of insight into local people's thinking that I could never have gotten otherwise.[45] Another self-employed person I came to know was a man who sold whatever fresh vegetables were in season to drivers who stopped at a busy intersection near where we lived. Some of the merchandising was clever, such as his selling baggies full of podded peas which we could just pop into a pot of boiling water at home. He told me that he, like many urban dwellers, had a family farm in the countryside tended by his wife and other women and that the produce he sold was what he was able to bring with him from the farm whenever he had been able to accumulate enough money for a weekend visit to the family.[46]

Figure 4.11 shows a Mexican woman who contributes to the family income by walking a city neighborhood selling drinks to pedestrians and people who come out of their homes to buy from her. She doesn't earn much, but as she says, "Every little bit helps."

Figure 4.11
Drink vendor, Mexico.

An analysis of data for eighteen developing countries has led one research team to label such people "penniless entrepreneurs" in one context and "reluctant entrepreneurs" in another.[47] Their businesses are small and unprofitable. Few skills, little or no capital, and a shortage of wage jobs are the reasons for the prevalence of such activities. Later, these same authors continued: "Nothing seems more middle class than the fact of having a steady well-paying job. While there are many petty entrepreneurs among the middle class, most of them do not seem to be capitalists in waiting. They run businesses, but for the most part only because they are still relatively poor and every little bit helps. If they could only find the right salaried job, they might be quite content to shut their business down."[48]

DEVELOPING COUNTRY LABOR MARKETS ARE USUALLY THOUGHT TO BE SEGMENTED

A segmented labor market has two defining features. First, for workers of any given skill level, some jobs are decidedly better than others.

Second, access to the better jobs is rationed in the sense that not all who want those jobs and who are capable of performing them are able to get them.

The chief economist of the Inter-American Development Bank, Santiago Levy, stated it graphically for his native country, Mexico: "Of course, they all want to work for the telephone company." What Levy meant by this is that all workers, given their skills, would do better in terms of pay and/or working conditions if they were fortunate enough to be hired by the telephone company. The reason the telephone company pays so much better in Mexico is that labor unions are very powerful there. Some developing countries are like Mexico in having strong unions in some parts of the economy, but in most, labor unions are much less influential.

Of course, the telephone company does not want to hire all who would like to work there. Those workers not hired by the telephone company then have to do the best they can elsewhere. Often, the best alternative is to take paid employment in small enterprises, which typically pay less than larger enterprises do. Other times, it means entering self-employment, which also is lower-paying. In other countries, substantial pay differentials are found between the public sector and the private sector.

For a labor market to be segmented, *comparable* workers must be paid more in some parts of the labor market than in others. Using statistical techniques, researchers have tried to establish comparability by controlling for other wage-determining factors that can be observed in the data such as education, firm size, sector of employment, and so on. (Workers who are comparable in this way are said to be "observationally equivalent.") When such controlled studies have been done, wage differentials— often very large ones—have been found for observationally equivalent workers in various jobs in a developing country.[49]

Based on such evidence, most analysts including me regard developing countries' labor markets as being segmented. But such evidence is not accepted unanimously. Some argue that the differentials are found because workers who look comparable to researchers have unobservable characteristics that make them different from one another in fact.[50]

There are alternatives to thinking of labor markets as being segmented. One is to regard conditions as essentially the same in the different sectors of the economy for workers of comparable skill. Another is to suppose that the various sectors are open to all who would like to work in them but workers differ in terms of their relative abilities in one sector versus another, and therefore some workers willingly choose one sector while other workers choose the other.

In summary, there is widespread but not universal agreement among labor economists that the segmented labor market model—which assumes that some jobs are demonstrably better than others for workers of a given skill level and that not enough of the better jobs are available for all who want them and who could perform them satisfactorily—is the best way to understand developing countries' labor markets.

SOME CHOOSE NOT TO BE WAGE EMPLOYEES

Not all microenterprise operators and family workers are doing such work involuntarily, however. Some could be working as wage employees but choose not to. One such person is a man interviewed by my research team in San José, Costa Rica. For thirty-seven years, he had been selling a peanut-sugar-butter candy called "melcochas" in the city center, as his father had done before him. He was very insistent that he was there voluntarily, doing what he likes to do, and that it pays better than any wage job he might have gotten. He also reported that his brother had at one time started up a melcocha factory, but that he later gave up melcocha making because he realized he could make more money selling in the streets himself.

I have met many working people who reported that they had left wage employment voluntarily to set up their own small enterprises. Among them were one of Angela's brothers, who voluntarily left a job in a Ford garage to set up his own backyard auto mechanic shop in Oaxaca, Mexico (Figure 4.12); a noodle vendor outside a factory gate in Jakarta, Indonesia, who previously had cooked in a hotel restaurant; and a free-lance tourist guide in Chennai, India, who could have remained as an employee with a local travel company but chose to set up operations on her own.

There can be no doubt that some of the people working in self-employment are doing so by choice. What is unsettled is how large the proportion is. On the one hand, World Bank economist William Maloney and the World Bank as an institution both maintain that the proportion is quite large, particularly in Mexico but also in Latin America more generally.[51] This view is a minority one, and the "penniless entrepreneur" view reported earlier dominates the literature. New research, as yet unpublished, estimated for Côte d'Ivoire that 55% of those working informally have a comparative advantage in informal employment and so work informally by choice, while 45% of informal employment is involuntary.[52] More such work is needed.

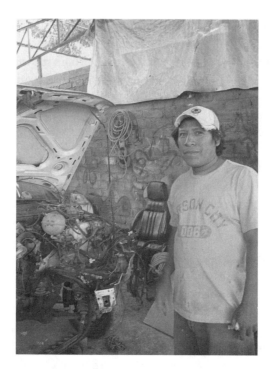

Figure 4.12
Backyard auto mechanic, Mexico.

MANY JOBS ARE MISERABLE

Apart from low earnings and lack of social protections, a large number of jobs are really awful. On April 4, 2008, my hometown newspaper, the *Ithaca Journal* ran the following story from the Associated Press datelined Gorakhpur, India: "When Durga Prasad heard of the mysterious job with the hefty paycheck, he jumped at it, no questions asked. The work could be risky—Prasad figured he'd be asked to smuggle drugs into Nepal—but for the itinerant laborer from Uttar Pradesh, one of the poorest states in India, the money was worth it: 250 rupees a day, about $6. 'I knew it must be some illegal work because no one pays so much money to an illiterate person like me,' Prasad said. The salary turned out to be part of a trap that ensnared Prasad and 14 other poor laborers, who were held captive while their blood was drained for sale to private medical clinics."[53]

Some of the jobs in which the poor in the developing world work are outrageous. Sex workers are found all over the world, of course. In Kenya, a female sex worker earns more money if the client does not use a condom than if he does. Sex workers in developing countries do not engage in unsafe sex out of ignorance. They do so because they are so poor that the risk of AIDS is worth the extra money they can get from unsafe sex. A seventeen-year-old Kenyan sex worker named Alice said, "I try to use condoms every time, but sometimes they refuse or offer much more money if we don't. If I am offered 200 [shillings] for sex with a condom or 1,000 [shillings] for sex without, then I don't use condoms. I have to feed my baby."[54]

Worse than the fact that economic conditions force women like Alice to engage in unsafe sex by choice is the sex slavery found throughout the world. Women (and a lesser number of men and children) are kidnapped, trafficked (that is, forcibly moved to another location), locked in rooms or buildings from which they cannot escape, and forced to perform sex without payment.[55]

Yet another outrage is the phenomenon of child labor. According to the ILO, some 218 million children in the world are working at any given time.[56] Figures 4.13 and 4.14 show two young boys working in Turkey's garment industry. Figure 4.15 shows an incense stick workshop in India. The overseer swore that all of the girls working there had papers certifying

Figure 4.13
Child laborer, Turkey.

Figure 4.14
Child laborer, Turkey.

Figure 4.15
Child laborers, India.

Figure 4.16
Boy plowing fields with oxen, Ethiopia.

that they are at least fourteen years of age. My wife and I had our doubts about the veracity of these work papers. Figure 4.16 shows a young Ethiopian boy in the family field holding a plow pulled by two oxen—this, at an hour of the day when he should have been in school.

All child labor is bad, but even worse than the fact that hundreds of millions of children are working is that millions of children are engaged in the worst forms of child labor. The ILO defines the worst types as (1) all forms of slavery or practices similar to slavery, such as the sale and trafficking of children, debt bondage and serfdom, and forced or compulsory labor, including forced or compulsory recruitment of children for use in armed conflict; (2) the use, procuring, or offering of a child for prostitution, for the production of pornography, or for pornographic performances; (3) the use, procuring, or offering of a child for illicit activities, in particular for the production and trafficking of drugs as defined in the relevant international treaties; (4) work which, by its nature or the circumstances in which it is carried out, is likely to harm the health, safety, or morals of children.[57] India alone is reported to have some 1.2 million child prostitutes.[58]

I have seen and read a lot about outrages in the labor market, but I will tell you about one particularly reprehensible incident. When my wife and I visited a textile museum in Ahmedabad, India, we were shown a dazzling display of truly beautiful works of art. At the end of our tour, the museum official encouraged us and the other guests to stop at the museum shop and buy the products on offer. What amazed and appalled me was the reason she gave for why we should purchase these products. The textiles on display in the museum, she said, had been woven by children as young as age eight who, by the time they were fourteen, had become blind from the fine handwork they had been performing in low-light conditions over a number of years. A portion of the proceeds from our purchases, she continued, would be used to support these teenagers who would never be able to work again. We left at once. I regret that I did not say what was on my mind: that if blinding children is what it takes to produce such textiles, then the world would be better off if we did not have the textiles and the museum and the industry that supports it were closed down.

DEVELOPING COUNTRIES HAVE AN EMPLOYMENT—NOT AN UNEMPLOYMENT—PROBLEM

In developing countries, poverty among those who work is a more serious problem than is unemployment.[59] According to the latest ILO statistics, more than 200 million people in the world are unemployed. By contrast, some 1,300 million people (i.e., 1.3 billion) belong to the working poor, defined as workers who lived in families earning less than the $2 per person per day poverty line. That is, six-and-a-half times as many people in the world are working poor as are unemployed (and indeed many of the unemployed live in well-to-do families). In other words, 85% of the poor are working. In the 2009 recession, conditions got worse according to three measures of labor market outcomes—unemployment, vulnerable employment (defined as own-account workers plus contributing family workers), and working poverty[60]—because working poverty is so much larger than unemployment, unemployment is the tip of the proverbial iceberg. By far the greatest part of the world's employment problem is low earnings among the employed, not zero earnings among the unemployed.

There is one important exception to this generalization, and that is South Africa. South Africa has a frightful unemployment problem. Using the standard ILO definition, that country's unemployment rate is 25.2%. When discouraged workers are included—those who are not working, who are not actively looking for work, but who report that they would take a job if one became available—the so-called broad unemployment rate reaches 32.5%. An estimated 46% of the labor force—about seven million people—earned less than a South Africa-specific low-earnings line. The unemployed, defined broadly, make up about half this group, and the working poor make up the other half. South Africa's one-to-one ratio of working poor to unemployed is of an entirely different magnitude from the six-and-a-half-to-one ratio in the world as a whole. This country is so different from the rest of the world because of the enduring effects of apartheid.[61]

IN SUMMARY: CORRECTING SOME MISIMPRESSIONS

I hope that the evidence presented in this chapter has cleared up some common misimpressions about whether the poor in developing countries work and how they work:

Misimpression: Poor people do not want to work.
Fact: Poor people want very much to work.

Misimpression: Poor households are poor because nobody in the household works.
Fact: The great majority of poor households have workers who despite working long hours do not earn enough to raise the household out of poverty.

Misimpression: What most developing countries have is an unemployment problem.
Fact: What most developing countries have is an employment problem.

Misimpression: Most workers making less than $2 per day or some other low earnings line are unemployed, earning nothing.
Fact: Most low earners are employed, but they have too little work and/or very low hourly earnings to be able to reach $2 or some other low earnings line.

Misimpression: Most low earners work as paid employees.
Fact: Most low earners are self-employed.

CHAPTER 5

Labor Markets in a Globalized World

DIFFERENT TYPES OF LABOR MARKETS

Economists define a labor market as the place where labor services are bought and sold. Two types of employment are distinguished: (1) paid employment, in which workers sell their labor services to others in exchange for wages or salaries, and (2) self-employment, in which workers sell their labor services to themselves. Provided that the idea of "labor market" is understood as comprising both paid workers and the self-employed, it is as relevant to analyze labor markets in the low-income countries of Africa and Asia as it is to analyze them in the middle-income countries of Latin America, the Middle East and North Africa, and Eastern and Central Europe or in the high-income countries of Europe and North America.

Labor markets in developing countries range from very organized to very idiosyncratic in nature. Here are some examples.

• Well-organized labor markets: The best-organized labor markets are ones in which workers seeking jobs and employers seeking workers can easily meet one another. In China, I visited the Xiamen Employment Service Centre. There, job seekers scanned a computerized job board on which job details were posted, including job category, job title, number of job openings, minimum and maximum age qualification, gender requirement, education qualification, wage, and other benefits. ("Gender requirement" is not a typo.) This type of open labor market represents a marked change from China's previous system, in which all workers were assigned to specific jobs. Such well-organized labor markets are rare in the developing world.[1]

- Well-structured casual labor markets: In Bogotá, Colombia, I learned about certain well-structured labor markets that existed there (and, I learned later, in many other places). Throughout the city, in different neighborhoods, would-be construction workers congregated to be hired for jobs as they arose. At a plaza near the city center, people with trucks would queue up to transport goods as needed. In other countries, well-structured casual labor markets can be found in union hiring halls, at the docks, at home care service centers, and at part-time home teaching service centers. What makes each of these labor markets casual is that workers are hired to perform specific tasks, which may last as long as a few days or weeks or as little as a few hours; when the task is completed, the job is over, and the search for work begins all over again.
- Being in the right place at the right time: When my wife and I went to live in Nairobi, Kenya, we were a graduate student couple living on a stipend which, by American standards, was quite low but by Kenyan standards was quite high. As soon as we moved into a rented cottage, local people knocked on our door many times a day seeking jobs as house workers. We resisted, more out of a sense of guilt than because of the going wage, which we could afford. Our resistance ended the first time we went to the neighborhood laundromat, where we found that each load of machine washing or drying cost more than it would cost to hire a person for a day to wash clothes in our sink. We quickly decided that we would much rather pay the money to a local person who needed the income than to the Speed Queen Corporation in Ripon, Wisconsin. That very day, we hired the next job-seeker who came along. His persistence paid off in more ways than one.[2]
- Word-of-mouth hiring: Throughout the world, employers put out calls for new workers and rely on referrals from existing employees. In China, for example, one's social network is very important in job searches in the sense that individuals exchange word-of-mouth information on job openings, and people can get opportunities for an interview or even an offer from word-of-mouth recommendations by one's friends or relatives. A Chinese student at Cornell University relates the following story: "My uncle had been searching for a job for a long time after he graduated from high school. He had a hard time finding a satisfactory job because he did not have a college degree. My aunty, who worked in a pharmaceutical company, recommended my uncle to the manager of the company's marketing department. My uncle got a job as a salesman in the company and earned a salary higher than that of his counterparts who did not have a college degree and ended up in low-salary jobs."

Thomas Friedman has famously told us that "the world is flat." As he explains, "It is now possible for more people than ever to collaborate and compete in real time with more other people on more different kinds of work from more different corners of the planet and on a more equal footing than at any previous time in the history of the world—using computers, e-mail, networks, teleconferencing, and dynamic new software."[3]

The world, says Friedman, is now in the third era of globalization. The first was about how much power—human power, horsepower, wind power, and steam power—your country had and how it deployed it. The second was about multinational corporations and the movement of goods and information from continent to continent to bring about essentially a global market with global arbitrage in products and labor. The third is about the ability of individuals to collaborate and compete globally, enabled not by horsepower or by hardware but by software.

Yale University's Center for the Study of Globalization puts it this way:

> Globalization is a relatively new term used to describe a very old process. It is a historical process that began with our human ancestors moving out of Africa to spread all over the globe. In the millennia that have followed, distance has been largely overcome and human-made barriers lowered or removed to facilitate the exchange of goods and ideas. Propelled by the desire to improve one's life and helped along by technology, both the interconnectedness and interdependence have grown.[4]

More concisely, says the Boston Consulting Group, globalization is about businesses "competing with everyone from everywhere for everything." [5]

Globalization has been described in essentially the same terms by, among others, Joseph Stiglitz (Nobel Prize–winning economist and professor at Columbia), Jagdish Bhagwati (one of the world's leading international trade economists and also a professor at Columbia), Anne Krueger (former first deputy director of the International Monetary Fund and now a professor of international economics at Johns Hopkins University), and Martin Wolf (prize-winning journalist at the *Financial Times*).[6, 7] While these and other analysts share a common idea of what globalization is, they are in fundamental disagreement about what should be done about it—contrast the title of Bhagwati's book *In Defense of Globalization* with Stiglitz's *Globalization and Its Discontents* and *Making Globalization Work*.[8]

What does globalization mean for labor markets? The answer, exaggerating only somewhat, is that it is possible for employers almost anywhere in the world to hire workers almost anywhere in the world to manufacture goods and produce services that can be sold almost anywhere in the world. Although some employers, workers, and products are excluded from global markets, so many *are* involved with global markets that it is much better to think in terms of *global* opportunities and *global* challenges than in terms of *local* ones. Indeed, workers, employers, consumers, producers, and sellers are connected to one another and dependent upon one another to an unprecedented degree.[9]

Here is one small globalization story. On a visit to Ethiopia, I was given a copy of a magazine called *The Big Issue*. This magazine is a street paper sold by homeless or marginalized people under the banner, "Working, not begging." I opened the magazine and found an article entitled "Google Goes Amharic." (Amharic is the language of the country's majority ethnic group.) Talk about a globalized world![10]

LABOR MARKETS IN TODAY'S GLOBALIZED WORLD

Globalization has important consequences for labor markets. In today's highly globalized world, labor markets have a number of features that must be considered by management, workers, and policy makers alike.

The first point is a fact staring us in the face, but it sets the stage for all that follows:

- *For the most part, poor people in the developing world are not able to sell their labor where it will command the highest return.*

In previous chapters, we met the workers building Lenovo laptop computers in China, a woman who hand-rolls cigarettes in India, a craftsperson in South Africa, a farmer in China, and a fireworks maker in Mexico. The most fortunate of these workers earn in a day what a minimum wage worker in the United States earns in an hour.

The poor people in the developing world are acutely aware of the great disparities in earnings levels between where they are and where they might be. The traditional way of learning about conditions elsewhere was for some of the more pioneering members of a community or a family to undertake a lengthy voyage, discover what it was like in the destination, and send back personal reports. Stories abounded to the effect that "life is good here, and with hard work you can do better than in the old country."

By comparison, the process of learning about migrants' experiences today is now enormously compressed in time. In today's globalized world, physical travel to a potential destination is no longer required.

The obvious way in which the poor learn how the more advantaged live is, of course, through television. Television requires supporting technology—in particular, electricity and the technology for sending and receiving signals. These supporting technologies have been put in place in nearly every corner of the world, permitting the poor to see how the more advantaged people in their own country live as well as more advantaged people elsewhere.

On a visit to China, my wife and I were taken to Weihan village in Yunnan province in the south of the country. This village had been half a day's horseback ride away from the nearest main road. Not surprisingly, because of their isolation, the villagers were quite poor. However, a year before our visit, a road had been built to the village, reducing the travel time from the main road to just one hour. As we wandered around, we were taken to the home of the poorest family in the village. The log walls and dirt floor provided little protection against the biting winter cold. And yet even this poorest family in the village had a television, which they regularly watched, enabling them to see how the more fortunate in China and elsewhere in the world lived.

The spread of technology—not just television, of course, but also the internet, cell phones, and smart phones—is the big difference between the developing world today and the way it was when I first went to Nairobi as a graduate student. Now, every day of their lives, even the very poorest of the poor can see and hear what it is like all around the world.

Given this knowledge, it is not surprising that significant numbers of the poor try to move to where the opportunities are better: to the nearby towns and cities, to the growing industrial and commercial areas of their own countries, and to the richer countries. It is also not surprising that some of the poor take independent action, voting with their feet whether they are welcomed into new countries legally or not. Despite the efforts of the richer countries to control their borders and limit the flow of immigrants, the poor keep coming—disparities in standards of living are simply too large for all of them to be content where they are.

In short, context is all-important. Whether a worker is absolutely poor or not is determined to a large extent by where that person is able to work.

• *Labor markets throughout the world are linked by an unprecedented degree of labor market competition.*

Offshoring—the movement of production to other countries—is surely about labor costs, but it is also about more than that. Accessing global talent, wherever in the world it is, and penetrating other countries' product markets are also major factors for global companies such as IBM, Lenovo, and GE.[11] Sam Palmisano, the head of IBM, describes three stages in the development of multinational companies. The first was when firms were based in their home country and sold products overseas. The second was the multinational firm that created smaller versions of itself around the world. The third—what we have now—is a "globally integrated enterprise" in which "work flows to the places where it will be done best . . . based on the right cost, the right skills and the right business environment." With the advent of globally integrated enterprises, labor market competition is enormously heightened.[12]

Two main factors are responsible for heightened global labor market competition. One is political, the other technological.

The political factor is the doubling of the world's labor force from 1.5 billion to 3 billion. This doubling is owing to the incorporation of China, India, and the former Soviet Union into the world economy.[13]

In China, a two-stage process of transition from a socialist command economy to a market economy was begun in 1978. In the first phase, to dismantle the command economy and achieve economic growth, markets were introduced throughout the economy, ownership was diversified, and competition created. Then, in the second phase, the institutional setup was made compatible with a market economy, the state sector was sharply reduced in size, and conditions were introduced for fair competition among market participants. Before 1996, nearly all workers were assigned to jobs, so there was no real labor market. Since then, employers have had to find and attract workers, and workers have had to seek out jobs, in most of the same ways that they do everywhere else in the world.[14]

In India in 1991, the government embarked on a broad program of economic reforms. These were aimed at placing greater reliance on the private sector, opening the economy to foreign trade and foreign direct investment, reorienting government activities toward those not likely to be performed by the market, and ensuring macroeconomic balance and a well-run financial sector.[15]

Turning from political to technological factors, the costs of accessing labor elsewhere in the world are very much smaller than they were even ten or twenty years ago. Because of cargo containerization and cheaper air freight, it costs much less to import raw materials, parts, or finished goods from overseas. With today's telecommunication technologies, international collaboration in services is feasible, rapid, and efficient for many tasks including call centers, check processing, x-ray reading, accounting services, translation services, computer-aided design, and many others.

Similar gains have been made for certain kinds of goods including custom-produced clothing, fresh produce, and cut flowers.

Production can shift more easily than before to take advantage of the available labor when it is cheaper elsewhere, adjusted for productivity differences, and indeed it does:

- In 2000, an array of products were made in Tijuana, Mexico, including telephones, tuners, PC monitors, batteries, lighters, printers, vacuums, hard discs, keyboards, printed wiring board assemblies, low noise block converters, synthesizers, cathode ray tubes, transistors, wire harnesses, and others. The factories producing these products are now gone, mostly to China.[16]
- We all know that companies have left North America and Europe and moved their production to China. What you may not know is that companies are now moving *from* China because of lower labor costs elsewhere.[17] Unskilled workers in China earn US$120 a month for a forty-hour workweek. In Vietnam, though, factory workers earn US$50 a month for a forty-eight-hour workweek including Saturdays. As a result, companies like Canon, Nissan, and Hanesbrands have recently built new factories in Hanoi.[18] More generally, higher labor earnings in China present new opportunities for workers in such low-income countries as Indonesia, India, and Ethiopia, as indeed workers in China benefited a generation ago from rising labor earnings in Hong Kong, Taiwan, and South Korea.
- Colombian flower growers have come to dominate the U.S. market, having attained a market share of 90% compared to virtually nothing two decades ago. Juan Maria Cock, the president of Uniflor, one of the region's biggest flower exporters, says: "We have the advantages of labor and a tropical climate with lots of light and sun. There was no way you could compete with us, *or any good reason why you should want to*" [emphasis added].[19] For similar reasons, 25% of the flowers sold in Europe are grown in Kenya, and another sizable percentage comes from Ethiopia.[20]
- Chinese companies are now investing in Africa in a big way. Average labor costs are lower in Africa than in China. A semi-skilled worker is paid US$100 per month in Africa but twice that in China. Moreover, social security is paid in China but not in most of Africa. A survey of 5,000 private companies in China found that more of them were looking to invest in Africa than any other continent because of the low labor cost.[21]

Because of the possibilities for production to move where labor is cheaper, the ability of any given group of workers to raise their earnings is severely restricted by the greater availability of other workers who would like jobs working for *the same company* producing those same products and who are prepared to work for less.

Very few jobs are secure in today's globalized labor market. As a tenured university professor, I am well aware that I am very fortunate to be in one of them. Also, because I live in a country where mandatory retirement has been banned, I can continue to do work I love for as long as I love doing it and am able to. Not having to think about whether my job will be there next week, next year, or next decade gives my wife and me enormous peace of mind compared to nearly everyone we know. (The only others we know who have the same sense of job security are also tenured professors in our small university town.)

- *Labor markets are highly competitive because numerous industries face an unprecedented degree of product market competition on the global level. Such globalization increasingly limits the scope for national, subnational, and local action, for example, individual country governments and individual labor unions.*

Many industries today are competitive on a global scale. In *consumer electronics,* the very success of RCA and GE led Japan's Sony and Panasonic to compete against them, and then led Korea's LG and Samsung to compete against them, and now is leading China's Haier and Lenovo and India's Videocon and Onida to compete against them.[22] In *autos*, the story is similar: first the United States' GM and Ford, then Japan's Toyota and Nissan, now Korea's Hyundai and India's Tata (thus far, primarily domestically) have taken on established competitors and prospered. In *textiles,* first it was British manufacturers, then U.S. ones, then Japanese ones, and now Chinese and increasingly Vietnamese ones. And in *airlines*, the U.S. legacy carriers (United, American, Delta/Northwest, and others) have been in deep financial trouble while domestic upstarts such as Southwest and overseas competitors such as British Airways and Australia's Qantas are taking their place.[23] The list of examples could go on and on.

What has always been there is the possibility that the work done by Kalavati and the tens of thousands of other bidi rollers of Ahmedabad might be moved within India or mechanized. What is new today is that so much other work could be outsourced to others. Major cities in India such as Bangalore and Hyderabad are thriving on such outsourcing.

Globalization of this kind has implications for everyone. Countries are limited in the social programs that they can put into effect because of what others might do. State and local governments face competition within their own countries and have to adjust their own positions accordingly. Labor unions are less able to push for higher wages and improved working conditions because workers in other countries are able to compete for their jobs—and so on.[24]

Let me venture a prediction. Our youngest child is a 2008 graduate of Cornell University, where I teach. It would not surprise me if, when she reaches my age, she will look back and say, "Do you remember when we at Cornell were so smug as to believe that we were immune from challenges from the Chinese, the Koreans, and the Indians?" At Cornell, nearly all of our graduate students in some technical fields like engineering and half of them in less technical ones like economics come from overseas, mostly from Asia. It is just a matter of time before the Asians develop world-class universities of their own. In fact, it is likely to happen in my own field. Ten years ago, the Korea Development Institute created the KDI School, which offers master's and Ph.D. degrees in public policy and management. One of China's top universities, Tsinghua University, has now opened a master's degree program in international development. As a result of new universities and programs like these, Asian students will stop seeking advanced degrees in the United States in such large numbers, and our faculties will shrink as a result. Because of the tenure system (which, I forecast, will remain in place, at least for decades to come), existing faculty will not lose their jobs. What will happen, I suspect, is that many fewer spaces will be available for those Americans who do complete advanced degrees and hope to enter academia.

- *In today's globalized world, few competitive advantages are sustainable; most advantages are likely to be short-lived.*

"Sustainability" is much in vogue these days. We hear and read about sustainable energy, sustainable enterprise, sustainable agriculture, sustainable architecture, and so on.[25] My own university has the Atkinson Center for a Sustainable Future, which serves as a focal point for new efforts in energy, environment, and economic development.

One of the hot topics in the management field is "sustainable competitive advantage." Economist Jay Barney is one of those who has elaborated on this idea at length over the years.[26]

Sustainable energy, as in windmills and solar collectors, makes sense to me. So too does sustainable environment, as in the clean air in my hometown of Ithaca, New York. And it is good to think of social entrepreneurship projects as sustainable if they can last after the first year without further support from donors. But it may shock you when I say that with rare exceptions, I do not believe in sustainable competitive advantage.

Why don't I believe in it? Jay Barney defines sustainable competitive advantage as occurring "when an organization is implementing a value-creating strategy that is not being implemented simultaneously by any current or potential competitors, and when other organizations are incapable of duplicating the benefits of that advantage." [27] This is a good, clear definition. The problem, though, is that according to this definition, most competitive advantages are not in the least sustainable. Let me explain.

In the electronics, auto, textile, and airline industries mentioned previously, the very success of one company acted and continues to act as a magnet for others to enter the industry and try to compete. Whenever there are supernormal profits to be made ("supernormal profits" are those that are above the level needed to induce firms to enter the industry in the first place), outsiders have a strong incentive to come in. To the extent that these outsiders can enter, any competitive advantage will be short-lived. Success invites competition. Competitive advantage can *not* be sustained.

Although I have maintained that most competitive advantages can not be sustained, there are some exceptions. It is helpful to put them into three categories: insurmountable barriers to entry, historically conferred advantages, and network economies.

An insurmountable barrier to entry arises when nobody else can get into a particular product market. In many countries of the developing world, monopoly rights have been granted, protecting the monopolist against any and all competitors. Examples are the wireless telephone company America Movil owned by Carlos Slim, one of the three wealthiest men in the world along with Bill Gates and Warren Buffett;[28] Russian telecommunications services, a state-run monopoly that controls local fixed line and long distance telecom providers and dominates their respective segments;[29] legal protection on patents, such as the TRIPS (Trade-Related Aspects of Intellectual Property Rights) agreement, which allows the patent holder an effective monopoly on the production and sale of the patented product for the duration of the patent. An example of the last type is in pharmaceuticals where an Italian-based multinational corporation sells raw materials to its Pakistani subsidiary for seventy times more than the prices in the international market.[30] In each of these cases, the incumbent firm's competitive advantage is sustained by law.

As an example of historically conferred advantage, consider U.S. universities. We have endowments that arise from gifts (usually from wealthy alumni) and that enable us to fund programs. A typical endowment pays out at an annual rate of 5% or so, leaving the principal intact in perpetuity. Cornell University, where I teach, has an endowment per student of $191,000.[31] The other university in our town, Ithaca College, has an endowment of just $36,910 per student,[32] and the State University of New York (SUNY) has essentially no endowment at all other than the sustaining funds it gets year-to-year from the state legislature. Cornell University can do things that Ithaca College cannot do. But lest you think that Cornell is at the top of the pecking order, consider that Harvard University has a total endowment seven times that of Cornell and Princeton University has a per-student endowment nine times that of Cornell. Harvard is able to offer free university education to students coming from families with incomes less than $60,000 a year. Princeton is even more generous—their cutoff is $75,000. Cornell cannot afford to do this. The best we can do, and we are proud of it, is to offer needs-blind admissions—that is, we decide which students to admit without regard to their ability to pay and then offer financial aid packages to all admitted students whose families cannot cover the full cost of their education. The competitive advantages that Harvard and Princeton have compared to Cornell and that Cornell has compared to Ithaca College and SUNY are indeed sustainable.

Finally, some competitive advantages are sustainable because of what economists call network economies. A network economy arises when the benefits of doing something increase as more people do it. Years ago, my colleagues and I switched from Apple to Microsoft operating systems so that we could exchange files with each other and with other Microsoft Office users and take advantage of certain specialty programs that then were available only for Windows—in our case, the Stata statistical software package. The value of subscribing to Verizon cell phone service increases as the number of Verizon users grows, because each Verizon user can call other Verizon users without charge—but not users of other cell phone services. And of course, it pays each of us to drive on the right-hand side of the road in the United States and China and on the left-hand side of the road in Britain and India.

To repeat, sustainable competitive advantages are exceptions. In general, advantages in the marketplace are temporary and cannot be sustained except in unusual circumstances.

A CONCLUDING WORD

I see market competition as both an opportunity and a threat. Thomas Friedman (2005, p. 114) repeats the following traditional African proverb:

> Every morning in Africa, a gazelle wakes up.
> It knows it must run *faster* than the fastest lion or it will be killed.
> Every morning a lion wakes up.
> It knows it must outrun the slowest gazelle or it will starve to death.
> It doesn't matter whether you are a lion or a gazelle.
> When the sun comes up, you better start running.

This proverb tells a lot in its own right. Equally striking is that it has been translated into Mandarin and posted in a factory owned by an American auto parts manufacturer operating in China!

Nothing is stopping the hungry lion from chasing after the self-confident gazelle, and indeed the opportunities have never been greater. It is not that the hungry lion will eat our lunch. It is that in today's globalized world, some of us will *be* the hungry lion's lunch.

PART TWO

Helping the Poor Earn Their Way Out of Poverty

As the chapters in Part I showed, despite the considerable progress that has been made, more than 3 billion people still live on less than two-and-a-half dollars a day. The labor market challenges facing the poorer half of the world's population are enormous. These people want to work, they do work, they work long hours, and they work very hard. And yet, they earn so little from their labor that their lives are marked by constant economic misery and unceasing economic peril.

Part II, which follows, is about development policy. As I see it, the essence of economic underdevelopment is severely constrained choices. In everyday English, we often say that someone had no choice, but in reality it is rare to have no choice at all. To give your money to a robber who holds a knife to your throat is a choice, though hardly a free choice. In the same sense, to take up an odious job is also a choice; economic underdevelopment is the metaphorical knife to the throat, and the choice is equally unfree.

Economic development is the process of relaxing such constraints. Creating more good jobs reduces the necessity for workers to take up odious ones ("necessity" in the sense that in the circumstances, it is better to work in odious conditions than in any other work that may be available). What matters is the choice setting itself. If you know the story of *Sophie's Choice* (Styron, 1979), you know that the horror was not what Sophie chose; the horror was the choice that she was forced to make.

More generally, in the terms used by Nobel Prize–winning economist Amartya Sen, economic development is about increasing capabilities and functionings.[1] A key question is, capabilities and functionings for whom?

My answer is a pragmatic one: capabilities and functionings of the poor. Why? Because the well-to-do have proven quite adept at caring for themselves and the middle class are not far behind.

It is much harder for the poor to care for themselves. They lack the means to make profitable investments that would improve their economic livelihoods. If my bicycle breaks down and I can no longer ride it to work, I can use a bank card to buy a new one immediately, if indeed I need a new one. In the event that I need to borrow, the bank card would provide me access to a loan at about 20% interest *a year*. But a poor farmer who uses a bicycle to transport himself or his inputs to distant fields or his produce from the fields to the market town almost surely does not have a bank card and, if he can borrow at all, he might well face an interest rate of 20% *a month*. Economists call such difficulties "market failures"; it is because of these market failures (and other failures) that interventions on behalf of the poor are needed.

Dr. Manmohan Singh, prime minister of India and himself a distinguished economist, has said: "Our biggest single problem is the lack of jobs *for ordinary people*. We need employment *for the semi-skilled* on a large scale, and it is not happening to anything like the degree we are witnessing in China. We need to industrialise to provide jobs *for people with fewer skills*. Why is it not happening on the scale we would hope? Because we are not as single-minded as China in pursuing our goals in a clear manner."[2]

Single-mindedness in the pursuit of goals—a great idea. For India or any other country, I would not presume to know what *all* of their economic development goals should be. But consistent with the prime minister's statement, I do know what I think *one* of the priority objectives should be in India and elsewhere: helping the poor earn their way out of poverty.

What *I* think is probably not as important as what the poor themselves think. We know that they see work as a primary means of escaping from poverty. We know that they want more wage jobs for people like themselves. We know that they want to earn more from their (usually) small-scale self-employment enterprises. And we know that they have many excellent ideas about what is constraining their livelihoods and what interventions might help overcome the most binding constraints they face.

Fortunately, there is cause for hope. We know in broad outline what policy actions would enable more of the poor to earn their way out of poverty.

What is needed is to focus policy efforts on this objective and to raise more resources so that the actions that have been shown to work can be undertaken on a greatly expanded scale.

The chapters that follow in Part II are about policies aimed at improving earning opportunities for the poor in both self-employment and paid employment. We will first look at policies that have an important bearing on the labor market and then at those that work directly in the labor market. These include economic growth, trade, aid, business environment and investment climate, corporate social responsibility and consumer movements, pay policy, protective labor legislation, education and skills, public sector employment, labor market information systems, increasing productivity, complementary inputs, off-farm employment, capital markets, and entrepreneurship.

It is not new to consider the effects that policies in these areas would have on economic development. What will be new to many of you is to examine such policies through the lens of creating jobs and raising earnings for the poor. Are tax cuts concentrated on the rich the best way to stimulate economic growth that will benefit the poor? Where should educational dollars be channeled: on world-class university education for the few or basic education for the many? Which problem is more deserving of attention: educated unemployment or unsteady work for the less educated? And so on.

What may also be new to some of you is to give serious attention to the role that the private sector can play in helping to solve these problems. I talked earlier about seeking win-win solutions. The president of one of the world's leading nongovernmental organizations, Ray Offenheiser of Oxfam America, has said,

> Once we get beyond the adversarial rhetoric and distrust to a place where civil conversation can began, both for-profits and not-for-profits must focus on a common set of questions. First, how do we find mutual interests in our core missions? Is that actually something that's possible? Second, how do we identify win-win outcomes that we can build upon? Is it possible for us to actually do a deal? And finally, how do we find systemic market-based solutions to fundamental social problems? Is that a pipe dream or is that something we might be able to pursue together?[3]

A guiding premise of this book is that the joint pursuit is more than worthwhile; it is essential, unless the system is changed fundamentally, which I don't see happening any time soon.[4]

By focusing on employment and earnings, we will not be looking at how to combat poverty through programs aimed at people as consumers and citizens rather than as workers. This is not to say that development policies in other areas such as housing, health, social services, and many others are unimportant. Rather, I think it best to leave the design of policies in those areas to others who are expert in them, which I am not.

CHAPTER 6

Setting Objectives, Facing Trade-Offs

THE OBJECTIVES OF LABOR MARKET POLICY

During my career, I have been privileged to write books and articles and advise governments and international organizations on economic development policy in a wide range of countries in Africa, Latin America, and Asia. In my policy work, I urge my clients to be explicit about what their ultimate development objectives are so that we can work together to design policies to try to achieve them. In what follows, I share with you some of the stated objectives that are at the forefront of current labor market policy.

I have seen different labor market policy objectives come and go. When I was first getting started, the energies of the labor economics profession were focused on reducing unemployment. I was enthralled by John Harris and Michael Todaro's two-part policy conclusion for Kenya: first, that a policy of urban employment creation would be expected to *increase* urban unemployment; and second, that the solution to urban unemployment would be a program of *rural* development.[5] Part of my Ph.D. dissertation research involved enriching the Harris-Todaro model by adding in other features that had not to that time been introduced or analyzed.[6] And yet, I continued to use Harris and Todaro's single criterion for evaluating policies—namely, the effect on unemployment.

Increasing employment was, and still is, one of the objectives of labor market policy. It is not, however, the *only* labor market objective. Today, three others also receive considerable attention among policy makers and analysts.

One additional objective is higher labor market earnings for those who are working. As detailed in Chapter 4, many hundreds of millions of people are working and are poor. These people mostly work very long work weeks at very low hourly wages, and therefore are low earners. Even when the earnings of all of the working members of the household are combined, together they are insufficient to enable the household to rise above the poverty line. A central objective of labor market policy is therefore to raise the earnings of those who work so that they and their families can achieve an acceptable standard of living.[7]

Another objective of labor market policy is to increase social protection. Social protection encompasses those public interventions that help individuals, households, and communities manage risk or provide support to the critically poor.[8] Some social protection programs operate through the labor market and protect against the loss of labor market earnings. As shown earlier, the United States and other rich countries have been able to provide protections for their workers, including unemployment insurance for those who lose their jobs, workers' compensation for those who are injured on the job, disability insurance for those who become unable to work, old-age pensions for those who want or need to retire, and earned income tax credits for those households whose working members do not earn enough to attain the minimal standard of living set by the country. Other social protection programs such as cash assistance, supplemental nutritional assistance, and subsidized housing address people as citizens, not as workers. The richer countries are able to supplement the incomes, housing, and food of the less fortunate among us. In addition, many countries, though sadly not mine as yet, provide health insurance for all members of society.[9]

The great majority of those who live and work in poor countries do not have developed-country social protections. They are entirely on their own or at the mercy of family members and villagers. Extending social protection to the masses is a great challenge facing the developing world.

Yet another objective of labor market policy is to assure that core labor standards are honored. In 1998, the International Labor Organization (ILO) adopted a Declaration on Fundamental Principles and Rights at Work. The declaration affirms that all ILO member states have the responsibility "to respect, to promote and to realize, in good faith and in accordance with the Constitution [of the ILO], the principles concerning the fundamental rights," which include the following:

(a) freedom of association and the effective recognition of the right to collective bargaining;

(b) the elimination of all forms of forced or compulsory labor;

(c) the effective abolition of child labor; and

(d) the elimination of discrimination in respect of employment and occupation. [10]

In 1999, the ILO set as a goal "Decent Work for All" which incorporates the declaration but goes beyond it. The aim of Decent Work is not just to create jobs but to create jobs of acceptable quality. The Decent Work agenda is pursued through four strategic objectives:

(a) full employment,
(b) improved levels of socio-economic security,
(c) universal respect for fundamental principles and rights at work, and
(d) the strengthening of social dialogue. [11]

The director-general of the ILO reports regularly on the decent work deficit. According to the ILO, among the elements of this deficit are that half the world's workers are unable to lift themselves and their families up to the US$2 per person per day poverty line, the continuation of a gender gap in much of the world, unemployment in general and among youth in particular, rising international labor migration, and the failure of global economic growth to produce poverty-reducing jobs.[12] (I would have said that there has not been enough economic growth to result in a sufficient number of poverty-reducing jobs, but I did not write the report.)

Today then, labor market policy makers around the world recognize the importance of employment for poverty reduction and aim to improve labor market well-being for the poor. There is considerable agreement, though not universal consensus, that each of the four factors discussed is important and therefore that labor market well-being depends upon the following:

1. The number of jobs, including wage and salaried employment as well as self-employment
2. How much workers earn in those jobs
3. The amount of social protection provided
4. The honoring of core labor standards

ULTIMATE OBJECTIVES OR INTERMEDIATE ONES?

Some organizations have a single overarching objective. For a typical company, it is to "be as profitable as we can be." For an atypical company, such as the social entrepreneurship organizations Ashoka and Acumen Fund or social businesses like Grameen Danone, it is to use entrepreneurial approaches to solve the problems of global poverty. For a sports team, it is to "win the championship." For the development banks, it is to achieve "a world free of poverty."

In cases such as these, the single objective is the ultimate objective, taking precedence over all others. The other objectives are intermediate objectives, serving as inputs to the ultimate goal.

Here are some examples of the distinction between ultimate and intermediate objectives. For a company, increasing market share may be an intermediate objective; maximizing profits (or in the case of publicly held companies, maximizing shareholder value) is the ultimate objective. For a sports team, having happy players may be an intermediate objective; winning the championship is the ultimate objective. For a development bank, accelerating economic growth is an intermediate objective; achieving a world free of poverty is the ultimate objective.

Some organizations are unclear about what their ultimate objective is or, if they have more than one, what their ultimate objectives are. As Lewis Carroll (1865) famously wrote in *Alice in Wonderland*:

> Alice: "Would you tell me, please, which way I ought to go from here?"
> "That depends a good deal on where you want to get to," said the Cat.
> "I don't much care where," said Alice.
> "Then it doesn't matter which way you go," said the Cat.

Why organizations do not state clearly what they are trying to achieve, I do not know—I just know that many organizations are not at all clear and that this confusion makes it difficult for the people working in such organizations to know what to do.

As I told you a few pages ago, I myself did not always focus on ultimate development objectives. However, now that I do, let me be explicit with you about what I am seeking.[13] My bottom-line objective for developing countries is to reduce poverty to the maximum possible extent. The means that I focus on are policies in and bearing on the labor market.

What then about the labor market objectives discussed in the last section: the number of jobs, how much workers earn in those jobs, the amount of social protection provided, and the honoring of core labor standards? What about the four pillars of the ILO's "Decent Work for All" agenda: full employment, improved levels of socioeconomic security, universal respect for fundamental principles and rights at work, and the strengthening of social dialogue? For me, each is important as an intermediate objective toward achieving the end that I have declared: minimizing absolute poverty. There is only one circumstance under which I am willing to forgo the maximum possible poverty reduction: when poverty reduction is achieved by violating a profoundly held value. Put differently, in certain extreme cases, I would rather not have people working at all than working in outrageous jobs—for example, the worst forms of child labor. Where to draw the line is, of course, an intensely personal matter; I urge you to think about it carefully for yourself and reach your own conclusions.

Another deeply personal matter is how much weight to give to relative inequality. I know there are those who give much more weight to inequality than I do. Some of these people have carefully considered the role of inequality vis-à-vis poverty in social welfare judgments, and I respect the difference of carefully considered views. Others, though, give inequality as much attention as they do because they know that they want to pay attention to distributional issues; they see that others have looked at measures of inequality such as Gini coefficients and 90:10 ratios, and so they do too. If you fall into this category, you might want to give this matter some additional thought.[14]

To the extent possible, governments and the development organizations that work with them would want to have more of *all* of their ultimate objectives. Occasionally, there are actions that permit more than one objective to be enhanced at the same time without any objective being sacrificed. For a time, the government of Singapore deliberately repressed wages in the mistaken belief that such a policy would improve the country's international competitiveness and contribute to its economic growth. It was only after businesses pressured the government to allow them to pay higher wages that the wage repression policy was relaxed. Happily for the state of labor market conditions and economic growth in Singapore, the removal of the wage repression policy led to higher employment and to higher earnings for those employed as well as a return to high economic growth.[15]

More often, policy actions that are helpful to one objective come at the expense of another. In these (normal) cases, policy trade-offs need to be addressed explicitly. The next section suggests how to do this.

CHOOSING AMONG OBJECTIVES: TRADE-OFFS ON THE POLICY SIDE

Higher employment and lower unemployment are presumed to be good for economic development in general and poverty reduction in particular. The problem is that some of the means for reducing unemployment are arguably bad for development. Based on statistical studies all over the world, economists have very good reason to believe that in the great majority of circumstances employment could be increased if wages or other types of compensation were to be lowered. This has led some analysts to make the following argument:

* We aim to lower unemployment.
* Reduced wages or other types of compensation would lower unemployment.
* Therefore, wages or other types of compensation should be reduced.

The problem with this line of argument is that although lower unemployment is arguably *one* factor in development, it is not the *only* factor that matters. How much people earn when they are employed is assuredly another important factor. A policy of reducing wages or other types of compensation hurts this aspect of development. Such a policy helps achieve one objective but it does so at the expense of another.

Consider an alternate policy: that of *increasing* wages, for example, by raising minimum wages. Such a policy follows from a different argument:

• We aim to increase the amount that poor workers earn.
• An increased minimum wage would raise the amount that the working poor earn.
• Therefore, minimum wages should be increased.

This second argument is also problematic—this time, for even more reasons. One problem is that, as in the first argument, an increased minimum wage is likely to reduce employment, causing fewer people to be working. A second problem is that some low earners belong to households that are not poor, and therefore an increased minimum wage is not necessarily well targeted to the poor as opposed to low earners.[16] And a third problem is that we do not know that an increased minimum wage would raise the amount earned by all workers *taken together.* What we do know is that an increased minimum wage would raise the amount earned *by each worker who keeps his or her job.*

Consider, then, a third argument:

• We aim to increase the amount that each employed poor worker earns.
• An increased minimum wage would raise the amount earned by each of the working poor who keep their jobs as the minimum wage is increased.
• Therefore, minimum wages should be increased.

This third argument is problematic as well. In my view, it is ethically indefensible to be concerned only about those who remain employed while not also being concerned about those who become unemployed or who do not get jobs as the result of the policy under consideration.

Comparing these different arguments, you probably already noticed that they lead to diametrically opposed policy conclusions: the first calls for minimum wages to be *lowered* and the second and third for minimum wages to be *raised*. This policy disagreement arises because the first argument is based on one express aim: to lower unemployment; the second and third arguments are based on another: to increase the earnings of poor workers.

The preceding arguments are flawed, and so too are the conclusions derived from them. Invalid arguments do not produce valid policy implications. The correct conclusion, I submit, is that neither lowering the minimum wage nor raising it is obviously the right thing to do. The ambiguity is reflected in the following:

- We aim to (1) lower unemployment and (2) increase the amount that each employed poor worker earns.
- A lower minimum wage would likely reduce unemployment.
- A higher minimum wage would raise the amount earned by each of the working poor who keep their jobs as the minimum wage is increased, but fewer people would have jobs.
- Therefore, whether the minimum wage should be raised or lowered depends on the balance between the employment objective on the one hand and the desire for higher earnings for those employed on the other.

Now we have a full-fledged policy dilemma because we have two policy objectives—lowering unemployment and increasing the amount that each employed poor worker earns—and these call for opposing policies. An analyst or policy maker who recognizes both objectives but who is unable or unwilling to weigh the objectives cannot reach a policy conclusion about whether the minimum wage should be raised or lowered. Actually, this ambiguity is a good thing: worse than saying "I cannot say, because there are offsetting effects, and here is what they are" is to say "here is the answer" when no unambiguous conclusion can be reached. Such pseudo-policy conclusions are irresponsible, even dangerous, and should be avoided.

If poverty reduction is the ulitimate goal, the only way out of this dilemma is to weigh the trade-offs among the labor market objectives in terms of their ultimate effects on poverty. When there are multiple factors like this, policy making is not easy. Advancing one of these objectives may come at the cost of harming another. The analyst needs to work out how a given policy intervention affects each factor and try to assess the gains and the losses. It is difficult, but it is nonetheless worth trying: whenever faulty arguments like those presented above can be avoided, better policy conclusions are more likely to result.[17]

CHOOSING AMONG OBJECTIVES: TRADE-OFFS ON THE BUDGETARY SIDE

Every day, thousands of decisions have to be made about how to allocate scarce development resources among the many alternative uses to which they might be put. Earlier in this chapter, we examined trade-offs that might be made in terms of alternative objectives: whether to seek increased employment, higher earnings for those employed, or something else. This section concentrates on a different trade-off: how to allocate a given budget among two or more alternative uses in order to achieve *one single objective*—for example, higher earnings for those employed.

Here are two different arguments that are often made. First:

- We want to help the poor.
- The poor work mainly on family farms and in family businesses.
- Therefore, we should invest our development resources in improving incomes where the poor are, on family farms and in family businesses.

Alternatively,

- We want to help the poor.
- The poor will remain poor as long as they remain in poor sectors.
- Family farms and family businesses pay poorly relative to wage employment, particularly when the wage employment is in enterprises registered with the government
- Therefore, we should invest our development resources in creating new wage employment in registered enterprises so that the poor can move to the parts of the economy where earnings are higher.

These last two arguments lead to precisely opposite conclusions. According to the first, the available resources should be used on family farms and family businesses. According to the second, the available resources should be used to create new wage employment in registered enterprises so that the poor can get *out* of family farms and family businesses. What should be done? Just the first? Just the second? Some of each?

The simple answer is that *none* of these is *necessarily* the right thing to do. Raising self-employment incomes would contribute to reducing poverty. So too would creating additional wage employment at relatively high rates of pay. What neither of the preceding arguments recognizes, but what needs to be considered, is that to use more of the available resources for one purpose is to have *less* available for the other purpose. Economists use the term "opportunity cost" to recognize budgetary trade-offs—in this case, the cost of using resources to create jobs is to *not* have those resources available for raising earnings within jobs.

Opportunity costs need to be considered. The next section suggests how.

USING SOCIAL BENEFIT-COST ANALYSIS IN FORMULATING POLICY

I hear repeatedly from policy makers, public intellectuals, and the poor themselves that the poor want regular jobs providing steady pay. I have no doubts that more regular jobs are extremely important, which is why we will spend an entire chapter (Chapter 9) discussing policies that have been put into effect to create more of them. And I also hear repeatedly that most of the poor work in their own microenterprises because nothing better is available. As James Surowiecki, the *New Yorker*'s economics columnist, has written, "Just fourteen per cent of Americans, for instance, are running (or trying to run) their own business. That percentage is much higher in developing countries—in Peru, it's almost forty per cent. That's not because Peruvians are more entrepreneurial. It's because they don't have other options. What poor countries need most, then, is not more microbusinesses. . . . To be sure, for some people the best route out of poverty will be a bank loan. But for most it's going to be something much simpler: a regular paycheck."[18]

It is much more expensive to create a steady, regular paid job than it is to make a microloan to a microenterprise owner. Given the difference in costs, it is by no means clear that those who agree with Surowiecki have necessarily reached the right conclusion (which does not imply that they have reached the wrong conclusion either).

One good way of deciding on policy priorities is to think in terms of social benefits and social costs. The easier question is to decide whether to do one single thing or not do it. In this case, we can ask three related questions:

1. What are the extra social benefits if the activity is undertaken?
2. What are the extra social costs of the activity?
3. How do the extra social benefits and extra social costs compare?

When more than one option is possible, similar questions can be asked:

1'. What are the extra social benefits from each possible use of a development budget?
2'. What are the extra social costs from each possible use?
3'. For each possible use, how do the extra social benefits and extra social costs compare?
4'. For which activity is the difference between benefits and costs the greatest?

Here is an example of how the government of a developing country answered these questions.

Planners in the Gambia, a small West African country, had decided that they wanted to improve labor market outcomes by expanding the country's educational system. I was sent by the World Bank as a one-person mission to work with the government on setting priorities for an education sector loan. At the beginning of my mission, I asked the minister of education what was the most important educational need. Without hesitation, she answered that it was to build more secondary technical schools. I set out to see for myself.

What I found was appalling, yet typical of low-income countries. Elementary schools in the Gambia, I learned, existed for only 56% of school-age children. Some schools were just a teacher and students getting together under a tree (Figure 6.1). Looking at the children who were fortunate enough to have found spaces in the schools, I saw classrooms full of mismatched chairs and desks, most of which, I learned, had been made at home and brought to school, because the schools could not afford to buy furniture . Many of the children sat quietly while others worked. I discovered that the reason many students were just sitting is that they had no workbooks, pens, or paper to work with. I saw that many of the school buildings were made of corrugated iron (Figure 6.2), which made them like ovens in the equator sun. The technical schools had virtually no equipment. The metal shops were without metal and the wood shops without wood, so the students were taught

Figure 6.1
School under a tree, Gambia.

Figure 6.2
Corrugated iron school, Gambia.

the theory of metalwork and woodwork. The country's one institution of higher education, the Gambia College, had classrooms, dormitories, and a library that were heavenly by comparison. Alas, the chemistry lab had glassware but no chemicals, so the students learned the theory of chemistry.

Five educational challenges had been identified by government: improving the secondary technical schools, providing teacher training and upgrading, acquiring books and other educational software, completing the incomplete schools, and adding new schools. The government gave me cost data, which I then analyzed. Returning to the minister, I said: "Madame Minister, for a given addition to your budget, you could (i) educate a certain additional number of Gambia College students or (ii) educate 2.3 times as many additional students in secondary high schools or (iii) educate 5.3 times as many additional students in secondary technical schools or (iv) educate 7.6 times as many additional students in primary schools. Alternatively, you can divide the money, using some of it for one purpose and some for another. Which allocation of resources do you think would be best for your country?" Her instant answer: "Put all of the money into expanding the primary schools."

Implicitly, the minister had weighed the extra social benefits against the extra social costs, at least in a rough and ready way, and had decided in favor of primary education over secondary technical education. Her answer also illustrates a point made earlier in this chapter that bears repeating: within a given policy area—in this case, education—some expenditures are more likely than others to contribute to the ultimate objective—in this case, minimizing poverty. It is not that the minister had stopped thinking that expanding the Gambia College or building new secondary technical schools would be worthwhile. Rather, she had decided that using additional resources to expand primary schooling would be *more* worthwhile.

FINDING OUT SPECIFICALLY WHAT WORKS

The traditional way of discerning the effects of different policy interventions has been to carry out statistical studies using methods ranging from simple comparisons to highly sophisticated econometric analyses. These studies estimate such outcomes as the average treatment effect, the average treatment effect for those treated, and the distribution of treatment effects for different individuals. Their lessons are many and valuable.[19]

Take education, for example. Many interventions are possible: decentralization, incentives, vouchers, competition, pedagogy, teacher training, textbooks, class sizes, and so on. Which of these interventions would help the most, which a little, and which not at all?

The statistical/econometric approach has identified these broad areas that make a difference in developing countries: It has proven more cost-effective to spend on elements of infrastructure, recurrent inputs, and learning materials than raising teacher salaries or reducing class sizes. Increasing school quality has more of a development payoff than getting more students into poor quality schools. School quality is increased more by higher-quality teachers than by reduced class sizes. Putting more money into schools and hoping that it will be put to good use has not proven effective. But little is known about which policies will raise teacher quality.[20]

A newer approach is gaining wide circulation, most visibly at the Abdul Latif Jameel Poverty Action Lab at MIT (J-PAL), Innovations for Poverty Action (IPA), and ideas42. These organizations maintain that although we know the general areas in which development interventions are needed—education, health, and so on—there are relatively few areas where rigorous testing has shown specifically what works and what doesn't. Their mission is to add to the knowledge base.[21]

Two methods involving experiments are particularly promising for providing the answers: natural experiments and randomized experiments. In a natural experiment, some event affects particular individuals differently from others—in one example, it is that those individuals born just before a particular date got an extra year of schooling compared to those born just after. On the other hand, in a randomized experiment, interventions are applied to a randomly chosen experimental group and not applied to a randomly chosen control group. If the sample sizes are large enough, the differences in outcomes between the two groups cannot be attributed to prior differences in the groups but rather to the differences between the two groups because of the intervention itself.

Continuing with education, here are some of the lessons from these experiments:

- Teacher absenteeism is endemic in India. It is common for salaried teachers to simply not show up at school, often for days, weeks, or even months at a time. Working in conjunction with Seva Mandir, a non-governmental organization (NGO) in Udaipur district in India, 120 single-teacher schools were selected to participate in a teacher monitoring program. Half of these schools were chosen randomly as treatment schools, the other half as control schools. In the treatment schools, the teacher was given a camera with a tamper-proof date and time function and told to take a picture of himself or herself and the students at the beginning and end of each school day. Teachers were paid based on the number of days they actually came to school. The evaluation results showed that the absence rate in the treatment schools (22%) was half of that in the control schools (42%), which the researchers attributed to photographic monitoring.[22]

- In Kenya, educators found that schools that used flip charts had better student outcomes than those that did not. Did the use of flip charts cause higher student outcomes or were the districts that could afford flip charts also the ones that could afford other inputs that would raise student performance? Researchers conducted a randomized experiment in 178 schools, putting flip charts into a randomly selected half and not putting flip charts in the other half. The result was that using flip charts made no difference at all at that time in that place.[23]

- In many countries, although school is nominally free, students are expected to attend school in uniforms, which are costly relative to students' family incomes. In Kenya, students were randomly selected to receive free uniforms costing $6 each, a substantial benefit for students in a country with a per capita income of $340. Research showed that those who received the free uniforms were 6% more likely to attend school on any given day, 13% less likely to drop out of school, and (in the case of teenage girls) 10% less likely to bear children while they were school-age. The research also showed that what mattered for school attendance was receiving a first school uniform but not an additional one.[24]

- Smaller class size is often advocated as a way of improving student performance. In Israel, the government follows an ancient principle known as Maimonides' rule: no more than forty students in a class. When a class size exceeds forty, the class is automatically broken into two smaller classes. Analysts there found higher student performance on standardized tests in the classes that had been divided into two than in the larger ones.[25] Similarly, in South Africa, smaller class sizes have been found to have strong positive effects on school enrollment, educational achievement, and test scores for numeracy.[26]

- Does education raise earnings? In the United States, the age for ending mandatory school attendance is sixteen. A study was done comparing those who were born just before the cutoff for starting school with those born just after. The students born just before the cutoff had to complete one more year of schooling than those born just after the cutoff. The research findings showed that those who were forced to stay in school one year longer earned more as adults.[27]

The point of all this is that many possible interventions seem plausible, but not all of them necessarily work. Experiments such as these tell us which specific interventions make a positive difference and which do not.

I wish I could tell you that many such studies have been done to determine which specific interventions matter for developing countries' labor markets, but unfortunately that has not yet happened. Unless and until such research is conducted, developing country governments and the aid agencies that help support them must base their decisions on other evidence, or failing that, on educated judgments.[28]

Let this *not* be taken as a call to inaction. I would conclude by quoting one of the pioneers of the randomized experiment movement, Esther Duflo, who was talking about fighting HIV/AIDS but equally well could have been talking about raising labor market earnings: "We need to spend money . . . not because we pretend to know what works, just because it seems the problem is so serious we have to try." [29]

IN SUMMARY

Here then is how I suggest formulating policy decisions to help the poor earn their way out of poverty:

First, policy makers have identified four key labor market policy objectives: create more jobs, raise the earnings of those working, increase social protection, and assure that core labor standards are honored. Policy makers need to keep all four in mind and not go after just one heedless of the other three.

Second, while each of these four objectives is important in its own right, the overriding objective in my view is reducing poverty to the maximum extent possible.

Third, policies aimed at helping advance one labor market policy objective may be harmful to another—for example, higher earnings and improved protections for those employed may conflict with generating more wage and salaried employment. Trade-offs on the policy side need to be faced explicitly.

Fourth, resources always have alternative uses. To use resources to achieve one labor market policy objective is not to have them available to achieve another. Trade-offs on the budgetary side also need to be faced explicitly.

Fifth, a good way to bring all these considerations together is to ask about the size of the extra social benefits, the size of the extra social costs, and how they compare for one or more uses of a development budget. Though it will often be impossible to answer these questions fully, it is better to answer the right questions approximately than to answer the wrong questions precisely.

And sixth, when the right questions are asked but the answers are not known, it would be good to carry out in-depth research to find the answers. Statistical/econometric studies and experiments both have an important place in showing what matters.

CHAPTER 7

Growth, Trade, and Aid

In Colombia, Luz Dari García waters flowers in a greenhouse operated by Uniflor, a flower exporter in Medellín. Ms. García earns Colombia's minimum wage of $250 per month, by no means a generous income, but far more than she and her family could earn raising fruits and vegetables in their village. What enabled Ms. García to earn her way out of poverty by obtaining such a job? As we saw in Chapter 5, her job arose because Uniflor figured out how to take advantage of the opportunities in today's globalized economy to penetrate the North American flower market, outcompeting growers in California and Texas.[1]

How typical is Ms. García's experience? This chapter presents evidence that stories like Ms. García's have been repeated hundreds of millions of times around the world. The proportion of the world's people living in poverty has fallen sharply. But as we will also see, because of population growth, we now have more poor people in the world than we did twenty-five years earlier. Much progress has been made, but even more remains to be done.

ECONOMIC GROWTH AND POVERTY REDUCTION

Earlier, we saw the results of the most recent global poverty calculations by the World Bank's Shaohua Chen and Martin Ravallion. When poverty is defined as living on less than US$2.50 per person per day in purchasing power parity units, 3.1 billion of the world's 6.5 billion people were in poverty in 2005. In that same year, the number in extreme poverty, defined as living on less than $1.25 per person per day, was 1.4 billion people.

In the 1981–2005 period analyzed by Chen and Ravallion, the world population grew by some 2 billion people, from 4.5 billion to 6.5 billion.

What has happened to global poverty during this quarter-century? Combining the Chen-Ravallion poverty estimates with world population data, we find six important changes.[2]

First, the number of extremely poor people in the world (defined as those living on less than $1.25 a day) *fell* by 600 million people. I calculate that if the rate of extreme poverty in the world had remained the same, the number of extremely poor people in the world would have *risen* by 800 million people.

Second, in percentage terms, the share of the world's people in extreme poverty *fell in half* from 41.9% to 21.4%.

Third, the number of poor people (those living on less than $2.50 dollars a day) *rose by 350 million*. Had the rate of poverty in the world remained the same, the number of poor people in the world would have risen by *700 million* people.

Fourth, in percentage terms, the share of the world's people living in poverty *fell* from 60.3% to 47.7%.

Fifth, the number of people in the world living above the extreme poverty line ($1.25 a day) *increased* by *1.5 billion* (i.e., 1,500 million). Had the rate of extreme poverty in the world remained the same, the number of *nonpoor* people in the world would have increased by just *800 million*.

And sixth, the number of nonpoor people in the world (those living on more than $2.50 a day) *increased* by *1.8 billion*. Had the rate of poverty in the world remained the same, the number of nonpoor people in the world would have increased by just *600 million* people.

Why were these reductions in world poverty achieved? The simple answer is that the world economy achieved sustained economic growth. In the 1981–2005 period, the world economy doubled in real terms (i.e., after adjusting for inflation), and China's increased nearly tenfold.[3]

In short, economic growth substantially outpaced population growth, and poor people participated in that economic growth. World poverty fell as a result.

Progress has been made in a great many of the world's countries, but sadly by no means all. The most striking success case is China, which not only is the world's largest country in terms of population but also has experienced the most rapid and sustained economic growth of any country in the world. In the 1981–2005 period, the percentage of Chinese living on less than $1.25 fell from 84.0% to 15.9%, while the percentage living on less than $2.50 per day fell from 99.4% to 49.5%.[4] Wang, the Chinese farmer whom we met in Chapter 3, and his family are among those who have earned their way out of poverty during this time.

The Chinese economy is one of the world's leading successes in terms of economic growth. Other countries whose economies have achieved sustained high economic growth over a period of at least thirty years include Botswana, Brazil, Hong Kong, Indonesia, Japan, South Korea, Malaysia, Malta, Oman, Singapore, Taiwan, and Thailand. India, the world's other most populous country after China, is excluded from this list because its economic growth rate has been high only for the last twenty years.[5]

Yet, as Paul Collier tells us, the world's poorest billion people are concentrated in fifty-eight countries, mostly in sub-Saharan Africa. Taken together, the economies of sub-Saharan Africa are so small that their total economic activity is of the same magnitude as Belgium's. Scattered countries in other regions make up the balance of the poorest billion including Haiti, Bolivia, Laos, Cambodia, Yemen, Burma, and North Korea. Writes Collier, "The problem of the bottom billion has not been that they have had the wrong *type* of growth, it is that they have not had *any* growth." At best, their economies have stagnated, and at worst they have declined. [6]

Analysts have advanced different theories about how economic growth would affect poverty. The more positive view is that economic growth enables countries to supply more publicly provided services, afford to create new social programs, fund existing programs more generously, and tighten labor markets so that employers compete more vigorously for workers, raising workers' earnings in the process. The more negative view is that economic growth enables the concentration of economic and political power so that those who start in advantaged positions are able to enrich themselves and others around them while leaving the poor out or even making their situation worse.

The evidence leads to two clear conclusions about the effect of economic growth on poverty in the developing world.[7] First, when economic growth has taken place, poverty has nearly always fallen. And second, when poverty has not fallen, it usually is because economic growth has not taken place (and, sadly, what has taken place is economic decline). Because the majority of developing countries have experienced economic growth, poverty rates have fallen in most of the developing countries for which we have data.

Taken together, these results show that in the world as a whole and in a majority of the countries of the world, economic growth has indeed taken place and poverty has indeed fallen. I conclude that economic growth is central to the quest for reducing poverty.

Notwithstanding the progress that has been made, the picture is far from uniformly positive. First, despite this progress, nearly half the world's population is still poor. Second, a considerable number of countries, especially in Africa, did *not* experience economic growth, and poverty did not fall in most of the nongrowing countries. And third, these aggregate statistics do not trace specific individuals and households. It is estimated that many hundreds of millions of individuals who started in poverty moved up and out of poverty, but at the same time a smaller number who initially were not poor fell into poverty.[8] Thus, both at the world level and at the levels of individual countries, a huge amount remains to be done.

THE LABOR MARKET AS A CRUCIAL LINK BETWEEN ECONOMIC GROWTH AND POVERTY REDUCTION

We know that economic growth is key to confronting the challenge of reducing poverty. What we will see in this section is that the labor market provides one of the crucial links between economic growth and poverty reduction. (Enhanced government-provided goods and services is the other.)

What matters to assure that economic growth actually leads to reductions in poverty is not only the *rate* of economic growth but also the *type* of economic growth. For workers to benefit from growth, labor market channels must be kept open. Specifically, the labor market may transmit economic growth and reduce poverty via a five-step path. First, people work in miserable conditions because working in such conditions is better than not working at all. Second, their conditions of work—in particular, their labor market earnings—will be improved if the competition for their labor is increased. Third, the competition for their labor will be increased if employers want to hire more workers. Fourth, employers will want to hire more workers if product market conditions improve. And fifth, what will help product market conditions improve is economic growth, often led by exports.

International comparisons show that in countries with the most rapid growth, labor market conditions have tended to improve the fastest:[9]

- *Developing countries that have achieved the highest rates of economic growth are the ones that have achieved the highest rates of real wage growth.* Three pieces of evidence support this point. First, a comparison across twenty-two low- and middle-income countries shows a strikingly high correlation between the rate of economic growth and the rate of increase in real (that is, inflation-adjusted) earnings in agriculture and manufacturing. Second, in the developing world, the region with the most rapid and sustained economic growth has been East Asia. There, the manufacturing sector was the engine of growth. Looking specifically at manufacturing wages, over a twenty-year period, real wages rose 170% in East Asia as manufacturing employment increased fourfold. Manufacturing workers in other regions did much less well: real wages rose by only 70% over the same twenty years in South Asia, by just 12% in Latin America, and not at all in sub-Saharan Africa. And third, the regions with the highest rate of reduction in working poverty— East Asia and Southeast Asia—are the ones with the fastest economic growth; the slowest-growing regions—sub-Saharan Africa, North Africa, and the Middle East—registered the slowest reduction in working poverty.

- *Countries that have achieved rapid economic growth have also seen a growth in manufacturing and service employment (relatively high-paying sectors of the economy) and a reduction in agricultural employment (a relatively low-paying sector).* The more rapid economic growth has been, the larger has been the compositional change. In Asia, where the world's highest growth rates have been recorded, the economies that grew most rapidly— those of China, Taiwan, South Korea, Malaysia, and Indonesia—all experienced marked reductions in agricultural employment and marked increases in manufacturing and services employment as percentages of the total. For example, in South Korea, over thirty-six years of high growth, agriculture's share of total employment fell from 64% to 11% while services' share rose from 28% to 69% and manufacturing's share rose from 8% to 20%. In Bangladesh, India, and Pakistan, which experienced slower growth rates over this period, the changes in the composition of employment, though in the same direction, were much smaller in magnitude. The patterns are similar in Africa and in Latin America.[10]

- *Real wages tend to rise faster when exports grow.* The positive association between export growth and wage growth appears clearly in a comparison of forty-nine countries. However, the link with wage growth is not as tight for export growth as it is for national income growth. Further examination shows that the countries that grew rapidly and made the most progress in terms of wages and employment are the ones that were export-oriented. The leading countries were China, South Korea, Thailand, Indonesia, and Malaysia. On the other side, the big losers were Jordan, Ghana, and Nigeria.

The inescapable conclusion is that workers benefited most when rapid, export-oriented economic growth occurred.

For a smaller number of countries, economic growth has been linked both to changes in the labor market and to the rate of poverty reduction. A comparison of Taiwan and Brazil reveals a pronounced contrast.[11]

Taiwan has been one of the world's fastest growing economies and also one of the world's most export-oriented ones. Over thirty years, its real national income per capita increased sevenfold. In just fifteen years, Taiwan was able to reduce its poverty rate by 75%. What happened in the labor market to bring about the sharp reduction in poverty was that the unemployment rate never rose above 3%, workers moved from lower-paying to higher-paying sectors and occupations, and real earnings increased in parallel for all labor force groups (men and women; trade, manufacturing, and service workers; public and private sector employees; public sector and private sector employees).

In contrast, Brazil's economy grew by just 25% in per capita terms in the last quarter of the twentieth century—just 1% per year—in part because of the inward-looking policies pursued by the economic management team. Because of the very slow growth in Brazil, the poverty rate did not fall. Alas, the labor market exhibited only small changes as well: unemployment crept up, the composition of employment improved somewhat, but real earnings barely moved.

Comparing Taiwan and Brazil, Taiwan's labor market transmitted the rapid, export-led growth that took place in that economy into an impressive reduction in poverty. In Brazil, as in Taiwan, the labor market was also the intermediary between macroeconomic growth and poverty reduction; but unlike Taiwan, Brazil's poor growth performance was linked to a poor poverty performance by a poor labor market performance.

From the point of view of creating a growth process that involved the poor, it helped that Taiwan started with one of the world's most equal distributions of income; it did not help that Brazil had and still does have one of the world's most unequal income distributions. But what also helped working people in Taiwan is that economic growth and exports were much higher there than in Brazil.

Another place where economic growth has been accompanied by rising real labor earnings is India. There, from 1983 to 1993–94 and again from 1993–94 to 2004–05, average daily earnings in real (i.e., inflation-adjusted) rupees increased for all sixteen population segments tabulated (rural males in regular employment in agriculture, urban females in casual employment in nonagriculture, and so on).[12] The main factor responsible for higher earnings in agriculture was the increased demand for rural labor both in agriculture and in off-farm employment and the consequent rise in agricultural earnings.[13] These movements are attributed to new opportunities and not to distress migration.[14]

The country studies in the World Bank's *Making Work Pay* series present a mixed picture. In Bangladesh, economic growth, improved labor market conditions, and falling poverty went hand in hand. In Nicaragua, despite economic growth, poverty fell only modestly. In Madagascar, though, despite the absence of economic growth, real earnings rose at the bottom and the middle of the earnings distribution, causing poverty to fall.[15]

Can economic growth *not* reduce poverty and improve labor market conditions for low earners? Sadly, the case of the United States in the thirty-five years up to the Great Recession is instructive. Real national income grew by 113% between 1973 and 2008. Yet, the typical worker is earning only about 10% more in real terms than was the case earlier. As for the poverty rate, it had been below 12% of the population throughout the 1970s, but it exceeded 13% in 2008. The poverty rate reached 15.1% in 2010.

Another case where economic growth did *not* reduce poverty and improve labor market conditions is the Philippines.[16] Transparency International estimates that Ferdinand Marcos embezzled between five and ten *billion* dollars during his fourteen-year presidency. Yet, Marcos is only number two on the list of embezzling leaders. The dubious distinction of being number one belongs to Indonesia's former President Suharto, who in thirty-two years as president is estimated to have embezzled somewhere between fifteen and thirty-five *billion* dollars.[17]

The experience of the United States and a handful of other countries should convince us that economic growth does not reduce poverty in every single case.[18] Fortunately, though, these few countries are exceptions to the general rule that with economic growth comes lower poverty.

Finally, what happens when economic growth goes into reverse? As we all know, the world economy entered a serious economic recession in 2008. According to the latest data available at the time of this writing, the world economy contracted by 1.1% in 2009. Economic growth rates were negative in three regions of the world: non-European Union (EU) Europe and the Commonwealth of Independent States (CIS) countries (–6.5%), the developed economies and the European Union (–3.5%), and Latin America and the Caribbean (–2.5%). But other regions had positive growth, ranging from 0.5% in Southeast Asia and the Pacific up to 6.1% in East Asia. Negative world economic growth would be expected to have hurt labor market outcomes, and indeed according to one labor market indicator, it did: the International Labor Organization (ILO) reports that the world unemployment rate increased by 0.8 percentage points for women and 0.7 percentage points for men. Note how much smaller these percentage changes in the world are than in the United States and Europe: the U.S. unemployment rate jumped from 5.8% in 2008, to 10.0% in December 2009, while in the Euro area, the jump was from 8.2% in December 2008 to 9.9% in November 2009. In short, those regions with the most negative economic growth had the greatest increases in unemployment.[19]

From a labor market point of view in addition to many other reasons, economic growth needs to get moving again. The next section discusses some of the main messages on this topic.

STIMULATING ECONOMIC GROWTH

The lessons of what helps economic growth and what hurts it have been summed up recently by a blue-ribbon Commission on Growth and Development, chaired by Nobel Prize–winning economist Michael Spence.[20] The Growth Commission reports that thirteen developing economies have achieved sustained and rapid economic growth over three or four decades. These thirteen—Botswana, Brazil, China, Hong Kong, Indonesia, Japan, South Korea, Malaysia, Malta, Oman, Singapore, Taiwan, and Thailand— have a number of features in common:

- *The rapidly growing economies made the most of opportunities in the world economy.*

For them, the global market was seen as more than an opportunity; it was regarded as essential to success. For example, in the case of transistor radios, the Sony Corporation of Japan became the world leader by licensing RCA's technology and then exporting radios in large quantity to the United States, the home of RCA. As the Growth Commission described the approach taken by the rapidly-growing economies, "They imported what the rest of the world knew and exported what it wanted."

- *The rapidly growing economies maintained macroeconomic stability.*

Economic volatility and unpredictability deter private sector investment and hence growth. Steady inflation is not necessarily problematic; but when inflation is volatile, periods of high inflation are often followed by policies aimed at slowing growth in order to bring inflation down. Fiscal responsibility was also a big plus.

- *The rapidly growing economies achieved high rates of savings and investment.*

In the 1970s, Southeast Asia and Latin America saved at the same rate. Twenty years later, Southeast Asia's savings rate was twenty percentage points higher. Higher savings translate into higher investment and in turn into a higher growth rate of productive capital and faster growth of national income.

- *The rapidly growing economies relied on markets to allocate resources but also intervened to affect what people brought to markets.*

A functioning market system provides price signals that indicate to current and potential producers which goods and services are in demand and therefore which ones to provide. It also decentralizes decision making, so that businesses of all sizes can seek economic advantage. In all of the economies that achieved sustained high economic growth, property rights were secure enough that firms and entrepreneurs felt they had a strong claim on their resources, and therefore it paid to invest heavily in them. Resources were mobile enough that capital and labor could move rapidly between sectors, industries, and even geographic locations.

But at the same time, the high-growth economies did not just simply leave it to markets to determine what people brought to them. Among the important areas of intervention were infrastructure, education, health, and social safety nets. When good roads and utility grids are in place, when young adults enter the labor market with solid educations and mature workers can be retrained, when people are generally healthy and well-nourished, and when those who take risks or are dislocated have social protection programs on which to fall back, economic growth can take off. As the Growth Commission states, "Government is not the proximate cause of growth. That role falls to the private sector, to investment and entrepreneurship responding to price signals and market forces. But stable, honest, and effective government is critical in the long run. The remit of the government, for example, includes maintaining price stability and fiscal responsibility, both of which influence the risks and returns faced by private investors." (Commission on Growth and Development, 2008, pp. 4—5).

- *The rapidly growing economies had committed, credible, and capable governments.*

For the last four decades, the government of Singapore has been committed to economic growth. In exchange for the government delivering on its promise, the people of Singapore have returned the same political party to office over and over. The people of Singapore believe that they and their children will benefit from the policy measures taken. Singapore's government has been exceptionally honest and devoted to social improvements; its record differs in degree from those of other high-growth economies.

On the other hand, many well-intentioned policies have proven harmful for economic growth. Among the "bad ideas" identified by the Growth Commission are these:

- Subsidizing energy in a general manner, not a targeted one.
- Relying on the civil service as an employer of last resort (as opposed to rural employment schemes, which serve as a safety net).
- Reducing fiscal deficits by cutting expenditure on investments that yield large social returns in the long run.
- Providing specific sectors, industries, firms, or jobs with open-ended protection.
- Fighting inflation through price controls.
- Banning exports to try to keep domestic prices low.
- Resisting urbanization and consequently underinvesting in urban infrastructure.
- Dismissing environmental issues as unaffordable.
- Measuring educational progress by school construction or enrollments rather than by extent of learning and quality of education.
- Paying civil servants less than they could earn elsewhere in the labor market.
- Regulating the banking sector poorly.
- Allowing premature increases in the exchange rate.

The Growth Commission's report was published in April 2008. The global financial crisis followed a few months later. The Growth Commission then reconvened and issued a new report in September 2009 asking what should be done in light of the changed circumstances. The main conclusions were that the characteristics of "economic miracles" cited in their earlier report continue to hold, that an outward-oriented strategy remains feasible and worth pursuing, that financial systems need to be changed in light of some of the failures that came to light in the financial crisis, and that the need remains for people to be protected through improved safety nets. The Commission also came up with an additional list of bad ideas:

- Assume that we will return to a pre-crisis pattern of growth, capital costs, trade, and capital flows.
- Micromanage the financial sector.
- Abandon the outward-looking, market-driven growth strategy because of financial failures in the advanced countries.
- Allow medium-term worries about the public debt to inhibit a short-term fiscal response to the crisis.
- Adopt counter-cyclical fiscal policies without concern for the returns on public spending, and without a plan to restore the public finances to a sustainable path over time.
- Ignore the need for more equitable distribution of gains and losses.
- Continue with energy subsidies.
- Treat the financial industry like any other, ignoring its external effects on the rest of the economy.
- Focus monetary policy on flow variables without attention to sources of instability from the balance sheet.
- Buy assets whose risk characteristics are hard to understand.

This is a long list of things to do and not to do. Many economists exhibit humility about knowing what should be done to achieve economic growth in a particular context. Robert Solow, who won the Nobel Prize in economics for his work on economic growth, wrote, "In real life, it can be hard to move the permanent growth rate; and when it happens . . . the source is a bit mysterious even after the fact."[21]

Still, there can be no doubt that both the rate of economic growth and the type of economic growth matter for poverty reduction. The evidence presented in this chapter has shown that as long as policy makers keep their eyes on the goal of poverty reduction via improved labor market conditions, economic growth has been and can continue to be a potent force creating new opportunities for the poor to earn their way out of poverty.

ACHIEVING FREER AND FAIRER TRADE

One of the most powerful theoretical results in economics is the principle of comparative advantage. One country may be better than another at producing many products or even all products. Nevertheless, according to the principle of comparative advantage, if the two countries trade according to what they are relatively good at, international trade will make both countries as a whole better off. These national-level gains from trade in the theoretical models are what have led many international trade experts to favor freer trade in the real world.[22]

What does the pro–free trade school of thought have to tell us about how poor workers would be affected by opening up to freer trade? The answer is, not much, for the simple reason that mainstream international trade theory does not have poor workers and rich workers, wage employees and self-employed, or workers covered by social security and workers left out. It has only workers. The results that have been derived using standard international trade theory have been developed to fit a highly stylized set of labor market conditions, not ones that hold in the real world. A task for the future is to develop an international trade theory based on more realistic labor market characterizations.[23]

In the meantime, it is best to focus our attention on empirical studies. What do the data show? One review highlighted five empirical lessons about globalization and poverty: (1) The poor in countries with an abundance of unskilled labor do not always gain from trade reform. (2) The poor are more likely to share in the gains from globalization when there are complementary policies in place. (3) Export growth and incoming foreign investment have reduced poverty. (4) Financial crises are costly to the poor. (5) Globalization produces both winners and losers among the poor.[24]

Two fears have been expressed. One is that the Great Recession of 2008 would encourage more protectionist behavior among countries. This does not seem to have happened to any serious degree so far, and I hope it does not.

The other fear is that in today's globalized world, in order to achieve outward-oriented economic growth, labor must be repressed so that wage costs remain low and exporting countries retain their competitive advantages. If this pessimistic view were correct, we would be finding that in highly open economies—that is, those that go in heavily for exporting and importing—economic growth would be accompanied by stagnating or at best slowly rising real earnings in the labor market, and therefore workers would be observed to have gained little or nothing from the growth process. But as we saw earlier in this chapter, the exact opposite happened: workers' real earnings grew the most when economic growth was high, and economic growth tended to be high when export growth was high. Nowhere has this growth-trade-poverty reduction nexus been more potent than in the most export-oriented developing economy of them all, China.

Such statistical evidence, as well as countless individual stories like those of the Lenovo workers with which this book began, has convinced me of the potential benefits of more open international trade if carefully managed. I do not say this because I am a doctrinaire free marketeer;

I most assuredly am not. Nobel Prize–winning economist Amartya Sen has said repeatedly that free markets can produce perfectly understandable outcomes which are perfectly hideous.[25] Nor do I say this because economists have shown that the country as a whole will gain; that is not the right policy criterion for me. Nor do I say this because I believe that freer trade will benefit every worker; nobody who follows the plight of the U.S. auto workers (which I, as a three-time graduate of the University of Michigan, learned to be attuned to) could possibly believe that all workers benefit from globalization and freer trade.

The reason I favor a more open international trade regime is that I see it as offering great possibilities for more of the poor to earn their way out of poverty by working in the export sectors. What first convinced me of this was a study I conducted in the 1980s of seven small open economies. The results showed the remarkable labor market gains that had been achieved in terms of employment and unemployment, earnings and poverty, in four export-oriented East Asian economies, and the much slower progress that had been made in three Caribbean economies that were less trade-oriented.[26] None of the research I have seen since then has caused me to change my position; in fact, the research results have reinforced it. One leading analyst wrote about the developing world's two greatest success cases: "China and India increased their reliance on market forces, of course, but their policies remained highly unconventional. With high levels of trade protection, lack of privatization, extensive industrial policies, and lax fiscal and financial policies through the 1990s, these two economies hardly looked like exemplars of the Washington Consensus."[27] And then there are countless stories about specific groups of workers who have benefited from exporting. One of my favorites is about many thousands of Mexican potters who switched from leaded to lead-free glazes at the urging of a government handicraft-promotion entity, Fonart, so that they could sell their wares in the United States and Europe. Their incomes have risen from less than US$1,000 per year to as much as US$40,000 as a result.[28]

But opening up to international trade cannot be done willy-nilly. For involvement in the world economy to fulfill its promise for poor people and poor countries, it must be carefully managed. Freer is not necessarily fair.[29] Many issues concern me in this regard, but I will talk here about just two.

The first is developed-country trade subsidies. I'll cite just three examples, all in the agricultural sector:

• In 1994, the United States, Canada, and Mexico signed the North American Free Trade Agreement (NAFTA). One provision of NAFTA was to open up the Mexican market to imported corn. Subsidized U.S. corn flooded the Mexican market, devastating local corn farmers.[30]

- The United States and Europe give heavy subsidies to their cotton farmers. About 25,000 U.S. cotton farmers receive a total of $4 billion in subsidies. Four billion dollars is three times the amount of U.S. aid given to all of sub-Saharan Africa. Despite a 2005 World Trade Organization ruling that U.S. cotton subsidies violate global trade rules, the subsidies persist, harming cotton farmers in developing economies around the world.[31]

- Then there are cattle subsidies. Nicholas Stern, the former chief economist at the World Bank, has often noted that each European cow is subsidized at the rate of two-and-a-half U.S. dollars a day. Even more extreme is that each Japanese cow is subsidized at the rate of seven U.S. dollars a day. Remember: some three billion people in the world live on less than two-and-a-half U.S. dollars per person per day. I would not be the first to say that it is better to be a cow in Europe or Japan than a person in Africa or South Asia, and I am sure that I will not be the last.[32]

Agricultural subsidies by the United States, Europe, and Japan total $350 billion a year—seven times the foreign aid provided by all developed countries.[33] It has been estimated that 140 million people could be lifted out of poverty if the 148 member countries of the World Trade Organization (WTO) were to end farm subsidies and lower barriers to agricultural trade.[34] Trade can hardly be called free when some governments can and do subsidize their products, others cannot and do not, and then the subsidized and unsubsidized products compete in a global marketplace. Trade needs to be made fairer.

The organization responsible for setting the rules for international trade in the world is the World Trade Organization. In 2001, the WTO launched its latest round of trade talks in Doha, Qatar—hence the commonly used name, Doha Round. In 2003, the developing countries stood up to the developed countries at the WTO talks in Cancun, Mexico, saying that unless the developed countries acted seriously to reduce agricultural subsidies and otherwise make trade fairer, they (the developing countries) would refuse to consider further reductions in tariff and nontariff barriers to the flow of goods and services into their markets. The developed countries refused to reduce their subsidies, the developing countries effectively refused to negotiate further, and trade talks are now stymied. I don't see the current situation as a happy equilibrium, and I hope that the developed countries will relent so that progress can be made.

The other trade issue I want to call your attention to is compensating the losers from freer trade, or more precisely, the failure to compensate the losers. Opening up an economy to trade necessarily entails reallocations of workers from some jobs to others. If, for workers in a given skill category, all jobs were the same, then a worker who loses his or her job in one sector could take up a comparable job in another with essentially no loss in pay. But as we all know and as the data presented in Chapter 4 documented, not all jobs are the same. The workers in good jobs who lose those jobs because of international competition may well suffer significant permanent earnings losses and other dislocation costs. As journalist and social commentator Martin Wolf put it in advocating freer trade: "It would be immoral for rich countries to deprive the poor of the world of so large an opportunity for betterment merely because they are unable to handle sensibly and justly the distribution of the internal costs of a change certain to be highly beneficial overall." [35]

It is worth mentioning that Wolf's point applies beyond the context of international trade; it applies equally to domestic disruptions in the context of Schumpeterian "creative destruction"; that is, "a process of industrial mutation that incessantly revolutionizes the economic structure from within, incessantly destroying the old one, incessantly creating a new one."[36] In the case of India, Montek Ahluwalia, the deputy chairman of the National Planning Commission, has said,

> We sometimes underestimate the extent to which our system can adjust to change. When you are making changes, it is easy to say, "Don't change this, because X or Y is going to get hurt." That is true of any system. But if the system moves to a higher growth path, many of the people whose lives are disrupted will get absorbed and eventually benefit because of that growth. The problem, really, is that this does not apply to everyone; there will be some disruptions where people will not get absorbed. In a modern society, we need to take care of such people by having a base of social security. We don't have that in India, and a lot of the nervousness about change comes from that fact. We can't tell people, "You can't make an omelet without breaking eggs" if they are among the eggs that will be broken. On the other hand, if you tell people that the economy is about to move to a higher growth path, and that will create opportunities for them, and you further combine that with some form of social security that can help them adjust to the change, you will be able to carry them with you.[37]

This is one of the reasons that Indian thinkers talk about a "leveling up" of social protection so that informal workers are included rather than a "leveling down."[38]

As a political matter, it is no longer acceptable to base trade policy on national aggregates alone, because even if the country as a whole is better off from opening up to trade, not all individuals within it are. For this reason, publications across the political spectrum including the *Wall Street Journal*, the *Economist*, and the *New York Times* and analysts of all political persuasions are now calling for policies such as expanded trade adjustment assistance and wage insurance to compensate the losers from globalization and otherwise overcome protectionism.[39]

FOREIGN AID

Foreign aid is an increasingly controversial issue these days. Its supporters say that not enough money is available for all of the worthwhile things that need doing. Its critics say that aid as currently practiced is doing much harm.

Since 1970, the nations of the world have repeatedly set as a target that the richer countries would channel 0.7% of their gross national incomes to the poorer countries in the form of foreign assistance. Jeffrey Sachs tells us that that amount of aid would be enough to eliminate extreme poverty in the world.[40] I don't know if he is right, but I do know that what the developed countries have delivered—0.19% in the case of the United States, 0.20% in the case of Japan, 0.29% in the case of Australia, 0.38% in the case of France, and 0.45% overall—falls far short of what they have promised. Even though the richest countries gave $121 billion in foreign aid in 2008, the continued shortage of funds for development binds tightly in the poorer countries.[41]

I support increased foreign aid. Done well, it can make more resources available for stimulating development endeavors in general and for improving labor market outcomes in particular. I am sure that more worthwhile things are waiting to be done in the fight against global poverty and that the benefits from the good things outweigh the costs of achieving them. More of the good kind of aid is needed.

Many aid organizations are doing fine work. To cite just one that is particularly impressive to me, the Bill and Melinda Gates Foundation not only has identified pressing development gaps but has put massive resources into efforts to remedy them. The Gates Foundation insists on measurability and scalability of results in all that it does. For example, they have promised that once an effective vaccine against malaria is developed, they will purchase millions of doses for distribution worldwide. Contrast this with the ordinary approach of giving grants to researchers in the hope that something worthwhile is discovered.

But there is also a bad kind of aid, which comes in for lots of deserved criticism. That it goes to nasty governments, which pocket a chunk of it for themselves. That it serves geopolitical interests rather than development aims. That it is tied to purchases from the donor countries. That it pushes for the wrong things. That recipient countries lack absorptive capacity. Et cetera. Et cetera. How leaky must the leaky bucket be before we decide not to use it any longer to carry water?[42]

Major criticisms of current aid efforts come from three very different directions:

Jeffrey Sachs laments not only how little goes into aid efforts but also that, as he sees it, the money is not being used on the right things to break the cycle of poverty. On the resource issue, he calls for a doubling of foreign aid. On the question of what the resources should be used for, he urges on-the-ground solutions for ending poverty by finding out what the poor themselves believe they need. In the case of a group of eight villages in the Sauri area of Kenya, the community identified five major needs: agricultural inputs; investments in basic health; investments in education; power, transport, and communication services; and safe drinking water and sanitation. Sachs urges the international donor community to think about this question: how can such interventions be expanded on a massive scale? He calls for amalgamating the aid efforts of the United Nations, the World Bank and the International Monetary Fund (IMF), and other organizations into a super-agency, to be led by the secretary general of the United Nations.[43]

William Easterly is a harsh critic of these ideas. He asks, why is it that despite the West having spent trillions of dollars on foreign aid, it has still not managed to get twelve-cent medicines to children to prevent malaria, four-dollar insecticide-treated bed nets to poor families to keep them from being bitten by disease-carrying mosquitoes, and three-dollar treatments for new mothers to prevent millions of child deaths? What is needed, says Easterly, is not planning but searching. Searching among plausible interventions for what works and what doesn't. Not a big push but a piecemeal approach. Not hubris but humility. The subtitle of Easterly's book sums up his position: "Why the West's efforts to aid the rest have done so much ill and so little good."[44]

Abhijit Banerjee and Esther Duflo, whose work we encountered in Chapter 6, have a third criticism about foreign aid: although we know the general areas in which development interventions are needed, we know few specifics about what works and what doesn't. Aid could support many possible interventions, all of which are plausible a priori. Banerjee, Duflo, and their J-PAL colleagues urge that rigorous tests of effectiveness be carried out to decide where aid should go. They write, "[t]he ladders to get out of the poverty trap exist but are not always in the right place, and people do not seem to know how to step onto them or even want to do so."[45] This is as much true of aid in the labor market area as aid in any other area.

Here is a judgment I feel confident in venturing: efforts focused directly on the poor are much more likely to contribute to poverty reduction than are general purpose interventions. Imagine a sizable amount of aid being disbursed under the banner of "helping the poor earn their way out of poverty." How different the composition of aid would look from what it does now!

Grants from aid agencies and loans from development banks are being made every day. Let them not be made in the same way as now simply because we are not sure what will work. Not to decide is to decide.

IN CONCLUSION

This chapter has made five major points about growth, trade, and aid.

First, economic growth has been a force for enormous good in the fight against global poverty.

Second, the labor market is a crucial link between economic growth and poverty reduction, transmitting aggregate gains to the poor in the form of more and better job opportunities and higher earnings levels.

Third, we have a good idea of what helps economic growth and what hurts it.

Fourth, freer trade if managed well can contribute to faster economic growth and improved employment outcomes for the world's poor.

And fifth, international aid, if increased in amount and changed in character, can make a big difference to the working lives of the poor.

We turn now to the role of the private sector.

CHAPTER 8

Harnessing the Energies of Private Companies

Now, the true engine of job creation in this country will always be America's businesses. But the government can create the conditions necessary for businesses to expand and hire more workers.
  —President Barack Obama, *State of the Union Address*, January 27, 2010

PROFIT MAXIMIZATION AND GLOBAL POVERTY

We saw in Chapter 4 that 90% of workers in the developing world are in the private sector. Their job types range from steady, regular wage employment to casual wage employment to operating microenterprises, with or without paid employees.

The private sector has the potential to be a potent force in the fight against global poverty. The International Finance Corporation, the private sector development arm of the World Bank Group, exists for this very purpose; its mission is to "promote private sector investment in developing countries, which will reduce poverty and improve people's lives." We will concentrate in this and the following chapters on private companies, household enterprises, and self-employment activities. Other types of private sector institutions—nongovernmental organizations, religious groups, clubs, and other civil society entities—also have important roles to play, but because their primary impact lies outside the labor market, they are not dealt with in this book.

Private companies make many contributions to economic development: producing essential (and not-so-essential) goods and services, paying taxes, creating "good jobs" in paid employment, producing goods and services that raise the productivity of the poor, providing training to workers, maintaining commercial links with microenterprises, making capital available to ongoing and potential new businesses, transmitting technological and organizational improvements, and many others.[1] For example, in Indonesia alone, the Dutch consumer goods company Unilever supports 300,000 full-time jobs, creates a total value of $630 million, and pays $130 million a year in taxes. Those who are concerned about the fight against global poverty will want these contributions to be as large as possible.

Yet contributing to the fight against poverty is *not* a bottom-line objective of Unilever or other private companies. Much is written about the private sector supposedly serving multiple stakeholders: owners, customers, workers, and communities. Frankly, as a way of understanding how companies behave, the multiple stakeholder approach leaves me cold. It is highly debatable what companies *should* do, and this is not an issue that needs to be taken up here.[2] As to the question of what companies *actually* do, I have already told you what I think: that the great majority of them strive most of the time for higher profits. However high profits are, I see most companies most of the time trying to raise them even higher. The way economists put this is to say that firms seek to maximize profits, specifically the present discounted value of profits.[3] Businesses are best understood as profit-maximizing institutions, not philanthropic organizations.

Profit-maximizing companies hire workers or not, pay them well or not, train them or not, employ "high road" human resource management practices or not, and make many other decisions based on the effects these decisions have on profits. Few companies do what they do primarily to help workers lead better lives. Robert Reich, a former U.S. secretary of labor, states unequivocally: "Don't believe for an instant that a company is going to sacrifice profits for the sake of social goals. . . . It's not business' business."[4] A Harvard Business School study says, "Without a clear pathway to profit, private investors are not normally motivated to meet the poor's basic needs."[5]

Thomas Friedman has written, "While covering the Arab-Israeli conflict, I learned that the way you get big change is by getting the big players to do the right thing for the wrong reasons . . . . The desire of corporations to avoid being the target of global protest in a flat world has made them much more open to working with social and environmental activists, who are collaborating with progressive companies in ways that can make the companies more profitable and the flat earth more livable."[6] I agree. Actions should be judged by their effects, not by their motivations.

Offering a balanced view on the role of companies, the Nobel Prize–winning economist Joseph Stiglitz wrote, "Businesses pursue profits, and that means making money is their first priority." But Stiglitz continued, "Yet corporations have been at the center of bringing the benefits of globalization to the developing countries . . . [by bringing] jobs and economic growth to the developing nations."[7] And when I read about "the fortune at the bottom of the pyramid," I see that it is not just about making money by selling to the poor but also about enabling dignity and choice through markets and using new technology to deliver profitable solutions that reduce poverty and protect the environment.[8]

To those who seek to help the poor earn their way out of poverty, I would say that good policies cannot be formulated on the basis of wishful thinking. To be successful, policies must be formulated on the basis of an unromantic, hard-headed look at reality.[9]

Let us start by looking at the role of the business environment and the investment climate in firms' decisions about where to operate.

BUSINESS ENVIRONMENT, INVESTMENT CLIMATE, AND FIRMS' LOCATION DECISIONS

In today's globalized world, businesses have more choices than ever before about where and how to operate. When the business environment is favorable for profits and growth, businesses will consider investing in a country and employing its workers.[10] This is why Silicon Valley took off—because it was so much easier to start a company in the United States than in South Korea or France.[11] But when the business environment is not favorable, there is a good chance that companies will go elsewhere.

One story that brought home this lesson vividly to me was told by Michael Manley, who was prime minister of Jamaica on two separate occasions for a total of twelve years. Throughout his career in politics, Mr. Manley said, he fought steadfastly for one objective: combating poverty in his country. During his first stint as prime minister, he stated his intention to raise resources for Jamaica's anti-poverty efforts by imposing a tax on bauxite and aluminum. (Bauxite is the raw material from which aluminum is made.) The leading aluminum companies, Alcoa and Reynolds Metals, said they would move to Guyana or other countries if the levy was imposed. The Manley government imposed the tax, and indeed the aluminum companies pulled out of Jamaica. In part because of this, Mr. Manley was voted out of office. Four years later, he was voted back in, serving four more years as prime minister. Shortly after completing his last term, Mr. Manley spoke to my class at Cornell and told us what changed for him during his twelve years in office: "My number one goal as prime minister was to eliminate the crushing burden of poverty among Jamaicans. In my first term as prime minister, I thought we in Jamaica could take on the aluminum companies and other multinationals on *our* terms, but I was wrong. Between terms, I realized that we had to fight for our people on *your* terms. The goal remained the elimination of poverty—it hadn't changed. What had changed were the means."

What Jamaica had done by imposing a bauxite levy was to create an unfavorable business environment. The aluminum companies responded exactly as economic theory said they would: when higher profits can be earned elsewhere, profit-seeking companies will move to where those higher profits can be earned.

Businesses' pursuit of higher profits is a fact and should be taken as a constraint on the policies pursued by developing country governments and others who work for economic development. Put differently, policy makers need to think how businesses are likely to respond to various policies that might be put into effect and make their policy choices with the likely responses in mind.

It is often said that what keeps profit-seeking businesses operating in high-cost locations like the United States is the high productivity of its labor force combined with excellent infrastructure. Turning it around, a poor-quality labor force or poor infrastructure could cause a company *not* to locate in a given place. Taking off from this line of thinking, economists have formulated the idea that for economic development to succeed, many factors must be operating well and that the failure of *any one* of them could cause the entire development effort to fail. This way of understanding development or nondevelopment has come to be called the O-ring model, so called after of the explosion of the Challenger spacecraft because of the failure of a simple part called an O-ring, or the last straw model.[12]

What can go wrong in the creation of formal sector jobs? A study of Latin America found that small firms do not create as many jobs as they might because of insufficient access to finance, competition from informal firms, and corruption; large firms are constrained by regulatory framework, labor laws, and skills shortages; and all firms report macroeconomic and policy instability as major obstacles.[13]

Turning our attention specifically to investment climate, improvements in investment climate have direct impacts on poor people as employees; as entrepreneurs; as consumers; as users of infrastructure, finance, and property; and as potential recipients of tax-funded services or transfers. These effects operate through a variety of channels that include promoting employment growth; reducing the cost of doing business and mitigating risks; lowering the cost of producing and distributing goods and thereby lowering prices to consumers; improving infrastructure, finance, and property rights; and increasing tax revenues to fund public services and make transfers to the disadvantaged in society.

By increasing growth in average income, investment climate improvements have contributed to reductions in poverty in the world's two most populous countries, China and India. As Deng Xiao Ping famously said, "Black cat, white cat, all that matters is that it catches mice." Following a period of experimentation, what Deng called "crossing the river groping for stones," Deng led China in 1978 in the Four Liberalizations—liberalization of agriculture, industry, technology, and defense—aimed at opening China to foreign investment, the global market, and private competition. In the agricultural sector, for example, a household responsibility system was put into place whereby the government charged farm households for using government-owned land but allowed them to keep much of the extra output they produced beyond what was needed to fulfill their contracts. Agricultural output growth shot up as a result.[14] Between 1990 and 2004, the *increase* in vegetable production every two years in China matched the annual vegetable output of California![15] More generally, due to the four economic liberalizations, economic growth in China took off, averaging 9.8% in the subsequent thirty years. But besides the improved investment climate, positive elements of the socialist legacy were also responsible. These include social infrastructure, rural electrification, land redistribution, regional economic decentralization, basic scientific research, active fertility control, and female labor force participation and education.[16] Some negative elements remain as well, though, including corruption and venality of local governments—in the words of an immortal Chinese proverb, "the strong dragon is no match for the local snake."

For its part, India in 1991 launched a market-oriented liberalization program that remains in effect today—in fact, the finance minister who designed those programs, Manmohan Singh, is now India's prime minister. Its elements included greater reliance on the private sector, opening the economy to foreign trade and foreign direct investment, reorienting government activities toward those not likely to be performed by the market, and ensuring macroeconomic balance and a well-run financial sector.[17] India too has grown rapidly since its reforms; its real national income in 2008 was three times what it was in 1991. The reforms in China and India helped drive the greatest reductions in poverty the world has ever seen. In China alone, 600 million fewer people are in poverty than a generation ago.[18]

High on the list of factors creating an unfavorable business environment is burdensome regulation. With (generally) the best of intentions, poor countries regulate business more than richer countries do in ten areas: starting a business, dealing with construction permits, employing workers, registering property, getting credit, protecting investors, paying taxes, trading across borders, enforcing contracts, and closing a business. From comprehensive studies, we now have a very good understanding of the extent of these regulations, what makes for a good investment climate, what makes for a bad one, and what the consequences of a favorable business environment are. A number of lessons follow.[19]

Businesses in poor countries face much larger regulatory burdens than those in rich countries. In the poor countries, administrative costs are three times as large, and twice as many bureaucratic procedures are in place. Here is how some rich and poor countries compare. It takes two procedures to start a business in Australia, fifteen in Bolivia, and nineteen in Chad. It takes fifteen procedures to enforce a contract in Denmark but fifty-three in the Lao People's Democratic Republic. It takes one procedure to register property in Norway and sixteen in Algeria. The reported consequences are harmful for the earnings of those involved:

- An entrepreneur in Indonesia wants to open a textile factory. It takes him 168 days to get government permission to open his factory. In the meantime, customers he had lined up have contracted with a competitor.
- A trader in the United Arab Emirates has a customer who refuses to pay for equipment that had been delivered three months earlier. It takes twenty-seven procedures, costly legal fees, and a year-and-a-half in time to resolve the dispute. The trader decides to limit his business to customers he knows well.
- Another trader, this one in Guatemala, also faces a customer who will not pay for equipment delivered earlier. Facing years of expensive challenges in court with an uncertain outcome, the trader settles for payment of one-third of the amount, leaving him with no money to pay taxes. He then officially closes his business and operates informally.
- The operator of a small laboratory in Turkey seeks to provide employment opportunities to women. If the business experiences a drop in demand, the entrepreneur will have to make a severance payment of two years' salary to each laid-off worker. As a consequence, she

chooses conservatively, employing fewer people than she would have otherwise.

- A food supply business in Burkina Faso operates informally. The owner would like to register his business so that he can serve larger customers, who demand value added tax receipts. But registering a business would require minimum capital equal to five times Burkina Faso's per capita national income. Taking out a bank loan would require putting up collateral, which the owner cannot do, because his property is unregistered. The reason his property is unregistered is that the registration fees amount to 16% of the property's value. The business remains informal and small.

On the other hand, while regulations are stronger in poor countries than in rich countries, property rights in poor countries are weaker. Property owners in poor countries have fewer than half the protections that property owners in rich countries do. Laws in Canada require seven types of disclosure to protect equity investors, but Cambodia and Honduras have no requirements at all. China is infamous for its insecure property rights.[20]

When regulations are excessive, a variety of unfavorable outcomes may result: more inefficiency in public institutions—in particular, longer delays and higher costs, higher unemployment and informality, greater corruption, less productivity and investment, and slower economic growth. For example, if employment regulations are too stringent, labor force participation is reduced, unemployment is increased, and workers are forced into the informal economy. Informality is caused by another factor: burdensome entry regulations, which businesses can avoid by simply not registering their enterprises at all and hoping not to be noticed or paying off inspectors so they will not be reported. When the enterprise is not registered, neither are the workers, so they are not covered by protective labor legislation such as health and safety regulations, minimum wages, and mandated benefits such as unemployment insurance or old-age pensions.

Reform of regulations has been shown to produce large payoffs. For example, in Mexico, regulation reforms cut the time to establish a business from fifty-eight days to twenty-seven. It was estimated that the results included a 6% increase in registered businesses, a 2.6% increase in employment, and a 1% fall in prices because of the competition from new entrants.

What should be done? The Doing Business Report concludes: "The optimal level of regulation is not none, but may be less than what is currently found in most countries, and especially poor ones."[21] Five steps are urged: simplify and deregulate in competitive markets, focus on enhancing property rights, use the internet more, reduce court involvement in business matters, and make reform a continuous process.[22] Specifically, in the labor market, three types of interventions are urged: fostering a skilled workforce; crafting market interventions to benefit all workers, unlike the present ones which often do not cover the unemployed, the low-skilled, and the informal; and helping workers cope with change.[23]

An unfavorable regulatory environment is one of the factors that can cause companies to decide not to do business in a country. Other factors also influence location decisions. One survey carried out among managers of transnational corporations and international experts found that two factors were of primary importance in determining foreign direct investment (when a foreign company invests directly in plant and equipment in a host country): growth of market was first, and size of market was second. That is, the principal reason for companies to operate in China is that they want to sell their products in China, and only secondarily because they want to produce for sale elsewhere. Other factors found to matter, in decreasing order of importance, were profit perspectives, access to market, political and social stability, legal and regulatory environment, quality of labor, quality of infrastructure, manufacturing and services environment, access to resources, cost of labor, access to high technologies, fear of protectionism, access to financial resources, and access to raw materials.[24] Another study found that controlling for other determinants of foreign direct investment, "soft infrastructure" (i.e., market-oriented institutions) was more important in determining foreign direct investment into China than was "hard infrastructure" (such as highways and railroads).[25] A third study found that capital-scarce countries are not attracting a larger capital inflow because the perceived risk of investment remains high, because the community of private investors does not find it worthwhile to learn about a small country, and because genuine reformers cannot be distinguished from bogus reformers. Consequently, it is much easier just to invest in China, leaving out the Haitis, Bolivias, and Equatorial Guineas of the world and the would-be workers in them.[26]

Several factors determine the countries in which companies contract. On the cost side, factors that matter are tax rates, labor costs, geographic proximity to markets, transaction costs, economies of scale, agglomeration effects, cultural similarity to investors, productivity and skill levels, and low risk. Another set of factors includes product quality and labor standards. The consulting firm A.T. Kearney evaluates countries based on various factors and publishes an index of overall market attractiveness.[27] The International Finance Corporation tells us, "Private enterprise will be more effective in moving people out of poverty as progress is made toward enforcing the rule of law, reducing the cost of doing business, and promoting economic policies conducive to rapid growth and openness to the outside world." [28]

One great success has been China's development of the Pudong section of Shanghai.[29] Incentives to encourage development there included reduced income taxes for Sino-foreign joint ventures, tax exemptions for foreign investments in infrastructure in the first five profit-making years, and a 50% tax reduction for the first five profit-making years after that. Pudong's economic output came to match that of all of Shanghai ten years earlier. Nine thousand foreign firms set up operations in Pudong, vastly increasing employment in the area. As for the those who had been working in Pudong previously, under China's Sunshine Relocation Policy, three hundred thousand farmers were relocated to new accommodations and compensated for the acreage they had lost. Many of these took up jobs in the newly built factories, often earning more as janitors than they had been earning as farmers.

Intel decided to build a $300 million semiconductor assembly and test plant in Costa Rica rather than in Brazil, Chile, Indonesia, Mexico, the Philippines, or Thailand, which were also in the running. What made Costa Rica attractive were its stable economic and political system, its central location within the hemisphere, its openness and liberalized economy, its receptive investment environment, its educated labor force, and its early attention to English language instruction and computer education in the schools. Investors always have a choice about where to put their operations. Intel also decided to build a large new semiconductor factory in China rather than the United States. Costa Rica and China are thriving because of the favorable conditions they have created for companies like Intel.

What questions does Intel ask when it decides where to invest? Says its chairman, Craig Barrett, "What inherent strength does the country bring to the table?" Explaining why Intel did *not* build a plant in the United States, the company's CEO, Paul Otellini, explains: "The things that are not conducive to investments [in the United States] are [corporate] taxes and capital equipment credits. . . . If I build that factory in almost any other country in the world, where they have significant incentive programs, I could save $1 billion. . . . The cost of operating when you look at it after tax was substantially lower [in China] and you have local market access." And why does Intel *not* build a plant in India? Says Barrett, "You don't have infrastructure. Your electricity goes off four times a day."[30]

On the other hand, a country that rates much lower on investment climate scales is South Africa. The challenge for South Africa is to find new niches in which South African producers can become world class and thereby increase the demand for the nation's labor. There is only so far you can go with metals, alloys, and precious stones. What characteristics would promote investment in South Africa? High productivity of workers. A cooperative work environment. The opportunity to make money. What impedes investment? Excessively restrictive labor practices. The labor hassle factor. An unsafe living environment for the business executives and their families.[31]

Multinational corporations do not need the workers of Costa Rica or South Africa or any other particular country, but the poor workers of these countries desperately need multinational corporations to employ them. What the poor need are more and better jobs. Decisions about business environment and investment climate need to be formulated accordingly.

CONSUMER MOVEMENTS AND CORPORATE SOCIAL RESPONSIBILITY

You have read throughout this book that a good way to understand what private companies do is to see them as trying to maximize profits. If this is the reality, it follows that those who wish to harness the energies of private companies in the fight against global poverty must support those activities of companies that contribute to poverty reduction and try to change those activities of companies that work against this objective. At times, this means working to change what is in companies' profit-maximizing interests to do. Let us see how the consumer and corporate social responsibility movements have made a difference.

A highly visible organization on campuses around the United States is United Students against Sweatshops. Students have organized anti-sweatshop campaigns, mandating that the clothes bearing their collegiate logos be manufactured under fair and ethical conditions.

In 2006, more than 200,000 University of California (UC) students committed to purchasing clothing bearing UC campus logos only from factories that pay a living wage, follow adequate labor standards, and allow workers to form independent unions or other worker-sponsored organizations. In response to such pressure, Nike examined the working and environmental conditions in 569 factories around the world that produce the company's apparel, equipment, and footwear. It then issued a Corporate Responsibility Report criticizing its own supply chain conditions and pledging to improve conditions.[32] Deciding that Nike hadn't upgraded factory conditions sufficiently, the University of Wisconsin-Madison discontinued its relationship with Nike in 2010.

Closer to home for me, in February 2009, Cornell University terminated Russell Athletics as a supplier of Cornell merchandise. An investigation conducted by the Fair Labor Association and the Workers' Rights Consortium found that Jerzees de Honduras, a Honduran textile factory owned by Russell Athletics, had shut its doors rather than accede to workers' demands to form a union. As a university spokesman stated, "Cornell is committed to respecting the rights of workers around the world, and we expect the companies that are licensed to produce Cornell apparel to share that commitment."[33]

To the extent that such consumer movements are important, they affect companies' enlightened self-interest. If consumers can credibly threaten to take their business elsewhere, as the University of California, the University of Wisconsin, and Cornell did, companies may realize that their brand is at risk[34] and respond by upgrading conditions of employment—in effect, doing well by doing good.[35]

For the workers of Honduras, the Russell story has a happy ending. In November 2009, after more than one hundred universities including Cornell severed their contracts, the company agreed to rehire 1,200 Honduran workers. And pressure from university students helped in the case of Nike too: in August 2010, Nike set up a $1.5 million relief fund, job training programs, and paid health care for workers who had been laid off from Nike subcontractors Hugger de Honduras and Vision Tex. A novel feature of this agreement is that it marks the first time a major corporation accepted responsibility for misconduct by a subcontractor.[36]

Most recently, a garment manufacturer in the Dominican Republic, Knights Apparel, decided to dramatically raise the wage it paid to its factory workers. Upon the advice of the Workers' Rights Consortium, Knights agreed to pay a "living wage" of US$2.83 an hour, an amount deemed sufficient for workers to be able to provide their families with food, clean water, clothing, housing, energy, transportation, child care, education, and health care. Compared to the Dominican Republic's minimum wage of US$.85 an hour, the living wage marks a dramatic improvement for the company's workers. The company's highly visible marketing of its Alta Gracia brand has resulted in orders for T-shirts and sweatshirts at 400 American universities including mine. Joseph Bozich, the CEO of Knights, says the company is willing to accept a lower profit margin—that is, profit per unit sold. But possibly the company will make up the difference in increased sales or higher prices because of its living wage campaign. The

CEO of Knights states, "We're hoping to prove that doing good can be good business, that they're not mutually exclusive." [37]

Looking at it the other way around, *not* to profess a concern for worker rights and working conditions may harm a company's image and hurt its profits. In this way, consumer movements may create a win-win scenario: workers benefiting from higher labor standards and companies benefiting from a better standing in the community.

Turning to corporate social responsibility, virtually every large company today has a department that deals with corporate social responsibility (CSR). The CSR movement has arisen for three interrelated reasons.[38]

One is the view, by no means universally accepted, that the responsibility of a corporation goes beyond earning higher profits and thereby providing financial returns to shareholders. Instead, the CSR movement maintains that corporations should also pursue other objectives such as sustainable growth, equitable employment practices, and long-term social and environmental well-being.[39]

Whenever I hear about multiple objectives, I ask how much effort is going into each one. One study reported, "Even companies with award-winning CSR programs limit their investment in CSR initiatives to (for example) 0.5 or 1 percent of net profits."[40] With numbers like that, it isn't exactly profit-maximization, but it comes very close.

A second reason for the rise of the CSR movement is that it is now in the enlightened self-interest of many businesses today not only to profess a concern for CSR but more important, to be seen as acting on that concern. In today's highly globalized world, consumer groups, civil society, and collectives of activists are potentially potent actors. One article put it this way: "The forces that have pushed companies to fret about sustainability—the scrutiny from the internet, multiple lobby groups, popular concern about global warming, the threat of lawsuits for misbehavior on human rights—are not about to disappear. . . . And if companies are not seen to take their social responsibility seriously, governments will intervene to change the rules by which they operate." [41] Another said, "Now there's a more sophisticated understanding that environmental and social practices can yield strategic advantages in an interconnected world of shifting customer loyalties and regulatory regimes." [42] The vice president for corporate citizenship at GE expresses similar sentiments: "No good business can call itself a good corporate citizen if it fritters away shareholder money. The company is simply moving in the direction in which it thinks social pressures will push it anyway." [43] And my Cornell colleague Robert

Frank writes, "Ben & Jerry's sells more ice cream because of its preservation efforts on behalf of Amazon rain forests . . . [and] The Body Shop sells more cosmetics because of its environmentally friendly packaging." [44] A wise company is one that realizes it must do more than just appear to be a good corporate citizen; it can actually engage in "strategic CSR" and turn it to a source of competitive advantage. [45] This is what Geoffrey Heal means when he writes about "When Principles Pay" at Citibank, Merck, Wal-Mart, Starbucks, Monsanto, Interface, and other companies. [46]

And third, being known as a good employer is an important competitive advantage in the fight to attract and retain top talent. The CEO of Goldman Sachs, Lloyd Blankfein, has said. "[Our] '10,000 Women' initiative aims to provide management education to thousands of women in poor countries, offering courses in subjects such as marketing, accounting and human resources. . . . [The] programme will not only train future generations of Goldman Sachs employees, but also helps retain current employees looking for public service opportunities." [47]

For all these reasons—appealing to multiple constituencies, increasing private and public support, and gaining an advantage in the labor market—it is important to companies to be perceived as acting responsibly. AT&T states in a corporate report, "If we aren't good corporate citizens as reflected in a Triple Bottom Line that takes into account social and environmental responsibilities along with financial ones—eventually our stock price, our profits, and our entire business could suffer." [48] Ignoring CSR is something that a company would do at its peril.

Corporate social responsibility movements take a variety of forms:

- *Company codes of conduct.* American companies such as Nike, Adidas, Gap Inc., Levi Strauss, Wal-Mart, Disney, Toys "R" Us, and McDonald's and British companies such as Sainsbury, Marks & Spencer, Safeway Stores UK, Tesco, the Body Shop International, and WH Smith are among those that have established company codes of conduct. Typically, the labor conditions prescribed in these codes of conduct involve paying minimum wages, establishing maximum work hours, eliminating child labor, improving unhealthy and unsafe working conditions, and (sometimes) allowing for unions to be formed. [49]
- *Social labeling.* Among the better-known labels are Rugmark and Fair Trade Coffee. Rugmark certifies that children are not involved in the production of carpets. [50] For its part, Fair Trade certifies that products are made under fair conditions, which in the case of coffee, means that the coffee must be purchased directly from farm cooperatives, the

cooperatives must be guaranteed a minimum price, and farmers must be offered credit by importers. Businesses gain from Fair Trade Coffee too. Michael Ellgass, the director of house brands for Sam's Club (a division of Wal-Mart), says the company could afford to pay Fair Trade's premium price because it has reduced the number of middlemen in the supply chain.[51]

- *CSR audits.* A number of organizations conduct social audits of factories around the world. Among the leading auditors are Social Accountability International, the Worker Rights Consortium, and the Fair Labor Association. There are also country-specific groups such as Better Factories Cambodia. While the primary goal of these audits is to assure that codes agreed to are in fact followed, several operational issues have emerged, including these: audits are only conducted infrequently and on a spot-check basis, some of the auditing organizations receive their revenue from the companies being audited, and the companies themselves have become more adept at concealing abuses.[52]

- *Licensing.* The Beanstalk Group is the world's leading licenser of brands. Numbered among its clients are Harley-Davidson motorcycles, Stanley tools, AT&T, Jack Daniel's whiskey, and Paris Hilton. Beanstalk has written literally thousands of licensing agreements, all of which include an abolition clause stating that the licensing agreement can be terminated if the factories in which the goods are produced are not wholesome places.

A well-documented case study is Nike.[53] Nike enjoys a leading position in apparel, shoes, sporting goods, and other product lines. Because of its high visibility, the company faced enormous pressure from consumer groups and their political allies about the "ruthless exploitation" that was taking place in their factories. While the role of the consumer movement cannot be claimed directly as the only cause, Nike's profits fell from $800 million in fiscal 1997 to $400 million in 1998. Whatever the reason, Nike launched a high profile effort to remediate working conditions in its factories. Nike now requires that all its footwear suppliers around the world adopt U.S. Occupational Safety and Health Administration standards for indoor air quality. With respect to child labor, Nike has raised the minimum age for footwear factory workers to eighteen and for all other workers to sixteen. Its community development efforts in Vietnam, Thailand, and Indonesia include making microloans so that women in the communities where Nike factories are located can start or develop their own businesses. (More will be said about micro-credit in Chapter 10.) A careful statistical analysis found that monitoring and corporate codes of conduct helped improve working conditions in Nike plants but only somewhat. The most effective change was in the organization of work—specifically, those innovations that enabled suppliers to better schedule their work and improve quality and efficiency.[54]

Another place where a careful statistical study has been carried out is in the textile, footwear, and apparel (TFA) sector of Indonesia where global companies such as Nike, Reebok, Adidas, and the Gap operate. The real wages of unskilled TFA workers rose by 30% to 40% in just six years, more than in other sectors. To determine whether anti-sweatshop activism provided the impetus for these wage increases, the researchers controlled for other factors and found that wage increases were systematically larger for exporting and foreign TFA plants in those districts of Indonesia where activists concentrated their efforts. They found too that contrary to expectations, employment grew significantly *more* within exporting and foreign TFA plants than in other plants outside that sector. How could wages and employment both have increased? After Nike mounted an expensive public relations campaign trumpeting the new conditions, its share of the global footwear market increased by almost 50%. In the researchers' words, "Anti-sweatshop activism in Indonesia was a 'win-win' situation."[55]

Another case study of interest is the pharmaceutical company GlaxoSmithKline (GSK).[56] In 2000, GSK and thirty-nine other pharmaceutical companies brought suit against the government of South Africa then headed by President Nelson Mandela for voiding patents on prescription drugs including those to treat HIV. A new CEO, Jean-Pierre Garnier, came into office and conceded that the lawsuit was "a public relations disaster." Garnier decided to have GSK lead the drive to make medicines available at cost to poor countries, resulting in licenses being granted to eight local companies so they could produce generic versions of these medicines. At present, GSK sells fully 90% of its vaccines at not-for-profit prices to developing world customers. Would they have done this without consumer pressure? No. But because of consumer pressure, it is now in their profit-maximizing interest to act differently.

Before we see corporate social responsibility as a panacea, we should raise this cautionary note. While adherence to CSR principles brings benefits to companies, it also entails costs. Studies have shown that the link between CSR and financial performance is positive but weak.[57] One book on the subject paints a mixed picture: "Precisely because CSR is voluntary and market-driven, companies will engage in CSR only to the extent that it makes business sense for them to do so. . . . In the final analysis, CSR is sustainable only if virtue pays off."[58]

Private companies play an essential role in economic development. Companies themselves are motivated by higher profits. In the pursuit of higher profits, they produce goods and services, create jobs, offer training, pay taxes, and do many other things that may contribute to reducing poverty. Those governments, development institutions, nongovernmental organizations, and ordinary citizens who are interested in helping the poor should explore ways of harnessing the energies of private companies toward mutually advantageous ends.

One way governments have made a difference is by creating a favorable business environment and investment climate so that firms will decide to locate in their countries and employ their people. Businesses do not operate in a location where conditions are not beneficial to them. In today's globalized world, companies have more discretion than ever before about where to invest and produce. Countries need to set their laws, regulations, and other institutions in view of this reality.

The consumer and corporate social responsibility movements have also made a difference. Pressure from buyers to take their business elsewhere has caused companies around the world to reassess what behavior is in their profit-maximizing interest. In today's world, it may be necessary to the pursuit of higher profits for a business to be responsive to consumer movements and act in a socially responsible fashion.

CHAPTER 9

Labor Market Policies for Generating More Wage Employment

We have seen in previous chapters that economic growth, international trade, foreign aid, and the contributions of private companies are crucial for poverty reduction. We have seen too which public policies and private actions could contribute to faster economic growth—achieving freer and fairer international trade, enhancing the contribution of aid, and encouraging private companies to make an even more substantial contribution to poverty reduction.

In this chapter, we will look at different policies—labor market policies. As a reminder, the labor market is the place where labor services are bought and sold, including not only wage and salaried employment but also self-employment.[1] Labor market policies are those that work directly in the labor market, as opposed to those such as economic growth policies that impinge upon the labor market. Labor market policies include policies to affect the number and types of workers that employers want to hire, the number and types of people who are willing and able to work, and wage and non-wage compensation.

Remember that the great majority of workers in developing countries are *not* paid employees. In India, in a labor force of 470 million people, just 35 million are formal sector employees, where "formal sector" is defined as employees in establishments registered with the government. Of these, 21 million are employed by the government and only 14 million by the private sector.[2]

In India, as in other developing countries, there is an enormous labor pool able and mostly ready to move into paid employment if more jobs as paid employees were offered. As economist Joan Robinson famously said decades ago, "It's a terrible thing to be a worker exploited in the capitalist system. The only worse thing is to be a worker unable to find anyone to exploit you." And as *New York Times* columnist Nicholas Kristof said in 2009 (and before), "The central challenge in the poorest countries is not that sweatshops exploit too many people, but that they don't exploit enough."[3] Among the reasons given for the relatively slow growth of labor-intensive manufacturing employment in India are inadequate long-term finance for small firms, infrastructural deficiencies, limiting the manufacture or sale of a large number of products to small-scale firms, and rigid labor laws.[4]

Suppose policy makers in a country decide a top priority is to increase the number of jobs in paid employment. What would be an appropriate package of policies for them to pursue in the labor market? We will see that to create more paid employment, countries can take several actions:

- Set the rate of pay and other elements of the compensation package so as to avoid prematurely high labor costs.
- Remove undue barriers to hiring that arise from excessively protective labor legislation.
- Increase employees' skills and productive abilities to the extent that skill deficiencies are causing jobs to go unfilled.
- Establish programs for government to be an employer of last resort for the poor.

These are in addition to policies outside the labor market including the growth, trade, aid, and investment climate policies discussed in earlier chapters.

As you read about policies in each of these areas, please keep two things in mind. First, some of the policies to create more paid employment run counter to the attainment of other labor market objectives such as higher earnings or greater social protection for those employed, and therefore a policy that would lead to more jobs is not necessarily the best policy to be followed within the labor market. Second, once the best policies for creating more paid employment are determined, these policies need to be balanced against other uses of limited resources. You may want to revisit the messages on setting priorities and facing trade-offs detailed in Chapter 6.

AVOIDING PREMATURELY HIGH LABOR COSTS

By "prematurely high labor costs," I mean that labor costs at any given time may be higher than they would have been if they had been set by supply and demand in the labor market.[5] I am certainly *not* a believer in unfettered markets. What I am saying is that a predictable consequence of higher pay and other types of labor costs is that employment is likely to be smaller than it otherwise would have been, other things equal.[6] The reasons are straightforward. In the case of private companies, it will be in their profit-maximizing interests to hire fewer workers than they would have if labor costs were lower. In the case of public sector employers, unless governments can increase their budgets by the same amount that labor costs have increased, they have no choice but to hire fewer people.

Five forces have been shown to affect compensation levels in some developing countries (but not in others):[7]

- *Minimum wages* aim to assure an "adequate" standard of living to workers. Although minimum wage laws have been passed in many countries, their effects differ greatly. Some countries such as Bangladesh, India, and Côte d'Ivoire have minimum wages that are higher than would otherwise be paid, and these laws are enforced at least to some degree. On the other hand, South Korea's minimum wage is higher than the market wage level for only 2% of workers. Taiwan also has a minimum wage, but it is said that no company has ever been fined for violating the law.
- *Trade unions* are often encouraged by public policy so that workers can receive a "just" share of the fruits of their labor. Unions are estimated to have raised the wages of their members by as much as 150% in Jamaica, 31% in Ghana, 24% in South Africa, and 20% in Malaysia. By contrast, in South Korea and Taiwan, unions have been repressed, and the union wage premium is at most 2% or 3%.
- *Public sector pay policies* may result in government workers being paid at a substantially higher rate than their private sector counterparts. Costa Rica, Kenya, and India are examples of this, and as a result, "everybody" tries to get a job in the government. I would say that the same is true in Mexico, though not all analysts would agree. In East Asia, in contrast, the public sector pays neither more nor less than the private sector does.
- *Multinational corporations* are often the most sought-after employers because they typically pay above-market compensation and other benefits. Sometimes, the multinationals pay above the market to get a more productive labor force. Other times, they do it to appear to be good corporate citizens. Still other times, they do it because governments, especially in Latin America and Africa, have "encouraged" them to do it by not so subtly threatening expulsion or expropriation if they do not.

- Finally, *labor codes* in some countries regulate hiring and firing, impose payroll taxes on firms, and mandate that employers provide certain benefits to their workers. Labor codes in Panama and Bolivia are estimated to have raised labor costs by 90%. In India, Zimbabwe, and South Africa, the labor codes not only raise labor costs but also prevent large firms from dismissing workers. Knowing this, large firms often do not hire workers in the first place, a point to which we return later in this chapter.

As an illustration of how higher labor costs can reduce paid employment, consider South Africa. Up to 1990, wages adjusted for inflation and paid employment rose together. After 1990, though, real wages continued to rise but paid employment fell. What happened in 1990 was that Nelson Mandela and the other African National Congress (ANC) leaders were released from prison, marking the imminent end of apartheid.[8] It was clear that Mandela would shortly be elected president and lead a black majority government in which the ANC, the Congress of South African Trade Unions (COSATU), and the Communist Party of South Africa would be formal partners. Since then, COSATU and the South African Department of Labor have pushed incessantly for higher wages and improved working conditions for as many workers as could be covered by good union contracts. As a consequence, pay did indeed rise but formal sector employment fell steadily. Whether the COSATU-ANC-Communist Party policies were good ones is a judgment best made by the South Africans themselves.

REMOVING UNDUE BARRIERS TO EMPLOYMENT DUE TO EXCESSIVELY PROTECTIVE LABOR LEGISLATION

Many developing countries have employment protection laws aimed at securing steady employment by restricting dismissals of workers. In some countries, the laws have the intended effect in that those workers who are fortunate enough to have jobs covered by the legislation do indeed enjoy secure employment. However, an unintended side effect of employment protection laws is that employers to whom the law applies may be reluctant to hire workers in the first place, knowing that they cannot dismiss them in the event of a business downturn or unsatisfactory job performance. This phenomenon has been studied most carefully in India.[9]

India's Industrial Disputes Act of 1947, as amended in 1976 and 1982, requires that firms employing 100 or more workers obtain government permission for retrenchments, layoffs, or plant closures. In practice, such permission is rarely given. Accordingly, companies have engaged in a variety of practices to circumvent the law or simply not abide by it. Nonetheless, studies have shown that the law has had significant impacts, not all of them positive. One study estimated that as employment protection laws were strengthened, paid employment fell by 17.5%. This was an early indication that India's Industrial Disputes Act might not be an unambiguously good thing from the workers' point of view.[10] Another study examined the results when different Indian states amended the central government legislation; the researchers found that employment, output, investment, and productivity were lower in states that amended the act in what was thought to be a pro-worker direction. This same study also estimated that urban poverty was higher in the states that had enacted pro-worker legislation—specifically, urban poverty would have been 11% lower in the state of West Bengal and 12% lower in the state of Andhra Pradesh had they not enacted substantial pro-worker legislation. In the authors' words, "The battle cry of labor market regulation is often that pro-worker labor market policies redress the unfavorable balance of power between capital and labor, leading to a progressive effect on income distribution. We find no evidence of this here—indeed the distributional effects appear to have worked against the poor."[11] A third study also found that legal amendments and the consequent increased use of contract labor hurt workers in India's organized sector and imposed substantial costs on society. The authors concluded: "Workers do not benefit from Employment Protection Legislation or Dispute Resolution Legislation as practiced in India."[12] A fourth study stated: "Pro-labor regulations hurt where it matters the most—industries which employ more labor."[13] A fifth study concluded: "At best, all these laws have a normative role: to provoke—and act as a rallying point for—mobilisation. At worst, the very laws supposedly protecting labour encourage capital to informalise it."[14] Finally, a study by McKinsey, the global consulting company, forecast that China would gain enormously from the impending opening of the world textiles market on January 1, 2005, as indeed subsequently happened. Why China? Why not India? The foremost factor according to McKinsey was that India's labor laws lead to inefficiently small firm size compared to China and discourage foreign investment.[15] The generally negative conclusions of these studies have not gone unchallenged, though.[16]

Turning from India to South Africa, I encountered that nation's protective labor legislation in a particularly poignant way. During one of my trips to South Africa, I needed sun block, so I entered the Rexall Pharmacy on Camps Bay Road along the seaside outside of Cape Town. On the wall of the shop was a newspaper article published two years previously lauding a ninety-three-year-old gentleman, Mr. Isaacs, for being the oldest practicing pharmacist in the world according to the Guinness Book of World Records. A minute later, Mr. Isaacs himself appeared, and after I made my purchase, we began talking about his work, his business, and the larger South African society. Mr. Isaacs told me that for many years, he had run his pharmacy with the aid of an assistant. Thirty-two years earlier, he said, he had taken her on for a month, and she had stayed with him for thirty-one years, until she got too old and too sick and had to retire. For the last year, he said, he had run the business all by himself. "Why," I asked, "do you do it yourself?" His answer: "You see, Professor, if I take on an assistant in these times and that person doesn't work out, I can't dismiss that person. I don't want to be stuck with somebody like that, so I'm doing business on my own." This from a ninety-five-year-old man in a country with (then) 34% unemployment![17]

Labor laws such as those in India and South Africa are undoubtedly well intentioned. But as exemplified by the experience of these countries, whether they are beneficial in fact is open to question.

INCREASING EMPLOYEES' SKILLS WHEN SKILL DEFICIENCIES CAUSE UNEMPLOYMENT

Policy makers and advisors to them often recommend investing more in education and training to increase paid employment. Two reasons are commonly advanced for this recommendation. One is that individuals with more education and training tend to work in better job categories and have higher labor market earnings. A second reason is that throughout the developing world, skills shortages are thought to act as a severe constraint on economic growth and employment.

Taking the point about higher earnings and better job categories first, we have to be careful not to confuse what is good for a single individual with what is good for all individuals taken together. If any particular child gets more education, there is good reason to believe that he or she will do better in the job market as an adult, and indeed this pattern has been established statistically all over the world.[18] On the other hand, it is also important to understand that if one person gets a given job, some other person has not gotten that job. One more *qualified* person does not necessarily mean one more *employed* person.

Does increased education necessarily result in increased employment of the educated? Evidence on this point is far from encouraging.[19] In Africa, when school enrollments expanded, paid employment grew by nearly the same amount in just two countries, Botswana and Zimbabwe. Elsewhere, the number of newly educated individuals entering the labor force was four times larger than the growth of paid employment in Senegal, Kenya, and Malawi and between ten and twenty-nine times larger in Lesotho, Burkina Faso, Ghana, Uganda, and Sierra Leone. In Africa at least, the great majority of the newly educated do not find paid employment; unfortunately, where they do end up is either in low-level self-employment or in unemployment.

However, skills are often said to be in short supply among the workforce, especially in Africa. There, skills deficits are consistently ranked among the top five factors limiting manufacturing activity, along with unreliable electricity, high tax rates, costly finance, and corruption. Fifty percent of manufacturing firms in Mozambique state that skills shortage is a serious constraint, as do 30% or more of manufacturing firms in Ethiopia, Uganda, and Zambia.[20] If employers in countries like these want to hire workers but cannot find enough persons with the desired characteristics, the case is much stronger for investing in skills development so as to create the supply of skilled workers to match the demand for them.

What can be done to build skills? Let us first consider education in schools and then post-school training.

Education and skills remain appallingly low in the developing world. The primary school completion rate is 55% in Ethiopia, 54% in Papua New Guinea, 29% in Chad, and 21% in Haiti. Children from such countries do much worse on international tests than do students from richer countries. In Nepal, only 60% of children who had completed third grade could read a simple sentence. In Mali, the record is even worse: there, only 60% of those who had completed primary school (sixth grade) could read a simple sentence.[21]

Why are educational levels so low? Several factors are responsible:

- *Lack of schools.* In the West African nation of Gambia, only a little more than half of children of primary school age are able to secure school spaces. It is typical in low-income countries for many of the schools to be located miles away from where the children live and for no school buses or any other kind of transportation to school to be available.
- *Non-attendance in existing schools.* During a recent trip to Ethiopia, my wife and I traveled through the countryside on school days. We were struck by the large number of school-age children, mostly boys, who were herding goats, sheep, and cows within view of the road. These children were supposed to be in school—primary school attendance is compulsory in Ethiopia as it is in most other developing countries—but they did not go to school that day or any other day. Their stories were very

much the same: they could not go to school because their labor was too important to the family's economic survival. The International Labor Organization (ILO) estimates that child workers in the world number in the hundreds of millions.

- *Poor school quality.* Even when schools are present, one factor leading children not to attend is that they and their families judge the schools not to be worth attending. One important factor in low school quality is the lack of trained and qualified teachers. Too many teachers are themselves barely literate or numerate.

- *Teacher absenteeism.* Reports abound that salaried teachers are routinely absent from school, often for months at a time. Indeed, in the case of Masibisi whom we met in Chapter 3, her youngest son had not been to school in two months because his classroom had neither a regular teacher nor a substitute.

- *Insufficient resources.* The schools in developing countries have pathetically little to work with. The lack of physical infrastructure (buildings, roofs, desks, chairs) and materials (textbooks, notebooks, pens) is endemic. Everywhere in the developing world, children run up to people like me asking for school pens, and I have learned always to have a supply of them with me.

One study of youth education policies analyzed a wide range of policy interventions in the developing world to see what worked, what might work, and what is unlikely to work.[22] Some were judged to have been *proven successful*, including enacting compulsory schooling laws (Venezuela), allowing private sector entry and private-public partnerships (Colombia), providing quality assurance and information (Chile, South Korea), fostering competition (Chile), ensuring teaching quality, providing continuous needs-based teacher training with follow-up, using well-designed and negotiated performance-based pay (Chile), offering conditional cash transfers (Mexico), and providing vouchers for beneficiaries (Colombia). A second group of policies were judged to be *promising but unproven*. In this category are moving vocational tracks to upper secondary school (Chile), having no terminal vocational tracks (South Africa, Tunisia), offering part-time schooling (Argentina, Russia), making the curriculum more relevant, teaching practical thinking and behavioral skills (South Africa), blending vocational and general curricula (Chile), introducing school accountability, disseminating information on school performance (Chile), making income-contingent loans (Thailand), and offering individual learning accounts (Mexico). A third group were labeled *unlikely to be successful*. They include doing early tracking and selection (Tanzania and Thailand), maintaining an unregulated private sector (Cambodia), instituting teacher incentives based on narrow test scores (Chile, Kenya, Mexico), and offering supplementary teaching parallel to regular classes provided by the same teachers (Cambodia).

Judged particular promising is a new type of intervention called conditional cash transfers (CCTs), which have been put into effect in a number of developing countries. These programs include Bangladesh's Food-for-Education Program, Mexico's Progresa Program (now called Oportunidades), and Brazil's Bolsa Escola Program (succeeded by Bolsa Familia), among others. The essence of CCTs is that payments are made to parents—often specifically the mother—provided the recipient fulfills certain desired and verifiable behaviors; examples are a pregnant mother appearing for pre-natal check-ups, as certified by a health clinic, or a child attending school regularly, as certified by a teacher.[23] Evaluation studies have concluded that CCTs have been effective in improving children's schooling and health care while also providing material aid to poor families.[24] In an interesting reverse flow of ideas, New York City created its own CCT program called Opportunity NYC modeled on the successes in developing countries; as advisor to the program, the city brought in Santiago Levy, creator of the program in Mexico and now the chief economist of the Inter-American Development Bank.

In Chapter 6, I talked about the importance of social cost-benefit analysis in deciding how to allocate development resources among alternative uses. In the case of stimulating additional school attendance, Oportunidades costs $1,000 per extra year of school, school uniforms cost an additional $100 per year, and deworming students costs $3.50 per extra year. In terms of cost effectiveness, CCTs and school uniforms are effective but deworming is the clear winner.[25]

Turning from education in schools to post-school training, developing countries are often criticized for paying insufficient attention to specific vocational skills for which there is a labor market need. One successful training program is the In-Service Training Component of Mexico's System of Training Workers, known by its Spanish acronym SICAT (and previously known as PROBECAT). A particularly interesting feature of SICAT is that the subject area of the training is chosen by employers rather than the government. Workers receive training in such skills as lathe operating and air conditioner repair, which are not areas that would likely have been chosen by ministry officials in Mexico City. The government pays the Mexican minimum wage and other benefits to workers undergoing the training. The firms offering the training but not paying the trainees are obligated to hire at least 70% of those who complete the program. For most groups in the labor market, SICAT graduates have fared better than comparable individuals who did not undergo such training.[26]

As another example of the difference skills can make, take the international market for knockoff oil paintings. In Dafen, China, in a space of just four square kilometers, 9,000 workers produce 60% of the world's cheap oil paintings. Each artist produces on average 1,000 paintings a year. Why was this industry established in China and not some other country? One reason is that all the painters in Dafen are art academy graduates—all 9,000 of them. Which other country in the world would have so many workers with such a high and specific level of training?[27]

By the way, the Dafen story also illustrates both the advantages and the perils of participating in the world economy. When the global economic downturn hit in 2008, many of the Dafen factories lost their orders in the United States and simply closed down. As I have said before, few competitive advantages are genuinely sustainable.

CREATING JOBS FOR THE POOR

Given the shortage of good work opportunities, governments around the world are under enormous pressure to create jobs to employ the poor, the unemployed, and the underemployed. Many of these job creation programs have been designed to be self-targeting—that is, everyone is offered a program in which they may *choose* to participate. If the aim is to create opportunities for the poor, incentives can be created so that the poor, and only the poor, opt to join.

Among the government jobs programs in the developing world are Argentina's Program for Heads of Households (Plan Jefes y Jefas de Hogar), Bangladesh's Food for Work Program, the Employment Guarantee Scheme in the Indian state of Maharashtra, and India's National Rural Employment Guarantee Act.

Argentina's Program for Heads of Households (Jefes y Jefas). Jefes y Jefas is aimed at reducing poverty by providing short-term work at relatively low wages to unemployed workers from poor families. The wage rate was set at a maximum of $200 per month, an amount low enough to assure good targeting performance and to encourage workers to take up regular work when it became available. One evaluation study found that more than half the beneficiaries were in the poorest 20% of the income distribution, household heads who had been out of the labor force were drawn into the labor force by the availability of jobs; the unemployment rate fell by 2.5 percentage points compared to what it would have been without the program.[28]

Bangladesh's Food for Work (FFW) Program. The major objectives of the program are to provide income to the rural poor during the slack period when the unemployment rate in rural areas increases, as well as to mitigate losses due to natural disasters. Therefore, the target group for FFW includes anyone who is poor, willing, and available to do basic construction work like digging and earth-moving in exchange for payments of food. It is estimated that the net income gains of workers from the FFW program amounts to 10% to 11% of annual wage income and 7% to 8% of total annual income.[29]

The Employment Guarantee Scheme (EGS) in the Indian state of Maharashtra.[30] In the former Maharashtra program, which has since been merged into a nationwide rural employment guarantee act (discussed later), public works jobs were offered to all who wanted them, but the wage was deliberately set low so that only those with poor outside opportunities would find the EGS jobs attractive. Participants were put to work on such projects as road building, irrigation, soil conservation, and forestation programs. As an illustration of the effectiveness of the self-targeting feature, more than 90% of the participants in the Maharashtra program came from households with incomes below the poverty line. An important benefit for these workers was that employment was available particularly when it was most needed—in slack seasons and when other opportunities were most limited. As a result, income variations for the poor were reduced.

India's Mahatma Gandhi National Rural Employment Guarantee Act (NREGA).[31] NREGA is the largest employment guarantee scheme in the world. Begun in 2005 and expanded to all districts of India in 2008, NREGA is "an act to provide for the enhancement of livelihood security of the households in rural areas of the country by providing at least one hundred days of guaranteed wage employment in every financial year to every household whose adult members volunteer to do unskilled manual work." NREGA makes employment on demand a right. If an entitled worker demands employment and does not receive it within fifteen days, that worker becomes eligible to receive an unemployment allowance equal in amount to the NREGA wage.

Evaluation studies conclude that NREGA has had some noteworthy positive effects. These include reduction in distress out-migration; improved food security with wages being used for food, health, education, and repayment of loans; employment with dignity; greater economic empowerment of female workers; and sustainable asset creation.

However, NREGA also has some major problems, of which two stand out. One serious problem is that NREGA households are getting only about forty-three days of employment per year on average rather than the one hundred guaranteed to them. The limited participation not because of disinterest on the part of potential participants but because of lack of information and sufficient work opportunities. A second serious problem of NREGA is the existence of "operational deficiencies," the most important of which is nonpayment of wages to persons who have performed work.

In 2008, a number of colleagues and I had the opportunity to visit an NREGA site in Phoolpari village, Gujarat state.[32] In the rainy season, the villagers grew corn, lentils, gram, and other crops, some as owner-cultivators on family plots and others as sharecroppers. (Remarkably, the sharecroppers' shares were just 20% or 30% of the crop.) However, we were there in the dry season, and without water, nothing could be grown. In the absence of NREGA, these people would have migrated to a distant provincial city in search of construction or other kinds of work. But with NREGA, twenty men and ten women remained in the village, digging a huge well twelve meters in diameter and ten meters deep. Using just hand tools for digging (men's work) and wok-shaped pans for carrying out the dirt (women's work), they were two weeks into this particular project and had two months to go.

Each participant had been issued a job card entitling him or her to one hundred days of work at a daily wage of Rs.60 (about US$1.25). NREGA workers are supposed to be paid every week, but so far none of the workers at this particular site had been paid at all. They said it was because the person in charge of the payments was ill. That may or may not have been true at their particular work site. Sadly, in talking to other NREGA workers, we learned the ugly truth.

We were taken to a large meeting being conducted under the auspices of the Eklavya labor union which in turn was being supported by a nongovernmental organization called Developing Initiatives for Social and Human Action (DISHA). Gathered under a large tent were hundreds of people who crowded in to meet and discuss with the sarpanches (leaders) of the local gram panchayats (the smallest governmental units in India) the difficulties they were having in getting what the government had promised to them under NREGA. One after another, they told how work that was to have been offered had not come and payments for work done had not been made. One villager said, "It doesn't matter how the money is allocated. We in the village won't get much of it." Another said, "The system of record-keeping is rife with fraud." Others explained that the money for their wages was supposed to have been sent directly from Delhi (India's capital) to bank accounts that were to have been opened for them, but the banks refused to open accounts with such small balances. The Indian Postal Service was of no help either. Several villagers said that the local officers would open postal savings accounts only if they were paid bribes, which the villagers could not afford. Many related stories of under-payment. Most heart-rending to me was a woman who told us she had worked at an NREGA site for a month and was supposed to have been paid daily. The job card she held up was empty.

"Deficiencies" such as these throughout India are well documented.[33]A study in the Indian state of Orissa estimated that the amount of money skimmed off by a program administrator amounted to somewhere between 150 and 1,000 *times* that official's government salary![34]

The government of India is well aware of these problems and is work-ing actively to overcome them. One study concluded, "Corruption can be eradicated from NREGA, and the way to do it is to enforce the transpar-ency safeguards that are built into the Act and the guidelines."[35] Another possible direction is to accelerate efforts to spread mobile money technol-ogies.[36] As one step in trying to remedy the situation in NREGA and other government programs, in 2009, the government of India appointed the co-CEO of Infosys, Nandan Nilekani, to a cabinet-rank position responsi-ble for developing a biometric Unique Identification Card. As I write these words in August 2010, the new cards are scheduled to be rolled out first in Andhra Pradesh state within months.

General lessons. Drawing on the lessons from these and other workfare schemes, some key design features have emerged: [37]

- Low-wage work should be guaranteed.
- The work should be proposed by bona fide community groups in poor areas.
- The government should contribute to non-wage costs only if the com-munity putting up the proposal is in a designated poor area.
- The project wage rate should be no higher than the market wage rate for unskilled labor in a normal year.
- There should be little or no administrative discretion in access to the program.

ON IMPROVING LABOR MARKET INFORMATION SYSTEMS

Before leaving the topic of increasing paid employment, I would like to touch on one issue briefly: improving labor market information systems such as online information centers, public employment services, job banks, and the like. Countries all over the world have put such systems in place to a greater or lesser degree. Yet I think that the developing countries should *not* emulate the developed countries by trying to develop such institutions, at least at public expense. To explain, labor market information systems are designed for situations in which employers want workers, workers want jobs, but the employers and workers cannot find one another—in Chapter 4 you learned this is called "frictional unemployment." But I don't see frictional unemployment as an important problem in developing countries. The problem, in my view, is deficient demand in the labor market, which results in open unemployment for some and underemployment for a much larger number. Labor market information systems solve the wrong problem: they confuse what would be good for *an individual* (getting one of the available good jobs) with what would be good for *all individuals taken together* (there being more good jobs, which is what this chapter has been all about). Improved labor market information is not a priority need for poor countries; scarce public resources are better used elsewhere.

IN CONCLUSION

In some circumstances, the highest priority for labor market policy is to create more paid employment. When that is the objective, which policies should be pursued in the labor market? (Policies outside the labor market were discussed in earlier chapters.) Drawing on the experiences of various countries around the world, this chapter has drawn four main policy lessons.

First, avoid prematurely high labor costs. In Part I, we talked about the inadequacy of current wage levels and the importance of higher labor market earnings for poverty reduction. Yet if wages, benefits, and mandated work conditions are pushed up by government legislation, a predictable consequence is that existing firms are likely to hire fewer workers and some firms will go out of business entirely or not come into existence at all. Just because some of the firms we see operating pay the high labor costs does not mean that the overall volume of employment is insensitive to what has to be paid.

Second, be careful about labor legislation that is either excessively protective, excessively costly, or both. Of course, workers should be protected against abusive workplace conditions. The problem is that if workers are overly protected or if the protections are too costly, employers may refuse to hire workers in the first place. Policies that at first seem to be pro-worker do not necessarily turn out to be.

Third, weigh the benefits and costs of investing in the skills and productive abilities of workers, especially in those circumstances where skills deficiencies are causing existing job vacancies to go unfilled and new jobs not to be created. But do not make the mistake of thinking that what is good for any one worker or any one group of workers is necessarily good public policy.

And fourth, establish self-targeted programs in which the government guarantees low-wage employment to all who want to work in such jobs. Much learning, both positive and negative, has taken place. Draw on it.

CHAPTER 10
Increasing Self-Employment Earnings

As we saw in Chapter 4, in the countries where the world's poor are concentrated, the great majority of working people are self-employed; this includes those who operate their own businesses or are engaged in household enterprises, working alone or employing others. The self-employed tend to be poor, and the poor tend to be self-employed. "Survival entrepreneurs" is a term frequently used to describe those who work this way.

Furthermore, of those who are self-employed, the great majority are in firms not registered with the government (termed "informal sector" in most of the world and "unorganized sector" in India). Thus, informality is ubiquitous in the developing world. For this reason, much attention is paid to self-employment in the informal sector by general purpose organizations such as the World Bank, the regional development banks, and the Organization for Economic Cooperation and Development (OECD) as well as special-purpose organizations such as the International Labor Organization and Women in the Informal Economy: Governing and Organizing (WIEGO).[1]

Given that the poor are found predominantly outside formal paid employment and that most of the new entrants to the labor market, if they are to work at all, will have to enter the informal labor market, typically as self-employed, it follows that an important component of anti-poverty efforts will be to increase the returns to self-employment—what is sometimes called raising labor productivity. As detailed in the rest of this chapter, such a program would involve policy actions in the following areas:[2]

- Design products to help raise the productivity and earnings of the self-employed
- Adopt a positive policy stance and avoid hassles.

- Provide the poor in agriculture with more to work with.
- Facilitate supplemental off-farm employment and self-employment.
- Make capital available to the poor.
- Build skills and business know-how.
- Stimulate micro-franchising.

DESIGN PRODUCTS TO HELP RAISE THE PRODUCTIVITY OF THE SELF-EMPLOYED

Poor people often are limited in what they can earn by their very poverty and by the technologies available to them.[3] Paul Polak tells how the organization he founded, International Development Enterprises, helped refugee blacksmiths in Somalia build and sell five hundred donkey carts to their fellow refugees. An unexpected problem was encountered with the carts: the dirt roads they traveled on were covered with thorns, the carts would get flat tires, and tools for fixing flat tires were unavailable. Polak duly went off to Nairobi, the capital of nearby Kenya, and bought a large quantity of tube-patch kits and lug wrenches. The lug wrenches he bought were a high-quality British-made model that would last a lifetime and cost $12 each. He also returned with a small number of low-quality Chinese-made lug wrenches that were unlikely to last more than six months but sold for just $6 each. Polak reports his initial amazement that the cart owners would only buy the cheaper models even though these would probably not last until the next year. The donkey-cart owners explained their choices to him. By operating their carts for one month, they could generate enough income to buy ten of the high-quality wrenches the next month. However, getting a flat tire now that could not be repaired would cause them to lose their income and maybe even their carts. The cart owners therefore bought the wrench they could afford today so they could stay in business and earn more for tomorrow. As Polak puts it, "affordability rules."[4]

As another example of how product design can make a big difference, take the case of irrigation. Around the world, farmers could benefit enormously if they could irrigate their fields so they could grow crops throughout the year without depending on rainfall, quickly earning back what the irrigation system costs. Unfortunately, the farmers have no savings to use to make the investment, they lack collateral with which to borrow, and credit if available is prohibitively expensive. They therefore do what their ancestors have done before them since time immemorial: plant their seeds, rely on the rain, and sell the harvest at the same time as everyone else.[5]

International Development Enterprises has designed an ingenious new product to help overcome this negative cycle: a garden drip kit that irrigates twenty square meters at a cost of just $3. Using this new system, farmers can earn much more in the dry season than they could have otherwise, then use the profits to buy more drip kits, irrigate more land, increase their profits, and so on. Using this technology in India, Mohan Nitin and family have planted sweet limes intercropped with eggplant and other vegetables and are now earning more than $1,000 in the dry season compared to the $150 they had been earning before. And in Nepal, Krishna Bahadur Thapa and family were able to install many of these drip-irrigation units to grow cucumbers and cauliflowers in addition to rice and other subsistence crops. Because these out-of-season vegetables sell for three times more than in-season, the Bahadur family was able to increase their net income twenty-fold in just five years.

Besides International Development Enterprises, other organizations with names like KickStart, Fuel from the Fields, One Laptop per Child, and D-Rev: Design for the Other 90% are helping the poor increase their earnings and otherwise improve their lives. Some of the products are ingenious. A WorldBike is designed especially for transporting cargo. A mobile water purification tool called LifeStraw enables people to suck water directly though a filter, thereby preventing water-borne diseases. A rolling water system called Q Drum allows large quantities of water to be rolled from place to place rather than carried on one's head or back. A pot-in-pot cooling system with wet sand inserted between the two pots lets tomatoes last for twenty-one days rather than two or three.

In Chapter 6, I talked about using social cost-benefit analysis to help decide what works. One new technology is a treadle pump resembling a Stairmaster but made of bamboo that lifts water to the surface from up to seven meters below the ground. A cost-benefit calculation for Bangladesh showed that when donors invested $12 million in treadle pumps and smallholders another $37.5 million, the *annual* net smallholder return on investment was $150 million. So socially profitable investments *can* be made; they need to be discovered and implemented.

Let us not forget: affordability rules. Technology for the poor needs to be designed accordingly.

ADOPT A POSITIVE POLICY STANCE AND AVOID HASSLES

A twenty-six-year-old Tunisian with a degree in computer science could not find a job in his field, and so in economic desperation he started selling fruits and vegetables from a cart in his rural town. On December 17, 2010, authorities confiscated his produce because he was selling without a license and allegedly slapped his face. Incensed, the young man, Mohamed Bouazizi, poured gasoline over himself and set himself on fire. On January 4, 2011, Bouazizi died of his injuries. His supporters took to the streets, the police cracked down on the protestors, and even more people came into the streets of the capital city and elsewhere protesting escalating violence and oppression. On January 14, the protests forced the country's president, Zine al-Abidine Ben Ali, to flee the country. Similar protests spread to other countries in the region, forcing the ouster of President Hosni Mubarak in Egypt and, as these words are being written (July 2011), casting doubt on the continuation in office of Libyan leader Muammar Gaddafi.[6]

Masibisi, the handicraft producer and vendor living outside Durban, South Africa, whose story you read in Chapter 3, was also selling goods on the street without a license. As you learned there, Masibisi had rented a beachfront stall from a friend so she could sell handicraft items to tourists. The permit for operating the stall was in the friend's name. After four years of earning her living in this way, Masibisi was confronted by a government inspector who asked for her permit, saw that the name on the permit did not match the name on her national identity card, and prohibited her from operating further at that location. Masibisi had no choice but to return home and operate from there, selling mostly to middlemen at lower prices than she could have earned by selling directly to tourists.

Masibisi's situation exemplifies the attitudes taken by local governments in South Africa. In the late 1990s, the city council of Johannesburg declared the entire center city a no-trade zone. In 2004, the city council of Durban followed suit.

The Durban story is instructive.[7] The city council budgeted 3.7 million rand (about US$500,000) to be spent on employing and equipping fifty new metro police officers to stop "illegal, unlicensed street trading." What made them "illegal" was that the government had issued just 872 permits, thus denying permits to the vast majority of street traders in the city. Without warning, the police removed traders' goods. One street vendor in the Warwick Junction section described it this way: "The police have been taking our stuff, putting it in a lorry [truck], taking it and dumping it. It's a lot more now since Christmas. They have repainted the squares on the sidewalks [the squares delineated where each vendor could operate] and the police are enforcing it harshly. Now they come all the time; it used to be Monday, Friday, and Saturday."

The official hostility exhibited toward the self-employed by the governments of Johannesburg and Durban is worse than needless; it is anti-development. These attitudes are precisely what I was talking about in Chapter 6 when I discussed the importance of setting clear bottom-line objectives and moving on from there. If the city councils were to think of poverty reduction as a top priority, recognize that most of the poor people living in their jurisdictions have no choice but to earn their livelihoods from self-employment, and adopt a more positive or at least less-negative policy stance toward the self-employed, the urban poor would have a better chance of earning their way out of poverty.[8] I wonder, whose interests are the present policies serving?

At a high-level workshop in South Africa on that country's employment problem, I asked this question of the government official responsible for carrying out these policies in Durban. He answered, "I am trying to protect you against people like them." I told the official then and tell you now, I neither need nor want such protection. I want them to be able to earn a living.[9]

A diametrically opposed attitude toward self-employment in South Africa can be found in the village of Nqileni. The village has no road, school, running water, flush toilets, school, clinic, or electricity—in short, it is traditional Africa. What makes the village so special is that in Nqileni a remarkable couple, Réjane Woodroffe and Dave Martin, have built an eco-tourist facility called Bulungula Lodge in one of the most spectacularly beautiful settings on earth. There, with Réjane and Dave's assistance and encouragement, the local people, who own 40% of the lodge, have created self-employment opportunities for themselves offering visitors such opportunities as experiencing a women's day, learning to ride horses, taking a canoe trip, and growing vegetables and lemongrass. Thirty-five people have achieved more productive lives and are living better because of these self-employment activities.[10]

The informal economy should be nurtured, not repressed.

PROVIDE THE POOR IN AGRICULTURE WITH MORE TO WORK WITH

Agriculture is the source of employment for 1.3 billion people worldwide, 97% of them in developing countries.[11] Three out of four extremely poor persons in the world (defined as living on less than one U.S. dollar per person per day in purchasing power parity units) live in rural areas.[12] Most of these poor rural residents rely on agriculture in whole or in substantial part for their livelihoods. Figure 10.1 shows workers cultivating sugarcane in Barbados.

Figure 10.1
Agricultural workers, Barbados.

The people working in agriculture include landlords, smallholders, tenant farmers, sharecroppers, cultivators of collectively owned land, and wage laborers. *Landlords* own land which they rent to tenant farmers. *Smallholders* own land which they typically cultivate using their own labor and that of other family members; sometimes they are assisted by hired labor. *Tenant farmers* cultivate rented land, for which they pay a fixed rent. *Sharecroppers* cultivate land that they rent from landlords in return for a share of the crop produced; the typical share in the developing world is 50%. *Cultivators of collectively owned land* abound in countries such as China and Mexico where the land is owned by the government and throughout Africa where the land belongs to the tribe. Finally, *wage laborers* are landless people hired as needed to work others' land.

A study of fourteen countries gives a good sense of the different types of livelihood strategies followed by rural households. Nigeria is the most farm-oriented of the fourteen. There, 60% of rural households are subsistence farmers and 11% are market-oriented farmers. The remaining households are 14% oriented toward nonfarm labor, 1% to migration, and 14% in diversified activities. Countries like Bangladesh, Pakistan, and Vietnam have very different patterns. In Bangladesh, just 4% of rural households are market-oriented farmers and 2% subsistence farmers. On the other hand, 40% of rural households are labor-oriented, 6% are migration-oriented, and 48% are diversified.[13] These data show that non-farm rural activities are more than significant—they can predominate—and so they are treated more fully in the next section.

Rural poverty rates have fallen over time in many countries including China, India, and Ghana. How did those who moved out of poverty manage to get out? For a limited number of countries (Bangladesh, Tanzania, Indonesia, and the state of Andhra Pradesh in India), data are available following the same individuals or households over time. These data show that those who moved out of poverty did so via several pathways, including earning more in agriculture, earning more outside of agriculture, and migrating.[14]

One important component of the fight against global poverty is providing the poor in agriculture more to work with. African farmers grow only one-third the amount of grain per hectare as farmers in other developing regions. They are hampered by lack of fertilizers, high-yielding varieties of seeds, and access to water. Because they are poor and cannot get credit, they use the inputs they have, earn insufficient yields, and remain poor.[15]

A study of pro-poor growth policies in eight countries found that five policy interventions helped raise agricultural earnings. These were improving market access and lowering transactions costs, strengthening property rights to land, creating an incentive framework that benefited all farmers, expanding the technology available to smallholder producers, and helping poorer and smaller producers cope with risk.[16]

A critical resource in agriculture is, of course, land. Contrary to what you might have thought (and what I used to think), the amount of good agricultural land is not fixed in supply. It can be diminished by being turned to other uses—industrial development or urban spread, for example. But it can also be expanded through agricultural research.

An "agricultural miracle" has taken place in Brazil, which is the first tropical country to have joined the world's traditional big five grain producers (the United States, Canada, Australia, Argentina, and the European Union). The Brazilian successes have been brought about through a mix of agricultural research, capital-intensive production, openness to trade, and new farming techniques. In Brazil's cerrado (i.e., the savannah), the Brazilian Agricultural Research Corporation, known by its Portuguese acronym Embrapa, has made soils highly productive in four ways: pouring industrial quantities of lime onto the soil to reduce acidity, creating a new variety of grass that yields many times per hectare what the native grass had yielded, turning soybeans into a tropical crop, and pioneering new farm techniques including no-till agriculture. Government involvement in these ways led to a huge improvement which would not have happened otherwise.[17]

But in Brazil and throughout the developing world, land is distributed extremely unequally, even among agricultural households.[18] In Bangladesh, the bottom 40% of households own less than 2% of total land, while the top 5% own almost 35%. In Chile, commercial farmers cultivate 61% of the farm area, while small farmers, who are three times as numerous, cultivate only 2% of the farm area. In Tunisia, 8% of the farmers own more than 50% of the land area, 62% of landowners are smallholders, and 25% of the rural population is landless. In Udaipur district, India, which is extremely poor, 99% of poor households own some land, but many of the holdings are tiny and much of the land is of such poor quality that it cannot be used for cultivation purposes.[19] Small farms (defined as those smaller than five acres, or two hectares) make up more than 90% of all farms in China, Bangladesh, Vietnam, the Democratic Republic of Congo, and Egypt and more than 80% in Indonesia, India, and Ethiopia.[20] The *average* farm size in Bangladesh, Egypt, and Malawi is less than two acres.[21] As a result of such land distribution, the great majority of landholdings in Africa, Asia, and Latin America are too small to permit a household to earn a comfortable livelihood.

The inadequacy of small landholdings for rural livelihoods is one argument for land redistribution. Another is the widespread finding of an inverse relationship between farm size and output per hectare, due primarily to the availability of family labor on small farms and the consequent reduction in supervision costs. One consequence of this inverse relationship is that land redistribution to smallholders and the landless is likely to raise national income.[22]

Although there have been some historical successes—most notably, in Japan, Taiwan, Mexico, South Korea, and China—efforts at land redistribution have usually had only minimal effects because the forces of resistance are just too strong. Consequently, other policies have borne the brunt of efforts to lift the agricultural poor out of poverty. These policies include improving price incentives, making product and input markets work better, improving institutions, increasing access to financial services, reducing exposure to uninsured risk, enhancing the performance of producer organizations, and promoting innovation through science and technology.[23] More specifically, farmers in developing countries suffer from two policies that together reduce the prices they receive for their crops. On the one hand, their own country governments tax them to obtain revenue for urban-oriented programs. For instance, in sub-Saharan Africa, the agricultural tax rate is about 10%. On the other hand, developed country governments provide large subsidies to their farmers. Farm subsidies, already detailed in Chapter 7, have led to a stalemate in world trade talks and the consequent loss of potential gains from trade for the poor and for others.

Turning to product and input markets, these markets frequently do not work well for the poor. Information about market conditions is limited. Commodity exchanges are underdeveloped or nonexistent. Prices are volatile. Climatic shocks are great. The prices of traditional bulk exports such as coffee and cotton had been falling for years, before turning upward in 2009 and 2010. Problems in markets for inputs such as seed and fertilizer include high transactions costs and risks and diseconomies of small scale.

Some interventions in markets have helped the poor in agriculture. Information technologies such as community-based cell phones are enabling farmers to gain information about market prices. These cell phones have also helped lower farmers' transaction costs, for example, by enabling farmers to use agricultural credit cards to purchase inputs. Low fertilizer use has been overcome in some countries through targeted vouchers enabling recipients to purchase inputs and stimulating demand in private markets.

In Kenya, an experimental study found that farmers did not use fertilizer because the recommended use—that is, at the time of planting—did not pay; the seeds often failed to germinate and had to be replanted. But it was also found that returns were very high—231% to be precise—if a small amount of fertilizer was applied after the seeds had germinated, a process known as top-dressing. And yet, after field officers visited every one of the farmers in the study area to inform them of the results of the study, the farmers still did not use fertilizer much: only 37% of the farmers used fertilizer in the second season following the study and just 29% in the fourth. The problem, it turned out, was that farmers were unable to save the money they earned in the harvest season to buy the fertilizer in the next top-dressing season. A nongovernmental organization, International Child Support, offered to do the saving for them, offering free delivery of the fertilizer soon after the harvest season. Fertilizer usage doubled as a result of this intervention.[24]

Despite the best efforts of agricultural extension agents around the world, the diffusion of best practices is often slow. Applying fertilizer at the time of germination rather than planting is one case in which farmers learned better ways of doing things. Another example is a program called the System of Rice Intensification (SRI) in which my university, Cornell, participates. SRI was the life's work of Fr. Henri de Laulanié, a French priest who was sent to Madagascar in 1961, worked with local farmers to learn what worked, and then disseminated the results. The techniques are quite simple: planting very young seedlings (8–12 days old) rather than more mature seedlings (3–4 weeks old); planting seedlings singly rather than in clumps of three or four; planting fewer seedlings more widely spaced; keeping the fields moist but never flooded; doing several weedings rather than one; and adding compost to improve the soil quality. The effects are remarkable: by following these simple steps, rice yields have been raised by 50% to 100% compared with the yields in traditional flooded paddies while using 40% less water and 50% less fertilizer—and the production cost is 20% lower. SRI is now being practiced in forty-one countries around the world.[25]

Many institutional problems are to be found in smallholder agriculture. They include incomplete and inefficient land markets, poor access to and information about financial markets, distorted input markets, and producer organizations which only now are beginning to represent the interests of poor smallholders. These institutional problems are starting to be overcome in a variety of ways: through improved and more transparent property rights for farmers, the spread of banks and other financial institutions to rural areas, improved targeting of subsidies to smallholders and away from large landowners, and more effective producer cooperatives. Progress is slowly being made.

Exposure to negative shocks such as drought and illness can trap a household in poverty. Rural households find it difficult if not impossible to undertake actions that are likely to help them over the long run but that also run significantly greater risk of failure. For example, when new high-yielding rice varieties were introduced in Asia, farmers resisted planting the new seeds. The reason for their resistance, it turned out, was not that they were captive to tradition but because experimental evidence showed that although the new varieties were higher-yielding *on average*, they were too risky. High-yielding varieties require consistent rainfall or irrigation during the growing season. In the event of inconsistent access to water—either too much rain or too little—yields would turn out to be lower than with the traditional seed varieties, possibly disastrously lower. Such a risk is simply unacceptable to poor farmers. Well-functioning insurance markets—in this case, crop insurance—would have helped protect vulnerable households against such perils, leading to greater adoption of the higher-yielding varieties. But two problems arise for the poor: (1) such insurance markets often do not exist, and (2) because of their poverty, the poor typically lack the ability to participate in such markets.

Access to financial services remains a severe problem for agricultural smallholders in developing countries. In the absence of property rights on assets to serve as collateral, poor people are prevented from getting formal credit and other financial services. For example, in India, a survey showed that 87% of marginal farmers had no access to formal credit, and 71% had no access to a savings account in a formal financial institution.[26] Improving smallholders' access to these services would make it easier for them to use new technologies and thereby achieve higher productivity and earnings. Access to finance has been enhanced through microcredit schemes; because this topic is so important and extends well beyond agriculture, it is discussed in its own section later in this chapter.

An instructive example of how earnings among self-employed farmers are being raised is the government of Turkey's Southeast Anatolia Project, known by its Turkish acronym GAP. A part of the State Planning Organization, GAP has been going on for the last twenty years. The money used to finance GAP comes from privatization funds and from the Turkish social security system.

An integrated rural development project, GAP encompasses investments in agriculture, industry, transportation, education, health, and rural and urban infrastructure. Its goals are ambitious: to irrigate 1.7 million hectares of land, generate 27 billion kilowatt hours of electricity per year, increase per capita income by 209%, and expand employment by 3.8 million people.[27]

The government recognizes the importance of attracting private sector investment to the region. So far, little such investment has taken place because locating there is not considered profitable. GAP aims to improve transportation, energy, industrial, and urban infrastructure services; facilitate firms' access to financial resources; build incentive mechanisms in line with the productive features of the region; make services by other agencies in the region more effective; and improve social life.

On a visit to the region in 2009, I saw the striking contrast between the lands that had been irrigated with GAP support and the ones that had not (Figure 10.2). Those farmers that have been helped have seen great improvements in agricultural productivity. Sadly, though, the reality on the ground is lagging behind the targets: according to a government report, only 15% of the planned investments in irrigation had been realized to date.[28] Government recognizes full well that its targets for crop diversification and development of agro-based industry cannot possibly be achieved until the remaining investments are made.

Gokhan Guder heads the Social Support Program of the GAP, known by its Turkish acronym SODES. The program is spending some $80 million for the period of 2008–2012 and has helped more than twelve million people to date in nine Turkish provinces. SODES endeavors to (1) contribute to solving the nation's employment problem through public works

Figure 10.2
Irrigated and non-irrigated lands, Turkey.

employment (which planned to cover 100,000 people in 2009) and vocational education for unemployed people; (2) promote social inclusion (in particular, trying to integrate the multicultural and multi-ethnic southeast with the rest of Turkey, and trying to integrate the poor parts of the major city in the region, Diyarbakir, with the rich); and (3) offer cultural and supportive activities. Says Guder modestly, "SODES is a program of opportunities for the most needy region of the country and for the most needy people of the region. It is a tiny touch to the worlds of little people with an aim to make their hopes real through better education, better jobs, and a better social and cultural life."[29]

GAP illustrates both how a serious constraint to earning opportunities for the self-employed is being overcome —in this case, the lack of water for agricultural activities— and how much more needs to be done for even the government's own targets to be realized.

The Bill and Melinda Gates Foundation has highlighted agricultural development as one of its priority areas. When the Gates Foundation decides on a priority, two things happen. The first is that massive resources are made available provided (and this is the second thing that must happen) it can be shown that the interventions proposed are actually effective. In this case, the Gates Foundation commissioned a study by the International Food Policy Research Institute to find out what works. Out of more than 250 candidate interventions, twenty were chosen as "proven successes."[30] To give you a flavor, they range from the green revolution in Asia, to improved maize production in sub-Saharan Africa, to growing pearl millet and sorghum in arid lands, to connecting the milk grid in India, to land tenure reform in Vietnam. This kind of evidence-based policy formulation is a great model for other aspects of development policy.

In summary, poor self-employed farmers lack land, water, other inputs, knowledge of best practices, access to product markets, protection against risk, and access to financial services. They are confronted by numerous institutional constraints, only some of which are beginning to be relaxed. But many lessons are known about what works, and the word is being spread.

FACILITATE SUPPLEMENTAL OFF-FARM WAGE EMPLOYMENT AND SELF-EMPLOYMENT

The standard picture that many of us have of rural workers in the developing world—I know that I did—is that their primary activity is family farming. The problem with the standard picture is that it incorrectly equates rural with farming. Omitted is something that is less readily obvious: rural households are also engaged in large numbers in off-farm employment. The share of the rural population engaged in nonfarm employment is more than 40% in Asia and 25% in Latin America. China has more than twenty million township and village enterprises (TVEs), which employ some 30% of the total rural labor force. These TVEs played a key role in China's excellent record on economic growth and rural poverty reduction.[31]

Rural nonfarm incomes are reported to be twenty times as important as incomes from agricultural wage labor in Africa and four times as important in rural India.[32] The data also show that rural nonfarm activities account for 42% of the income of rural households in Africa, 40% in Latin America, and 32% in Asia. In short, off-farm employment is crucial to rural livelihoods.[33]

What is common, though by no means universal, is for a household to have more than one activity.[34] In some cases, single individuals do two or more kinds of work in the same day or week. In other cases, members of a given household divide up, some working on the land and some working elsewhere. And in other cases, everyone in the household works on the family farm during the planting and harvesting seasons and works off-farm in the slack seasons.

The reasons for performing multiple employment activities are many. They include such "push factors" as risk reduction, diminishing returns to labor input in agriculture, reaction to crisis or liquidity constraints, and high transaction costs that induce households to provide for themselves rather than trade in markets. On the other side, there are also "pull factors" which include realizing complementarities between activities, such as integrating crops and livestock or milling and hog production, and specialization according to comparative advantage.[35]

When individuals and households have been followed over time in East Africa and Southeast Asia, the data show that large increases in nonfarm income have led to corresponding reductions in rural poverty rates.[36] In the Philippines, as per capita income increased significantly for farm households, the share of nonfarm income in total income nearly doubled. Over two years, the proportion of households that were poor fell from 50% to 31% among farm households and from 63% to 24% among landless households. Equally dramatic increases in nonfarm income and consequent reductions in poverty rates were recorded in Thailand.

What types of rural nonfarm work are people doing? In the village of Debre Berhan in Ethiopia, 89% of the households gather firewood in common woodlands and sell the wood both to local urban residents and to itinerant traders on their way to areas with scarce firewood.[37] In Bangladesh, women work in cottage industries (those that can be performed in the home) including such activities as rice-husking, mat making, net making, and coir products—work that could be performed in the home without breaking social custom. In Africa too, women dominate in activities that can be performed in the home: beer brewing in Botswana, Burkina Faso, Malawi, and Zambia; fish processing in Senegal and Ghana; pottery in Malawi; rice husking in Tanzania; and retailing and vending in general.[38] In Mexico, countless small rural enterprises manufacture terra-cotta plates for cooking tortillas.

Besides the more traditional activities just described, rural workers often engage in quite modern nonfarm activities. In the town of Pelileo in the Sierra region of rural Ecuador, some four hundred small enterprises are engaged in jeans tailoring; most of these firms are operated by women and children working in their homes and providing the completed jeans to a larger firm.[39] In countless villages around the world, village phone ladies operate small businesses selling cell phone minutes to locals. And in China's Township and Village Enterprises, rural workers' activities run the entire gamut from manufacturing to construction to services.

The ability of the poor to participate in nonfarm employment is constrained by many factors which include lack of liquidity and access to credit, lack of information about production methods and markets, lack of education or language skills, poor transportation infrastructure, insufficient land or labor, and lack of social capital. The poorest households are most constrained by insufficient assets (education, skills, and startup capital) and lack of access to both product markets and labor markets. The poorest regions are constrained by poor physical infrastructure (roads, electricity, and the like), lack of skills in the workforce, and limited or uneconomical access to raw materials.[40]

What types of policies would help overcome these constraints? Rural nonfarm activities are quite diverse, and therefore policies need to be somewhat finely tuned to the specific needs of different groups. Some needs, however, are quite general.

One is the need to overcome the disadvantages of location. Those who live far from markets have little opportunity to engage in viable off-farm activities. To overcome such disadvantages, investments are needed in "hard infrastructure" such as roads and electrification as well as "soft infrastructure," which includes banking systems and market information systems.

Another is the need for general education and specific skills. In the rural economy, not only do better-educated farmers earn more than less-educated ones but also earnings in nonfarm rural activities are higher for the better educated.

A third is the need for greater access to credit and financial savings. Lacking such credit, rural households are limited in their ability to diversify out of crop agriculture and get into livestock raising, acquire costly assets such as machinery, or establish remunerative nonfarm enterprises.

One instructive contrast is presented by the experiences of Taiwan and South Korea. The government of Taiwan chose a geographically decentralized development strategy. There, the growth of industry is spread rather evenly across the island, as is infrastructure. In South Korea, by contrast, manufacturing activity was concentrated in Seoul and Pusan, the agricultural sector was slow to mechanize, and infrastructure investments were heavily concentrated in the cities. Although both economies grew rapidly, Taiwan followed a much more egalitarian path than did South Korea.

MAKE CAPITAL AVAILABLE TO THE POOR

With a per capita income of just US$270 per year, Nepal is one of the poorest countries on earth. Several hours east of the capital city of Kathmandu, a group of twenty poor people in Chaurmuni village led by a man named Gure Sarki decided to expand their livestock herd. Together, they took out a World Bank–financed loan from the government of Nepal at an interest rate of 1% per year so that they could buy fifty-five goats at $50 apiece. Sarki plans to sell his goats after one year for a profit of about $25 each. Such profits are huge for a low-caste, underfed farmer in a location with a per capita income of just $90 a year.[41]

Studies in countries such as Mexico and Sri Lanka show high rates of return for borrowers with low amounts of initial capital. The *monthly* rates of return are 15% in the case of Mexico and 5% in Sri Lanka.[42]

Noted economist Jeffrey Sachs tells us that the extreme poor lack six kinds of capital:[43]

- Human capital, which includes health, nutrition, and skills needed for each person to be economically productive.
- Business capital, which includes the machinery, facilities, and motorized transport used in agriculture, industry, and services.
- Infrastructure, which includes roads, power, water and sanitation, airports and seaports, and telecommunications systems, all of which are critical inputs into business productivity
- Natural capital, which includes arable land, healthy soils, biodiversity, and well-functioning ecosystems that provide the environmental services needed by human society.
- Public institutional capital, which includes commercial law, judicial systems, government services and policing that underpin the peaceful and prosperous division of labor.
- Knowledge capital, which includes the scientific and technological know-how that raises productivity in business output and the promotion of physical and natural capital.

In Thailand, for example, one-third of households report that they would like to open their own business, but they are unable to do so because of lack of capital. The majority of Thai entrepreneurial households report that they would earn more if they could expand their business, but 56% of them do not have enough funds to expand.[44]

The lack of capital is particularly severe for micro-enterprises, which suffer from inadequate property rights and hence lack of collateral. To overcome these problems, the Peruvian economist Hernando DeSoto and others have advocated providing formal titles to land and clear property rights over assets so that the poor can put up collateral and obtain loans more easily.[45]

At first, it may seem puzzling that capital does not flow to the poor. Basic economics courses teach that a given extra amount of capital would produce a lower extra benefit for an enterprise that already has a lot of capital compared to one with only a little.[46] If this proposition were descriptively accurate, the poor enterprises with less capital would be able to benefit more and pay banks higher interest rates than the rich enterprises. Lenders would then be willing to serve the poor, and capital would flow from rich to poor borrowers. Indeed, Nobel Prize–winning economist Robert Lucas wrote a paper addressing this very issue with the provocative title "Why Doesn't Capital Flow from Rich to Poor Countries?" [47]

However, some features of the real world run counter to this basic economic model.[48] One set of reasons has to do with the low credit-worthiness of small borrowers. Because the poor lack collateral to offer as security to banks, loans to the poor are riskier.

A second set of reasons has to do with what economists call "market failures." One type of market failure is adverse selection, which arises when banks and other financial institutions cannot distinguish easily between safer borrowers and riskier ones, and so they raise average interest rates for all borrowers, thereby driving safer borrowers out of the credit market. Another type of market failure is moral hazard, which arises when borrowers do not undertake everything in their power to pay back their loans—for example, by defaulting opportunistically. A third type of market failure is transaction costs, which make it costlier for banks to process many small loans to poor borrowers than to make a single large loan to a rich borrower.

As a consequence of these real-world features, the poor have only limited opportunities to raise the capital they need to be able to make profitable investments that might help lift them out of poverty. First, poor households may borrow from families, relatives, and friends. Because those loans are made reciprocally, they carry little or no interest. On the other hand, the social networks of the poor include mostly other poor people, so this limits the amount of capital that can be raised from this low-cost source. Second, the poor may borrow from moneylenders who charge them very high interest rates. Kalavati, the bidi roller whom we met in Chapter 3, pays an interest rate of 10% *per month* on her loans. In the Philippines, under a system known as 5/6 loans, a lender makes available 5,000 pesos (about US$100) at the beginning of the month and expects the borrower to pay back 6,000 pesos by the end of the month, usually at the rate of 200 pesos per day. The going interest rate therefore exceeds 20% *per month*. Even worse, in Chennai, India, fruit vendors borrow 1,000 rupees at the beginning of the day from a wholesaler and repay

1,046.9 rupees at the end of the day—an interest rate of 4.69% *per day*.[49] In fact, lenders often hope that the loans they make will not be repaid, so that they will receive interest payments in perpetuity. In India, debts do not end at death but are passed on to one's heirs.[50]

Fortunately for the poor and for the development enterprise more generally, new microfinance institutions are being established and existing ones are being expanded. The major types of microfinance institutions are these.[51] *Credit unions* are owned and controlled by members, and profits are reinvested or shared among members. *Village banks* are member-based institutions that receive deposits and make loans. Village banks have been supported by a variety of nongovernmental organizations including FINCA (the Foundation for International Community Assistance), Freedom from Hunger, CARE, Save the Children, and others. *Microbanks*, by contrast, are owned not by their members but instead by individuals or legal entities. The primary purpose of microbanks is to serve the demand for financial services for micro- and small-scale entrepreneurs. Examples are the BRI in Indonesia, Bancosol in Bolivia, and Calpiá in El Salvador. Then, there are different *group retail models*. Acción in Latin America was the first major one of these. The most famous is Bangladesh's Grameen Bank.

The Grameen Bank and its founder, the Bangladeshi economist Dr. Muhammed Yunus, were awarded the Nobel Peace Prize in 2006 for their pathbreaking work in microfinance. The Nobel citation read in part, "Loans to poor people without any financial security had appeared to be an impossible idea. From modest beginnings three decades ago, Yunus has, first and foremost through the Grameen Bank, developed microcredit into an ever more important instrument in the struggle against poverty."

The approach taken by Dr. Yunus and the Grameen Bank works as follows. Five (previously ten) individuals, usually all women, form a group which may then borrow a small sum of money (around US$100) collateral-free at relatively low interest rates (on the order of 12% to 17% *per year*). (The Grameen Bank charges a lower interest rate than my credit card company does.) The bank makes loans to group members in sequence, extending a loan to another person in a group only after the previous loans made to group members have been repaid. Knowing this, group members have a strong incentive to choose others for the group whom they judge to be reliable, thus helping the bank overcome the problem of assessing credit-worthiness. (The group used to have a collective responsibility system whereby each group member would be liable for repaying a loan made to any member of the group, but that is no longer the case.) Through self-enforcement by group members, particularly risky projects and opportunistic defaults are kept to a minimum. As a result, the Grameen Bank's loan recovery rate exceeds 90%. Once all the loans in a given round have been repaid, the group becomes eligible for new, larger loans.

This basic model has been carried all over the world by organizations like Acción, BRAC (formerly, the Bangladesh Rehabilitation Assistance Committee), FINCA International, Opportunity International, Spandana, Kashf, and the Grameen Foundation—even to New York City, where Grameen America makes loans ranging from $500 to $3,000 to people like vendors, bakers, and barbers who have little or no access to credit.[52] Microloans go to more than 150 million borrowers a year.

Another type of microfinance is for-profit lending. In Mexico, organizations such as Compartamos ("Let Us Share" in Spanish) make small loans to the poor at interest rates starting at 6% *per month*. Angela, the Mexican fireworks maker whose story you read in Chapter 3, is one of the Compartamos borrowers. She and the others in her group each pay interest on the order of 90% per year. Moreover, Compartamos has a group liability clause which Grameen and most other not-for-profits do not—in Angela's case, she and eighteen other group members are collectively responsible for repaying the group's Compartamos loans each Wednesday for the term of the loan. Figure 10.3 shows the lending booklet for Angela and the others in her group indicating that each of them had paid the final installment leaving a balance of zero for all nineteen women.

The high interest rates charged by Compartamos result in high returns for the lender: 52.2% annual return on equity in the specific case of Compartamos, 33.2% on average for a group of twelve microfinance institutions in Latin America.[53] By comparison, the average return on equity for Mexican commercial banks is just 15%.[54]

Interest rates on small loans in poor countries do not need to be so high. India's largest microcredit company, SKS Microfinance, keeps costs low by standardizing loan-approval techniques and using technology to keep track of disbursements, enabling it to charge a relatively modest annual interest rate of 28.3%.[55] Despite the high interest rates charged, the default rate on these microloans is just 2%, which is quite low by international standards. The high repayment rate is attributed in part to the needs the poor have for capital and the many good uses to which they can put it. But another reason repayment rates are so high is the design of the loan mechanism itself: like other micro-lenders, SKS relies on group lending whereby five clients assume joint responsibility for timely payments, and

Figure 10.3
Document showing loan fully paid off, Mexico.

if any one group member's loan has to be written off, the other members of the group can no longer borrow.

Microfinance institutions (MFIs) are charging interest rates ranging from more than 100% in the case of for-profit lenders like Compartamos, to 28% plus fees and insurance premiums for SKS, to 12% to 17% for non-profits such as the Grameen Bank. It doesn't have to be this way, even in India.

A major transformation has taken place in the state of Andhra Pradesh. (Andhra Pradesh has a population of more than 80 million, comparable to that of Germany. If Andhra Pradesh were a country, it would be the fourteenth largest in the world.) In Andhra Pradesh, borrowers may take out loans from each other or borrow from banks at interest rates of 12% a year, which itself is a low rate for microlending. But beyond that, as an incentive for prompt repayment, those who borrow from the banks and repay on time pay just 3% interest. The remaining 9% is paid by the state government. More than 11 million women in Andhra Pradesh are able to take out loans on such terms.

During a visit to Andhra Pradesh in June 2011, I learned first-hand how the state achieved this remarkable outcome. Beginning in 1992, with encouragement from the Independent South Asian Commission on Poverty Alleviation and India's National Bank for Agriculture and Rural Development, women in Andhra Pradesh and elsewhere were encouraged to form local self-help groups (SHGs), each comprised of ten self-selected women. The SHGs in a village were then federated into village organizations, and the village organizations in turn into larger federations called mandals. With funding from the United Nations Development Program and the World Bank, the South Asia Poverty Alleviation Project was piloted in three districts of Andhra Pradesh in 1995, then later expanded to fifteen districts and then to all twenty-two. In 2000, the state government created the Society for the Elimination of Rural Poverty (SERP) as the organization responsible for a range of anti-poverty programs including microcredit.

The microcredit component works as follows. The members of SHGs meet weekly or monthly to collect savings from their members. As a group's savings balance accumulates, the group makes loans to its members in ways they themselves decide, typically at an annual interest rate of 12%. In addition, although the individual women are judged non-bankable, the SHGs may take out bank loans under the so-called SHG-Bank Linkage Model, using the group's accumulated savings as collateral. These are the loans for which the banks receive 12% interest, usually with 3% being paid by the borrowing SHG and 9% by the state. In turn, the SHG allocates the loan proceeds among members in ways they themselves determine, much as in Compartamos, Grameen, and most other microcredit schemes around the world.

At present, more than 11 million women are organized into one million self-help groups, the largest number anywhere in the world. The loans are now funded more by the SHGs' own accumulations than from banks. Enabling microloans to be offered at 12% annual interest or even 3% is a major achievement of the Andhra Pradesh program. In the words of SERP's head B. Rajsekhar, "[p]overty is an affront to human dignity, and a cost to the economy and the polity. SERP's model is to empower the poor, offer greater opportunities, and reduce vulnerabilities."[56]

A heated debate rages between those who take the not-for-profit and the for-profit approaches.[57] Says Muhammad Yunus, "Let them make money—

but why do you want to make money off the poor people? You make money somewhere else. Here, you come to help them."[58] Taking the opposing view, Carlos Danel and Carlos Labarthe, the heads of Compartamos, say, "Microfinance will help more poor people by tapping the boundless pool of investor capital rather than the limited pool of donor money."[59] The *Economist*, which has been publishing articles on microfinance for years, published an editorial subtitled "In Support of Profiting from the Poor," but the article itself went on to say, "Profiting from the poor can be wrong, when lending is predatory—when the lender expects that the borrower will be unable to pay the interest or repay the principal."

Several lessons emerge from the microfinance institutions' experiences. One is that on average it works best to lend money to women rather than men because women have proven themselves more credit-worthy. Second, beyond lending money, it works to provide poor people with the ability to save and invest. The director general of Compartamos, Carlos Labarthe, states: "People don't just need credit. They need financial services. They need savings accounts. They need insurance, life insurance, education insurance. These are things that no middle-class person, no poor person, has ever had in Mexico." A third lesson is that it does not work for the government to run such programs. As Mohammed Yunus explains, "Politicians are interested in the votes of the poor. [They] are not interested in getting the money back."[60]

Following a comprehensive review of various countries' experiences, one analyst has proposed thirteen rules for successful pro-poor credit: (1) Respect fungibility. (2) Focus extra lending on the poor, but not by targeting it directly on persons or households labeled "poor" by lenders. (3) Avoid lending rules that discriminate against the poor. (4) Poor people lack collateral, so protect lenders' capital by other means. (5) Keep down the transaction cost of lending. (6) To avoid covariate risks, adopted nested organization to diversify the lender's portfolio by size and sector. (7) Avoid monopoly of lending; formal lenders, moneylenders, and NGOs are complements. (8) Before the state acts to increase credit supply, ensure that unmet needs exist and that meeting such needs has satisfactory financial, private economic, and social returns. (9) Subsidize administration and transactions costs of lending agencies readily but temporarily, capital loans very sparingly, and interest rates hardly ever. (10) Don't politicize or otherwise soften repayment. (11) Good economic returns to credit and good repayment are likelier if there is adequate infrastructure and education. (12) Lending institutions gain by insisting that members save before they borrow. (13) Create incentives for lenders to expand where, and only where, they succeed.[61]

Evaluation studies have shown that the Grameen Bank has been successful in channeling credit to the poor at reasonable cost. For example, in Bangladesh, a loan of one hundred taka (the local currency) has been shown to raise household consumption by eight taka annually—a significant but not huge effect. Similarly, in other countries, the effects have typically been shown to be positive in direction but modest in size.[62]

Randomized experiments of the type described in Chapter 6 have produced mixed results in India, the Philippines, South Africa, Peru, Ecuador, Honduras, and Bangladesh. Spending on tobacco and alcohol was reduced in favor of durable goods. More businesses were started up. Villagers who received loans and business training did better than those who received loans alone. Using individual liability rather than collective liability did not reduce repayment rates. Combining village health banks with microcredit sometimes raised family income compared with microcredit alone. Poverty among participants fell in South Africa, but not in India or the Philippines.[63]

In sum, microcredit has succeeded in getting money into poor people's hands, producing favorable but not uniformly favorable outcomes. This is the best way known of creating opportunities for the poor to build up their own businesses and earn their way out of poverty.

BUILD SKILLS AND BUSINESS KNOW-HOW

The majority of self-employed workers in developing countries are characterized by low skills, low productivity, and low income. These individuals often lack basic life skills such as numeracy and literacy, problem-solving, decision-making, and negotiation skills. Lacking these skills, their confidence and capacity to explore and try new income-earning opportunities are severely constrained.

The situation in East Africa typifies the developing world. A national-level survey in Kenya of micro and small entrepreneurs (MSEs) showed that the formal educational attainments are limited: 10% had no education at all, 54% had only primary education, 33% had at least some secondary education, and just 3% had post-secondary education. Of the self-employed operating informally, 85% had received no training at all, and for rural and women entrepreneurs, the percentage was even higher. In Uganda, conditions are the same: national-level surveys of small and medium-sized enterprises show that the majority of those working in this sector are without skills.[64]

Besides basic education and life skills, self-employed workers often lack basic business skills. Among the gaps are the technical and entrepreneurial skills to operate and manage a business; the basic financial knowledge needed to manage money, save safely, obtain credit, and take out insurance; and knowledge of new technologies, access to information about their trades, and knowledge of marketing of produce and other products.

To overcome these limitations, many interventions have been put into place aimed at building up skills and abilities for self-employment. The organizations involved include labor unions, private companies, membership-based organizations, overseas volunteers, governments, and development banks. Here are some of their stories.

Shantabai was born into a poor and illiterate family in India.[65] She achieved only an incomplete elementary school education before entering into an arranged marriage at age thirteen. For years, she and her husband worked the family's small piece of land, while Shantabai shouldered the additional burden of caring for her children and her husband's elderly parents.

To try to improve her situation, Shantabai enrolled in several training courses operated by Srujan, a 3,000-member union which is a partner organization of the ILO's Workers' Activities programme (ACTRAV). The training that made the difference for Shantabai was a course in photography skills. As a child, she had dreamed of becoming a professional photographer, and this course opened the door for her to make photography a profession. Although her husband was supportive of her endeavor, the family elders were not. In the conservative village community where she lived, women were expected to cover their faces with veils, not work openly in the community. But Shantabai persevered, taking out a loan of US$125 to buy a used camera. Gradually, she built up a reputation, and her clientele grew. The fact that she is a woman works to her advantage in one important sense: women who would not bare their faces to male photographers agree to be photographed by her. She now earns about US$50 per month taking photographs at weddings, family functions, and village festivals. She also helps other women by teaching photography and by participating actively in local government. She says, "Women should be bold and gather as much knowledge and information as they can and excel in their respective fields. This will help them to be independent and confident to lead a decent life and contribute to the development of society." [66]

One corporate effort that aligns the training needs of small operators on the one hand with the marketing needs of a global company on the other is the experience of Coca-Cola Sabco (CCS). CCS is a multinational operating throughout southern Africa as well as South and Southeast Asia. ("SABCO" originally stood for South Africa Bottling Company, but that term is no longer used because of the company's geographic spread.) CCS found that it could not get its product distributed to rural areas because of the poor quality of roads, especially in rural areas and informal settlements. At the same time, unemployment and underemployment were widespread in the host countries. CCS responded by creating a system of manual distribution centers (MDCs), which are small businesses owned and operated by micro-entrepreneurs. CCS assisted the new owners by designing routes and methods of delivery, determining the frequency of delivery service required to keep the shelves stocked, working with local banks to arrange for credit for the entrepreneurs, helping with procurement of delivery vehicles such as custom-made bicycles, and offering financial training and other types of skills development. At present, there are 380 MDCs in Kenya generating over US$100 million in revenue and employing nearly 4,000 people. One MDC owner states, "I'm very happy with the opportunity that Coca-Cola has given me. I did not ever dream of being an investor, employing others, and supporting my greater family." For CCS, the benefits include increases in sales, access to smaller and harder-to-reach retail outlets, and further innovation in distribution methods. Ed Potter, the director for Global Workplace Rights at Coca-Cola, calls this a "marriage of company interest with individual interest."[67]

Another company, Goldman Sachs, has launched a global philanthropic drive called "10,000 Women" which, over five years, is aimed at empowering women through business education and training. Among the beneficiaries are Ngozi Okoli-Owube, a Nigerian woman earning a certificate in entrepreneurial management; Fatima Kazimi, who attended a management program in Arizona and now is the only female storeowner at the bazaar in her hometown in Afghanistan; and Iman Youssry, an Egyptian furniture designer, who attended a five-week course on basic business skills at the American University of Cairo.[68]

A world-renowned membership-based organization is India's Self-Employed Women's Association (SEWA). SEWA is an organization of poor, self-employed women. SEWA's information and communications technology initiative has been providing training to semi-literate and illiterate women, some of whom had been marginalized farmers, salt workers, dairy farmers, and artisans; many had never been to school or even held a pen in their hand. Once these women were taught the English alphabet, they could then be trained to use mobile phones in their micro-enterprises and even in selling agricultural products. Thus, sesame seed growers like Jasuben of Surendranagar district use their mobile telephones to get information on the market prices of produce in nearby markets. They can then make informed decisions ensuring the maximum revenue from their produce. Similarly, salt workers and tobacco rollers now use telephones and mobiles to get the latest market information and decide their selling strategy accordingly.[69]

An example of a government-operated training scheme for the self-employed is the Labor Force Training Support Project in Côte d'Ivoire, known by its French acronym PAFPA (Projet d'Appui a la Formation de la Population). The objectives of PAFPA are to contribute to an increase of labor force productivity and mobility through technical and basic skills training with special emphasis on small businesses and women's enterprises. Before this training project, the literacy rate of women in the area was only 10%, and for those in agriculture only 7%. This project focuses on micro-enterprises and women's training because the labor market is dominated by very small firms, and women represent 63% of informal sector employment. PAFPA's three components are micro-enterprise training, training of displaced workers, and training of female entrepreneurs. A careful econometric evaluation study found positive economic impacts in terms of increased earnings for several groups as a result of training received—namely, women, the agricultural and electronics sectors, and micro and small enterprises.[70]

As a last example, a program in Peru addresses the needs of the self-employed for both financial capital and human capital. Poor female micro-entrepreneurs who borrowed from FINCA (the Foundation for International Community Assistance) were randomly assigned to two groups. The control group had mandatory weekly meetings, as indeed is customary for the kinds of microfinance programs described in the previous section. The treatment group, on the other hand, received thirty to sixty minutes of entrepreneurial training during their mandatory weekly meetings over the course of a year or two. Clients were taught such skills as separating household money from business money, reinvesting profits in the business, maintaining records of sales and expenses, and thinking proactively about new markets and opportunities for profits. An evaluation study showed positive effects of the business training not only for the borrowers in terms of improved business knowledge, practices, and revenues but also for the lending agency in terms of higher repayment rates.[71]

STIMULATE MICRO-FRANCHISING

Marie-Claire Ayuwanda runs two small businesses in rural Rwanda. One of her businesses is a restaurant at which she serves grilled goat and

Irish potatoes. The other is a small cell phone business: when a customer or a passerby wishes to make a phone call, she sells minutes on her cell phone—one of the few phones of any kind in her village.

In Marie-Claire's case, the Grameen Foundation provided a loan so that she could literally buy a business in a box: not only the phone but also instructions on how to operate the phone, charge for minutes, and so on. Marie-Claire was able to repay her start-up loan in five months from the profits on her business; now the phone and the business she now owns generate about US$12 of income for her each week—this in a country with average income of around US$ 230 per year. Marie-Claire says, "In addition to paying school fees for my children, I bought the land and the foundation for my new home with the profits from my Village Phone. If I get some more business to do, in a few years I will die as a rich woman." (Sadly, the reason she expects to die in a few years is that she is living with HIV/AIDS.) [72]

The Rwandan program is modeled on the Grameen Bank's highly successful Village Phones program in Bangladesh.[73] The Village Phone ladies in Rwanda, Bangladesh, and elsewhere (so-called, because nearly all of them are women) are beneficiaries of an approach to development known as micro-franchising.

In India, an organization called Drishtee operates tele-kiosks offering telephone, internet, and computer services. The company operates in 4,000 villages, has created 5,300 jobs, and serves 7.5 million clients.[74]

Micro-franchising brings together micro-franchisors (entrepreneurs who wish to expand their businesses) and micro-franchisees (people who seek to operate their own self-employment activities but may be lacking in business know-how).[75] The micro-franchisors bring to the table knowledge of how to create numerous small businesses that can be replicated over and over. The micro-franchisees bring a drive for success and a willingness to work hard. The franchisors provide the franchisees with business placement support, tested operational guidelines, established suppliers, access to loans, and built-in support systems including business development help, mentoring, and a network of peers. When successful—and indeed there are hundreds of thousands of successes around the world—micro-franchising results in profitable involvement for both sides.

One type of micro-franchising is top-down. In top-down micro-franchising, the micro-franchisor grants a contract to the micro-franchisee to establish a similar business. After paying the franchise fees and agreeing to adhere to quality standards, the franchisee obtains the right to use the franchisor's trademark and receives marketing support, detailed manuals on how to operate the business, start-up assistance, staff training, equipment, procurement of raw materials, and regular visits by a representative of the franchisor. An example familiar to many readers is McDonald's, which operates on a top-down franchise model. A successful example of this type of franchising in the developing world is VisionSpring.

VisionSpring, formerly known as the Scojo Foundation, and Scojo Vision LLC operate now in El Salvador, India, and Guatemala and are planning to expand to Nicaragua, Honduras, Mexico, Bangladesh, and Afghanistan. VisionSpring creates self-employment opportunities for micro-entrepreneurs, especially women, to be "vision entrepreneurs." Scojo Vision LLC provides VisionSpring with reading glasses at low cost. The foundation in turn trains the vision entrepreneurs to administer basic eye exams and sell eyeglasses at affordable prices. The women own their small businesses, meaning that they buy the eyeglasses and retain the revenues from their sale. The women meet regularly to discuss business performance, new products, sales strategies, and other tips.[76]

Another type of micro-franchising is bottom-up. In bottom-up micro-franchising, small enterprises in the same sector decide to join forces under a cooperative or similar structure to enhance their performance and competitiveness by developing a number of shared services. These shared services include exchange of information on market conditions, joint lobbying of public authorities to ensure a more favorable business environment, knowledge-sharing and business upgrading, and services to achieve economies of scale. Regional dairy cooperatives operate under this model around the world.

A successful example of bottom-up microfranchising in the developing world is Honey Care Africa, a private sector social enterprise working with NGOs to promote sustainable community-based beekeeping in East Africa.[77] It costs about US$160 to purchase the four hives needed for beekeeping as well as necessary beekeeping equipment; microcredit is available for this purpose. Once established, the smallholder needs to work only thirty minutes every two weeks, earning enough money from the sale of honey to add US$200–$250 to his or her annual income. Honey Care Africa assists farmers in their beekeeping by providing them with access to loans, training, extension services, and a guaranteed market for the honey produced by smallholder farmers at fair trade prices. The company then processes, packs, and sells the honey for profit through supermarket chains and other industrial clients. Honey Care Africa has been able to help 9,000 small-scale farmers earn income through beekeeping in Kenya.

Experience in the developing world has shown that self-employment earnings can be increased through a variety of measures:

- *Designing products that have an immediate impact on the productivity and hence earnings of the self-employed.* A $3 irrigation kit has been designed and used successfully in much of East Africa and South Asia. Small farmers have been able to increase their profits in just one growing season and then invest their profits in additional irrigation kits, starting a cycle of higher profits, further investments, and still higher profits.
- *Adopting a positive policy stance and avoiding hassles.* Who is benefited when handicraft producer-vendors like Masabisi in South Africa are prevented from selling their wares? Policy makers often lose sight of the concerns raised in this book. The issue of the livelihoods of the poor needs always to be kept on the table.
- *Providing the poor in agriculture with more to work with.* Various constraints bind in different circumstances. Some of these have been overcome in various places including lack of land, water, other inputs, knowledge of best practice, access to product markets, protection against risk, and access to financial services. Much can be learned from policy interventions that have made a difference to the poor in various places.
- *Facilitating supplemental off-farm wage employment and self-employment.* The elements that help the poor participate in nonfarm employment are investments in roads and electrification, banking systems, and market information systems; general education and specific skills; and greater access to credit and financial savings. Here too, international experience offers many lessons.
- *Making capital available to the poor.* One microfinance approach is the not-for-profit model developed and refined in Bangladesh by the Grameen Bank and spread throughout the world through the Grameen Foundation and other organizations. Another approach is the for-profit model found, for example, in the case of Compartamos in Mexico (and used by Angela, the fireworks maker you met in Chapter 3). One way or another, the needs of the self-employed for business capital must be met if they are to have a chance of earning enough to cross the poverty line.
- *Building skills and business know-how.* Governments, companies, trade unions, and NGOs are all involved in providing education and training. General education like literacy and numeracy has its place. Specific skills may be even more important.

- *Stimulating micro-franchising.* Micro-franchising provides equipment, financing, and training to small businesses. Successful examples are the Village Phones programs in Bangladesh, Rwanda, and elsewhere; VisionSpring in El Salvador, India, and Guatemala; and Honey Care Africa in Kenya.

PART THREE

Taking Action

CHAPTER 11

What Can You Do?

Having read to this point, you have learned how the poorer half of the world's people work. You have also learned about many things that have been done in different countries to help the poor earn their way out of poverty.

In my classes and public talks, when we reach this point, students and audience members have often asked me, "What can I do?" In this short concluding chapter, I will tell you about some of the possibilities open to you.

One thing you can do is share with others the information you have learned. When I was an undergraduate student, one of the subjects I studied was poverty in America. It was only in graduate school that I started to learn about global poverty. Those of you who are ahead of where I was can share your knowledge about international issues with friends and family. You can post some of what you know online. You can seek out a global development club, a workers' rights organization, a microfinance club, or a regional studies program to find others who share your interests.

You can talk widely to others. You cannot know what useful information you will learn or what use will be made of the information you pass on. The first time I set foot in a development economics classroom was when I walked to the front of a classroom at Yale to teach a full semester course about it. Those early students urged me to write up the class notes as a book, which I did.[1] I had no idea at the time that one of those students would go on to become the president of Mexico, another would become the Mexican minister of commerce and negotiate the North American Free Trade Agreement (NAFTA) on behalf of his country, and another would become the head of the social protection unit for Latin America at the World Bank. Later, at Cornell, I taught and advised a succession of Ph.D. students from South Korea. The first of those students went on to become the chief advisor to the president of Korea; it was said that during that presidency, he was the second most powerful man in the country after the president himself. So talk about what you have learned and learn from others; you never know who will be listening and be influenced by your words or who will influence you.

You can take courses in which you work on problems that the poor face. Examples are development economics, design for extreme affordability, social entrepreneurship, or sustainable global enterprise. A wealth of online resources is available at www.pooreconomics.com.

You can follow the advice of Bill Gates: "The key thing is to pick a cause, whether it's crops or diseases or great high schools. Pick one and get some more in-depth knowledge."[2] (Gates himself left Microsoft to devote full time to the work of the Bill and Melinda Gates Foundation.) To find out about the range of causes, visit www.idealist.org, www.thelifeyoucansave.com, or www.halftheskymovement.org/get-involved.

You can get out into the world to see what conditions are like elsewhere, learn from the poor themselves, and give something of yourself to them. A soon-to-be Cornell graduate told me as I was writing this chapter that she had decided to take a job in India rather than work in the United States for a leading consulting company. She said, "There really could not be a better opportunity for someone my age with my interests." Many others have found a stint with the Peace Corps to be a great way both to learn and to give. Go take a look and see for yourself.

You can work for better public policies. Sometimes governments, aid agencies, and nongovernmental organizations do what they do simply because they haven't thought of trying something else. For years, I saw the development banks do their work with no apparent overarching principle. Later, I saw them profess a concern for distributional issues but then concentrate on inequality rather than poverty. I have seen them profess a concern for poverty but not have a labor markets unit, even though the poor derive all or nearly all of their income from the work they do. You can try to influence development organizations to be more focused on helping improve the earning opportunities of the poor and make that a top priority for policy.

Sometimes public policies are what they are because of powerful interests. You can join with others in trying to add a countervailing voice on the other side. Protectionism in the richer countries may help some of the workers there, but who is voicing a concern for the well-being of workers in the poorer countries? The farm lobby is an enormously influential voice on behalf of farm subsidies. You can add your voice to those who are trying to make governments and the world community more generally aware of the harm that farm subsidies in rich countries are doing to working people in poor countries. The forces of resistance are powerful, and change is often impossible, at least in the short run. But when change does occur, it is often because somebody had a good idea, the good idea spread, and as a result somebody in power decided to go down a different road.

You can push for new or expanded international efforts. You can try to influence the amount and structure of foreign aid by joining with others in trying to get our governments to meet their pledges and trying to get aid efforts to be more focused than they now are on improving earning opportunities for the poor. You can advocate for an international earned income tax credit. The possibilities are great.

Many of you are working for companies or will work for companies. Companies make important contributions to economic development: employing people, paying taxes, and so on. Besides helping the company you work for achieve its business objectives, you can also help harness its energies to contribute to reducing global poverty. Win-win actions are often possible. You can seek them out or even propose them. The company's human resources and corporate social responsibility departments may be good places to start. Your company may be involved with other companies in a network where ideas are exchanged and contacts made.

Your employer may be devoting money and efforts to social-impact projects. You can participate in these social projects. Not only will you feel good about doing it, but you will be helping your employer be seen as a good institutional citizen in the community. The company will like that.

You may not have thought about where other than companies you might deploy your talents. Every fall, when I teach a labor economics course that would-be human resource managers are required to take, a number of students come to me asking whether the skills they are acquiring at Cornell might be used in efforts against global poverty. They are surprised to learn that nearly all development banks, national aid agencies, international organizations, think tanks, social entrepreneurship organizations, social venture capital outfits, and advocacy groups have human resource functions (and also finance departments, legal departments, etc.). One word of caution: an organization's true bottom line is not necessarily what is in its mission statement, so before signing on with an organization that proclaims a lofty mission, make sure you know what the organization really does, values, and rewards its people for.

You might join a professional organization such as Engineers without Borders, Bankers without Borders, Potters for Peace, Business Leaders' Initiative on Human Rights, or the Institute for Responsible Investment. You will probably enjoy rubbing shoulders with like-minded people in your field. Your employer will probably be glad that you are spreading the good name of your organization in such venues.

If your employer is a multinational one, you may want to request an overseas posting. Your heightened sensitivity to the lives of working people less fortunate than you may help you do better work for the good of your employer, the employees, and yourself.

As a consumer, you can be more sensitive to the way the products you buy are made. You can patronize those brands and merchants that are certified to have decent working conditions. If you decide not to buy certain products because of how they are made, be sure to tell the manufacturer and the merchant why you are not buying from them. If you and enough others join a consumer movement, change might happen.

You can give money. Of course, you want to give your money to an organization that spends effectively on the things it said it would in its solicitations for contributions. Consider concentrating your contributions on a small number of organizations and try to monitor what they actually achieve. Organizations such as Charity Navigator and the American Institute of Philanthropy provide useful data for evaluating charitable organizations.

And last but by no means least, you can make the fight against global poverty your life's work. If you are thinking about doing this, let me offer you three bits of advice drawn from years of advising university students and graduates about career options. First, specialize in something that interests you deeply and get very good at it. The areas I chose were labor economics and development economics. I am well aware just how fortunate I am that the subject I chose to study because I liked it when I was a twenty-year-old is one that I still am passionate about many years later. Second, become skilled at analyzing data. Few people in the development field (or in most others) do it well. Many doors that would otherwise be closed will open for you if you become one of them. And third, go to law school only if you plan to be a practicing attorney or legal scholar. Policies to help the poor earn their way out of poverty are designed by economists, finance specialists, agriculturalists, educators, and many other specialists. Once the policies are chosen, the lawyers can draft the laws, regulations, tax bills, or contractual instruments to make them happen. You don't need to be a lawyer to do good policy work.

The possibilities that have been presented here by no means cover all the avenues that are open to you. I hope that I have given you a few useful ideas about where to turn.

People like Kalavati, Masibisi, Wang, and Angela need all the friends they can get.

NOTES

CHAPTER 1

1. Another multinational corporation operating in Shenzhen was in the news in May 2010 because of a raft of worker suicides. The company, Foxconn, employs 300,000 workers making products for such global companies as Apple, Nokia, Dell, and Hewlett Packard. You can view the conditions at Foxconn at http://www.cnn.com/2010/WORLD/asiapcf/06/01/china.foxconn.inside.factory/index.html?iref=allsearch, accessed 7/12/10.

2. United Nations (1997, p. 3) and World Bank, http://www.worldbank.org/poverty/data/trends/income.htm , 1999. Subsequently, the estimates were revised to 1.5 billion living on less than $1 per day and 1 billion living on $1 to $2 per day (Chen and Ravallion, 2010).

3. How well or badly a household lives is measured by the total amount spent per person adjusted for international differences in what money will buy. The technical name for this is "per capita consumption in Purchasing Power Parity dollars."

4. The World Bank, Inter-American Development, Asian Development Bank, African Development Bank, and European Bank for Reconstruction and Development are development banks. Unlike commercial banks and investment banks, they are not profit-seeking institutions. Their reason for being is to finance economic development—especially poverty reduction—in client countries. The interest earned on their loans and the repayments of principal are used to make fresh development loans.

5. See, for example, Azariadis and Stachursky (2005) or Bowles, Durlauf, and Hoff (2006).

6. Amartya Sen has written extensively about poverty as not only the lack of commodities but also the inability to function fully in society and enjoy basic freedoms; see, for instance, Sen (1999). Jeffrey Sachs (2005) tells us that the poor lack six major kinds of capital: human capital, business capital, infrastructure, natural capital, public institutional capital, and knowledge capital; they can face poverty traps in any or all of these dimensions. Stephen Smith (2005) lists sixteen poverty traps: family child labor traps, illiteracy traps, working capital traps, uninsurable-risk traps, debt bondage traps, information traps, undernutrition and illness traps, low-skill traps, high fertility traps, subsistence traps, farm erosion traps, common property mismanagement traps, collective action traps, criminality traps, mental health traps, and powerlessness traps. Paul Collier

(2007) discusses four poverty traps—the conflict trap, the natural resource trap, the trap of being landlocked with bad neighbors, and the trap of bad governance in a small country—as well as instruments to combat them. Abhijit Banerjee and Esther Duflo (2011) explore many aspects of the economics of poverty including health, education, savings, and so on; as regards the labor market, one chapter is devoted to entrepreneurship and wage employment, another to microcredit. Dean Karlan and Jacob Appel (2011) examine how a new economics is helping to solve global poverty in a number of areas: to work against poverty, to buy, to borrow, to pursue happiness, to cooperate in groups, to save, to farm, to learn, to stay healthy, to mate, and to give. The World Bank produces an annual World Development Report, each with a major theme. The 1995 report was on labor markets; the latest one on global poverty was the 2000 report.

7. Krishna (2007).

8. Pincus and Sender (2008).

9. Absolute poverty denotes a person's inability to attain a specified standard, often measured in terms of income or consumption, while relative poverty compares people's income or consumption levels. To learn more about the technical differences between absolute poverty and relative poverty and between poverty, inequality, and other aspects of economic well-being, see Fields (2001) and Ravallion (forthcoming). An article oriented toward laymen on these issues in the context of the United States is Cassidy (2006).

CHAPTER 2

1. The methodology used for these figures is somewhat revised from the earlier procedures. See Chen and Ravallion (2010) for details.

2. http://www.un.org/apps/news/story.asp?NewsID=35323&Cr=undp&Cr1=.

3. World Bank (2010).

4. Source for "poverty headcount ratio": Chen and Ravallion (2010).

5. http://www.un.org/millenniumgoals/bkgd.shtml, accessed 6/17/09. For an accessible discussion of the issues involved, see Besley and Burgess (2003).

6. An excellent introduction is Banerjee and Duflo (2007). In addition, publications presenting qualitative descriptions, statistical poverty profiles, and multivariate econometric analyses are available for nearly every country in the world.

7. The International Labor Organization maintains a photo gallery at http://www.ilo.org/global/About_the_ILO/Media_and_public_information/photo/lang-en/index.htm. Terms such as everyday life, poverty and exclusion, and agriculture can be accessed. My favorite large format book depicting workers and narrating their stories is Salgado (1993).

8. Where the poor do need to shoulder some of the blame is how some choose to spend their money. As *New York Times* columnist Nicholas Kristof tell us, "If the poorest families spent as much money educating their children as they do on wine, cigarettes and prostitutes, their children's prospects would be transformed. Much suffering is caused not only by low incomes, but also by shortsighted private spending decisions by heads of households." It is for this reason that government transfers are increasingly being made to women rather than men. See also Banerjee and Duflo (2007).

9. For one review, see Fields (1980).

10. A rich resource is the World Bank's *Voices of the Poor* series. The specific figures about the importance of employment come from Narayan et al. (2000, pp. 66–67).

11. South Africa is rather special in having systems of grants for the elderly and for children. These grants have had an enormous impact on poverty in the households where the recipients live. See http://www.sarpn.org.za/documents/d0000946/index.php for more information.

12. On the importance of remittances from family members living overseas, see http://web.worldbank.org/WBSITE/EXTERNAL/NEWS/0,,contentMDK:2064 8762~menuPK:34480~pagePK:64257043~piPK:437376~theSitePK:4607,00. html, accessed 7/7/09. Remittances made up more than a fifth of the GDP of some countries such as Jamaica, Jordan, Lebanon, Moldova, and Tajikistan.

13. The contrasts between coastal China and the interior are described graphically in Gifford (2007).

14. These words are taken from Emma Lazarus's poem "The New Colossus."

15. The following statistics will help put the limited extent of immigration into richer countries in perspective. The world has 3 billion (that is, three thousand million) poor people. In 2008, the United States, with its population of 300 million people, allowed one million immigrants to become citizens. For its part, Britain, with a population of 61 million, permitted the entry of some 600,000 immigrants in that same year. For details, see http://www.dhs.gov/xlibrary/assets/statistics/publications/natz_fr_2008.pdf and http://www.guardian.co.uk/uk/2008/apr/06/immigration.britishidentity.

16. It is interesting to speculate on what might lead to freer international migration and what its effects would be. Harvard economists Lant Pritchett, Richard Freeman, and Dani Rodrik address these questions in DeParle (2007), Clemens (2009), Freeman (2006), and Rodrik (2007). See also United Nations (2009).

17. See, for example, WHY, "Hunger Awareness: Economic Justice Not Handouts" (https://www.whyhunger.org/about-why/press-room/362-hunger-awareness-economic-justice-not-handouts.html, accessed 7/7/09) for a perspective from the left and Mark Levy, "Success Achieved by Hard Work and Perseverance, Not Handouts" (http://www.timesrecordnews.com/news/2009/may/31/levy-success-achieved-hard-work-and-perseverance-n/, accessed 7/7/09) for a view from the right.

18. For a time, a fierce political battle was being waged in the United States about immigration reform. Calls for immigration reform have been all but silenced since the onset of the 2008 financial crisis.

19. This is how I understand Lou Dobbs's nightly harangues on prime-time American television.

20. U.S. Census Bureau (2010).

21. http://www.alternatives.org/livingwage2009notes.html, accessed 6/3/09.

22. An authoritative and comprehensive source on federal government programs in the United States is the Green Book (U.S. House of Representatives, 2004).

23. Information at http://www.dol.gov/dol/topic/unemployment-insurance/.

24. For more information, see http://www.acf.hhs.gov/opa/fact_sheets/tanf_fact-sheet.html and http://www.acf.hhs.gov/programs/ofa/data-reports/caseload/2009/tanf_recipients.htm, accessed 10/07/09.

25. See http://www.fns.usda.gov/FSP/, accessed 10/7/09 and DeParle and Gebeloff (2009).

26. For more information, see http://www.ithacaha.

27. What I find more disturbing is the mobile soup kitchen that sets up each afternoon on the 1800 block of Pennsylvania Avenue NW in Washington, DC, two

blocks from the White House and directly across the street from the World Bank and International Monetary Fund headquarters.

28. See, for example, Gosselin (2008), Greenhouse (2008), Gautié and Schmitt (2009), Sherman (2009), and Krugman (2010).

29. "The Mountain Man" (2005).

CHAPTER 3

1. Efficiency wage is the idea that when a firm pays higher wages, its workers will be more productive, either because the current workers work harder and/or because the employer can attract a higher-caliber worker.

2. Interestingly, the SEWA leaders attribute the cutback in work to a recession in the bidi trade due to the advent of gutkha (a kind of chewing tobacco).

3. The vicious system of apartheid remains a raw wound in South Africa. Prize-winning novelist Damon Galgut tells us: "The past has only just happened. It's not past yet". (Galgut, 2003, p. 6).

4. The South African unemployment rate is 25.2% using the standard international definition. But the broad unemployment rate, including discouraged workers, is 32.5%. (Discouraged workers are those who did not work in the reference period, who were not looking for work, but reported that they would take a job if one were offered.)

CHAPTER 4

1. Excellent older books make many of the points presented in this chapter, but with data that are now obsolete. My favorites are Turnham (1971, 1993) and Squire (1981). A wealth of current information is published by the ILO, which is the source for much of the following data. The ILO publishes an online data source called *Key Indicators of the Labor Market,* which presents information on twenty indicators including participation in the world of work, employment indicators, unemployment indicators, educational attainment, wages and labor costs, the characteristics of job seekers, education, wages and compensation costs, labor productivity, and working poverty. This information is presented for the world as a whole, by region of the world, country-by-country, and year-by-year since 1980. The database, a guide to its use, and an executive summary of findings are available at http://kilm.ilo.org/KILMnetBeta/default2.asp, accessed 7/18/10. Another ILO source presenting an excellent overview of labor market conditions in the world is its annual publication *Global Employment Trends.* At the time of this writing, the latest available edition was published in January, 2011.

2. The Universal Declaration of Human Rights is at http://www.un.org/en/documents/udhr/index.shtml, accessed 10/23/09.

3. ILO (2009b, p. 9).

4. The source for these particular quotations is the World Bank's *Voices of the Poor* volumes; see Narayan et al. (2000, pp. 26 and 34). Other informative sources are World Bank (1995), Inter-American Development Bank (2003), Asian Development Bank (2005), and Chen and Vanek (2005).

5. Unemployment rates for the world and for different regions are taken from ILO, *Global Employment Trends*, January 2011.

6. Calculated by the author from data in "Economic and Financial Indicators," the *Economist*, August 14, 2010, p. 77.

7. Bourguignon (2005) and http://www.bls.gov/fls/flsfaqs.htm#developingcountries, accessed 1/27/09.
8. See, for example, Ghose et al. (2008, p. 59).
9. Fox and Gaal (2008, p. 3) and Turnham (1971, p. 74).
10. The source is the manager of the ILO Statistical Development and Analysis Group. See Peek (2006) for details.
11. Hamlin (2008).
12. U.S. Bureau of Labor Statistics (2007).
13. See Key Indicators of the Labor Market, Table 17, available at http://kilm.ilo.org/KILMnetBeta/default2.asp, accessed 1/18/10.
14. ILO, *Global Employment Trends*, January 2011, p. x.
15. ILO (2007c).
16. See http://www.ilo.org/global/Themes/Employment_Promotion/Informal Economy/lang--en/index.htm, retrieved 2/17/10.
17. Jütting and de Laiglesia (2009).
18. For a good introduction, see Chen, Hussmanns, and Vanek (2007).
19. Collins, Morduch, Rutherford, and Ruthven (2009).
20. Harriss-White (2003, p. 28).
21. These points come from World Bank (2007) and Chen et al. (2005, p. 8). Also see ILO (2009a), www.wiego.org, and Kristof and WuDunn (2009).
22. ILO (2009a) and Foster and Rosenzweig (2008).
23. Asian Development Bank (2005) and Fox and Gaal (2008).
24. The terminology in the text follows international usage as prescribed by the ILO. "Paid employment" includes those persons working for wages or salaries, with or without a formal contract. "Self-employment" includes two groups: "employers," who have at least one paid employee, and "own-account workers," who employ no one.
25. Kucera and Roncolato (2008).
26. Fox and Gaal (2008, pp. 3 and 11).
27. See ILO (2009a) for regional rates and Ghose et al. (2008) for country-specific data.
28. Fox and Gaal (2008).
29. NCEUS (2009, p. 59).
30. For overall data, see, for example, World Bank (2005, p. 32) and Millennium Challenge Corporation (2008, p. 3). Data for specific countries come from Tao (2006, p. 517) and Fox and Gaal (2008, p. 15).
31. For an overview and analysis, see Ahmad et al. (1991).
32. Smith, 2005, p. 91, emphasis in the original.
33. Levy (2008).
34. ILO (2008), p. 122.
35. NCEUS (2009). Following the lead of the International Conference of Labor Statisticians and the International Labor Organization, the following definitions are used. "The unorganized sector [also called the informal sector] consists of all unincorporated private enterprises owned by individuals or households engaged in the sale and production of goods and services operated on a proprietary or partnership basis and with less than ten total workers." "Unorganized workers consist of those working in the unorganized enterprises or households, excluding regular workers with social security benefits, and the workers in the formal sector without any employment/social security benefits provided by the

employers." The organization Women in Informal Employment: Globalizing and Organizing (WIEGO) has been influential in broadening attention to include informal employment in the formal sector. See www.wiego.org.

36. The ILO itself has launched a Global Campaign for Social Security and Coverage for All; see ILO (2007b). For more on social protection, the website of the World Bank's social protection unit at http://web.worldbank.org/WBSITE/ EXTERNAL/TOPICS/EXTSOCIALPROTECTION/0,,menuPK:282642~pageP K:149018~piPK:149093~theSitePK:282637,00.html, accessed 7/23/08, or the Asian Development Bank (2005, Section 5.2).

37. Felipe and Hasan (2006, p. 41).

38. Banerjee and Duflo (2008, pp. 18–19).

39. Sen, Mujeri, and Shahabuddin (2007).

40. Charmes (2009).

41. Luce (2007, pp. 50–52).

42. Abraham (2009).

43. Wittenberg (2002, p. 1194).

44. For a description of such jobs in Africa, see Fox and Gaal (2008, chapter 4).

45. One news item stated that the government of Kenya was threatening to bring charges against "unscrupulous merchants" who charged higher prices for milk in remote rural areas than the price charged in the cities. That the cost was higher to get the milk to the small rural shops and the sales were slower, and the storage costs therefore higher, was simply irrelevant in the view of the newspaper vendor.

46. And I learned too why families like his sent the men to the city and left the women in the countryside. In much of Africa, men do not do heavy physical work—that is women's work. If the men were to stay on the farm while the women went off to the city, the only task that would get done is supervision. So the men were sent to the city to earn whatever they could while the women tilled the land, fetched the firewood, hauled the water, and did all the other heavy lifting.

47. Banerjee and Duflo (2007, p. 162; 2011, chapter 9). Others call them petty entrepreneurs, microentrepreneurs, or the self-employed in the informal economy.

48. Banerjee and Duflo (2008, p. 26). These authors then added, "If the middle class matters for growth, it is probably not because of its entrepreneurial spirit." A special report in the *Economist* ("Bourgeoning Bourgeoisie," 2009, p. 17) reached a very different conclusion: "The middle class's . . . distinctive contribution to growth is its gift for entrepreneurship."

49. Examples are Appleton, Song, and Xia (2005) and Bardhan (2010) for China; Glinskaya and Lokshin (2005) and Hasan and Magsombol (2005) for India; and Stroll and Thornton (2002) for several African countries.

50. I have taken the predominant view in a variety of places, among them, Fields (2007a). A prominent dissenter to the segmented labor markets view is Rosenzweig (1988).

51. See Maloney (2004) and World Bank (2007).

52. Günther and Launov (forthcoming). In their study, all individuals who work in the public sector or who have a written contract with a company with formal bookkeeping are classified as formal employees.

53. An Indian reader told me: "I am doubtful if Indian readers would take this example seriously. There is a market for blood here and there are enough 'cheap blood sellers' who sell it at lower prices than the wages mentioned. I personally have

never heard of such instances of trapping workers for blood. There are umpteen number of people happily ready to sell blood. In fact there are professional blood sellers in the country that sell blood at fixed prices." Having to sell blood for a living is an outrage too.

54. Alice's story is told in United Nations (2007). See also Gertler, Shah, and Bertozzi (2005) for Mexico.
55. For a graphic account of sex slavery and other outrages against women, see Kristof and WuDunn (2009).
56. ILO (2006) and Edmonds (2008).
57. http://www.ilo.org/ipec/facts/WorstFormsofChildLabour/lang--en/index.htm, accessed 1/25/07.
58. BBC News (1998).
59. The term "employment problem" appears to have been originated by Turnham (1971) in an OECD study. The ILO picked up on the term in its 1972 Kenya report (ILO, 1972) and subsequent works on other countries (Thorbecke, 1973).
60. ILO (2010).
61. The figures in this paragraph come from unpublished joint work with Paul Cichello and Murray Leibbrandt. One good source on the legacy of apartheid in the South African labor market is Nattrass and Seekings (2005).

CHAPTER 5

1. One interesting aspect about the Xiamen job center: A sign at the entrance reads: "Attention: To rural-urban female migrants: Please show your Certification on Marriage and Fertility of Rural-Urban Migrants when you are seeking jobs. This is required by the policy of birth control." What this means is that a woman who has more than one child (the maximum allowed under China's family planning policy) can not use the government's job placement center. This is but one way in way the Chinese government uses carrots and sticks to regulate the economy and the society.
2. From which we learned the expensive lesson that one should verify and check references carefully.
3. Friedman (2005, p. 8).
4. Accessed at Yale Global Online, http://yaleglobal.yale.edu/about/.
5. Sirkin, Hemerling, and Bhattacharya (2008).
6. See Stiglitz (2006), Bhagwati (2005), and Wolf (2005, pp. 14 and 372).
7. But there is also another sense in which the term "globalization" is used. Many economic studies and journalistic accounts either define globalization or measure it as increased foreign trade or investment. To me, foreign trade and investment are consequences of globalization, but they are not globalization itself.
8. Leaders of global companies generally favor globalization because they view it as an opportunity. Jeffrey Immelt (2009, p. 141), the CEO of GE, lists six principles for globalization: "1. A strong international trade system is fundamental. 2. Continued economic liberalization enhances growth. 3. Protectionism must be resisted. 4. Global trade must be fair. 5. Governments must pursue domestic policies that allow their citizens to thrive in the global economy. 6. Each of us must contribute." And ArcelorMittal CEO Lakshmi Mittal (2009, p. 130) says, "What matters is that globalization has started and in my view it cannot—and indeed it should not—be stopped." Not surprisingly, the leaders of domestically protected companies and the workers in those companies take a very different view.

9. *Not* to be involved with the global trading system and the global labor market can be seriously problematic. See Ghose (2003).
10. "Google Goes Amharic" (2006).
11. See Engardio (2006) and "Just Good Business" (2008).
12. See "Hungry Tiger, Dancing Elephant," (2007, p. 67).
13. Freeman (2005).
14. Naughton (2007).
15. See Ahluwalia (2007) and Bardhan (2010).
16. Carrillo and Gomis (2004).
17. See Roberts (2008), Hamlin (2008), and "The Next China," 2010.
18. Bradsher (2008).
19. Faiola (2008).
20. "Roses Are Red"(2008).
21. See http://www.bdafrica.com/index.php?option=com_content&task=view&id=5871&Itemid=5822, accessed 2/2/09.
22. See http://www.chinadaily.cn/bizchina/2008-01/10/content_6384566.htm and http://www.emsnow.com/newsarchives/archivedetails.cfm?ID=13676 .
23. See http://premium.hoovers.com/subscribe/co/competitors.xhtml?ID=17160 and http://web.mit.edu/airlines/industry_outreach/board_meeting_presentation_files/meeting-oct-2006/7-Gittell%20Lean%20Production%20in%20the%20Air.pdf.
24. Economists refer to the greater responsiveness to wage pressures as "increased wage elasticity of demand for labor." The Hicks-Marshall laws lead us to expect that the demand for labor would have become more elastic (Ehrenberg and Smith, 2009). Empirical evidence shows that it indeed has; see Bertrand (2004) and OECD (2007).
25. See, for example, http://en.wikipedia.org/wiki/Sustainability.
26. Barney (2002).
27. Barney (1991, p. 102).
28. Wright (2009).
29. CSI (n.d.).
30. Oh (n.d.).
31. http://www.data360.org/dsg.aspx?Data_Set_Group_Id=992, accessed 3/22/09.
32. Calculated from data found at http://en.wikipedia.org/wiki/Ithaca_College, accessed 3/22/09.

CHAPTER 6

1. See, among others, Sen (1999).
2. Quoted in Luce (2007, p. 41). My emphasis added.
3. Quoted in Rangan et al. (2007, p. 9).
4. One visionary statement of what a fundamentally changed system might be like is provided by Ertuna (2009).
5. Harris and Todaro (1970).
6. Fields (1974, 1975).
7. The living wage movement in the developed countries, discussed in Chapter 2, is based on the premise that all full-time, full-year workers should be able to support themselves and as many as two others at an acceptable standard. For the developing countries, such a target is at best a distant dream.
8. For more on social protection, consult the website of the World Bank's social protection unit at http://web.worldbank.org/WBSITE/EXTERNAL/TOPICS/

EXTSOCIALPROTECTION/0,,menuPK:282642~pagePK:149018~piPK:149093~theSitePK:282637,00.html, accessed 7/23/08.

9. How best to provide social protection is itself under review. Denmark has become famous for its system of Flexicurity, which operates under six principles: flexibility in employment and compensation, robust security for workers, lifelong learning, customization, personal responsibility to make use of changing opportunities, and adaptability. For a nontechnical introduction, see Cohen and Sabel (2009).

10. http://www.ilo.org/declaration/lang—en/index.htm, accessed 2/22/10.

11. http://www.ilo.org/global/about-the-ilo/decent-work-agenda/lang—en/index.htm, accessed 2/22/10.

12. ILO, *Facts on Decent Work,* http://www.ilo.org/global/About_the_ILO/Media_and_public_information/Factsheets/lang-en/docName-WCM3_082054/index.htm, accessed 1/29/09.

13. For more on bottom-line objectives, see Fields (2009a).

14. I have written books and articles on the subject. For a sampling, see Fields (2001, 2007b).

15. See Fields and Wan (1989) for a description of the government of Singapore's policy and an explanation for why removing the wage repression policy led to increases in both employment and earnings.

16. In the United States, the minimum wage is not at all well targeted at the poor: an estimated 83% of minimum wage workers belong to nonpoor households. See Burkhauser and Sabia (2005) for details.

17. How precisely to weigh the trade-offs among objectives raises a number of technical issues. If you are interested in reading more about them, please see Fields and Kanbur (2007).

18. Surowiecki (2008).

19. Heckman (2001), Ravallion (2008), and Deaton (2010) are among those who present comprehensive overviews of the relevant issues and findings.

20. Hanushek (1995, 2009).

21. For introductions, see Bertrand, Mullainathan, and Shafir (2004), Duflo (2006a), Banerjee (2007), Blitstein (2009), Mullainathan and Shafir (2009), Banerjee and Duflo (2011), and Karlan and Appel (2011).

22. Duflo and Hanna (2005).

23. Glewwe et al. (2004).

24. Evans, Kremer, and Ngatia (2008) and Kremer and Holla (2009).

25. Angrist and Lavy (1999).

26. Case and Deaton (1999).

27. Angrist and Krueger (1991).

28. An illuminating and highly readable volume on educated judgments is Gladwell (2005).

29. Duflo (2007, p. 1048).

CHAPTER 7

1. Faiola (2008).

2. See Chen and Ravallion (2010, Tables I and II) for poverty figures and U.S. Census Bureau (n.d.) for world population figures.

3. Sources: Commission on Growth and Development (2008, p. 20) and United Nations Statistical Division, http://unstats.un.org/unsd/snaama/selbasicFast.asp, accessed 2/5/10.

4. Chen and Ravallion (2010, Table III).
5. For comparative studies of the experiences of China and India, see Chaudhury and Ravallion (2007) and Bardhan (2010), among others.
6. The quotation is from Collier (2007, p. 11), emphasis in the original.
7. For evidence on the developing world, see Fields (2001). It is not that I am disinterested in the developed countries but rather that the study of the developing countries is a big enough task in itself.
8. Chronic Poverty Research Centre (2008).
9. World Bank (1995, pp. 3, 19, 55, and 149), "Globalization of Labor" (2007), and ILO (2009b), pp. 29 and 39–47).
10. See ILO (2004, p. 111) and Asian Development Bank (2005, pp. 16–17 and p. 33).
11. See Fields and Bagg (2003), Paes de Barros (2006), and Lee (2007).
12. NCEUS (2009, p. 10).
13. Ravallion and Datt (1995).
14. Ahsan and Narain (2007, p. 297).
15. See Paci and Sasin (2008, p. 2) for Bangladesh; Gutierrez, Paci, and Ranzani (2008, p. 115) for Nicaragua; and Hoftijzer and Paci (2008, p. 7) for Madagascar.
16. Fields (1980).
17. "Indonesia: Suharto Tops List" (2004).
18. http://unstats.un.org/unsd/snaama/resQuery.asp, accessed 2/5/10, and www.census.gov, last accessed 1/11/10.
19. It is too early to have data on changes in other labor market indicators in the crisis, such as employment composition and real earnings or on changes in national poverty rates.
20. Commission on Growth and Development (2008) and El-Erian and Spence (2008).
21. Solow (2007, pp. 5–6).
22. A good exposition of the principle of comparative advantage in the context of labor market analysis is Ehrenberg and Smith (2009).
23. Textbook-level treatments of basic international trade theory abound; a good one is Krugman and Obstfeld (2003). Critics of economists and economists critical of free trade may be both enlightened and entertained by Davis and Mishra (2007). These authors regard the Stolper-Samuelson theorem, which is at the heart of standard international trade theory, as worse than a "theory crime"; it is a "theory felony." As they write, "theory felonies occur when we are so entranced by the elegance of our toy models that we lose sight of the question we are trying to answer, indeed come to believe that we have provided an answer even when clearly central aspects of the problem are addressed inappropriately." Speaking about the impact of trade liberalization on the wages of unskilled labor, they continue, "If we use it, as we so often have, as if it provides a reliable answer to this question of real human significance, then it is worse than wrong—it is dangerous" (Davis and Mishra, 2007, pp. 88–89).
24. Harrison (2007, chapter 1).
25. See, for example, Sen (1981).
26. Fields (1984, 1985).
27. See Rodrik (2006, p. 975), who also cites the earlier experiences of South Korea and Taiwan. See also the World Bank's (1993) *East Asian Miracle* study.
28. The story of the Mexican potters is told in "A Clean Plate" (2009).
29. See, for example, Stiglitz and Charlton (2005), Rodrik (2007), and Chang (2007).

30. Oxfam (2003).
31. "Special Report: The Cancun Challenge" (2003).
32. Stern (2002).
33. http://www.papda.org/article.php3?id_article=105, accessed 1/26/10.
34. Blustein (2004).
35. Wolf (2005, p. 170).
36. Schumpeter (1942).
37. "Montek Singh Ahluwalia" (2007, p. 4).
38. Kannan (2009).
39. See, for example, Bhagwati, Panagariya, and Srinivasan (2004), Kletzer (2005), Blanchard (2006), Scheve and Slaughter (2007), and Eizenstat and Cheek (2007). As Harvard's Dani Rodrik has said, social insurance and free trade are "two sides of the same coin," a concept entrenched in Europe but not in the United States (Uchitelle, 2007).
40. Sachs (2005, p. 288).
41. Gates (2010). The data on aid percentages come from stats.oecd.org/qwids.
42. Fisman and Miguel (2008).
43. Sachs (2005).
44. Easterly (2006a, b). Another highly visible critic of aid is Dambisa Moyo (2009).
45. The quotation is from Banerjee and Duflo (2011, p. 50). See also Banerjee (2007) and Blitstein (2009).

CHAPTER 8

1. See, for example, Klein and Hadjimichael (2003), Brainard (2006), and Rangan et al. (2007).
2. One classic and widely cited statement is by Milton Friedman (1970). For a wide range of views on this question, see John Templeton Foundation (2008).
3. In the United States, it is often maintained that the boards of directors of publicly held companies (those whose stock is owned by the public) have a fiduciary responsibility to maximize shareholder value, which is best achieved by maximizing profits, and that *not* maximizing shareholder value is not only wrong but also punishable by legal action.
4. Reich (2007, p. 86).
5. Rangan et al. (2007, p. 5).
6. Friedman (2007, p. 508).
7. Stiglitz (2006, p. 188).
8. "The Fortune at the Bottom of the Pyramid" is the title of an article by Prahalad and Hart (2002) and a subsequent book by Prahalad (2006). "Enabling dignity and choice through markets" is the subtitle of Prahalad's book. "Using new technology to deliver profitable solutions that reduce poverty and protect the environment" comes from the cover of Hart (2007).
9. I love the title of a book by Princeton economist Alan Blinder, *Hard Heads, Soft Hearts* (Blinder, 1987). Another brilliant phrase comes from Paul Collier who urges us to move "beyond the headless heart" by "accepting complexity" (Collier, 2007, p. 12).
10. This material is presented here in the context of increasing paid employment, but the points made are equally applicable to improving earning opportunities in self-employment, which is the topic of the next chapter.
11. Taber (2009).

12. Credit is due to Kremer (1993) for the terminology "the O-ring theory of economic development" and for the analysis of its implications. On last straw threshold effects, see Davis (2007).
13. Pagés, Pierre, and Scarpetta (2009).
14. Lin (1992).
15. Bardhan (2010, p. 44).
16. Bardhan (2010).
17. Ahluwalia (2007).
18. Chen and Ravallion (2010, Table III).
19. Much of what follows in this section draws heavily on the International Finance Corporation and World Bank's annual *Doing Business* reports and also *World Development Report* (2005).
20. The importance of secure property rights to economic growth is stressed by Acemoglu, Johnson, and Robinson (2001). Dam (2006) and "Beijing Plays Hedge Ball" (2009) detail China's weak property rights. One Chinese business owner put it graphically, "The law in China is something you can hang beside your toilet. In China, [success depends on] who you know and how much money you have. Anything else is a waste of time" (quoted in Roberts, 2009).
21. International Finance Corporation and the World Bank (2004, p. xv).
22. Klein and Hadjimichael (2003).
23. World Bank (2005, pp. 11–12).
24. Hatem (1997).
25. Fung et al. (2006).
26. Collier and Pattillo (2000).
27. Kearney (2004).
28. International Finance Corporation (2000, p. 24).
29. Khanna (2007).
30. For the Costa Rica story, see World Bank (2005, p. 139) and Spar (1998). The Barrett quotations are from Friedman (2005, pp. 322–323). The Otellini quotation is from Friedman (2010). For more on the poor state of infrastructure in India and its consequences for economic development, see Hamm (2007) and "An Elephant, Not a Tiger" (2008).
31. Chandra and Nganou (2001) and Kaplan (2005).
32. The story was reported in Dreier and Appelbaum (2006).
33. The quotation appears in Crowell (2009, p. 1).
34. See, for example, Compa (2008).
35. Birchard (1999).
36. The story is told in Stein (2010).
37. The quotation is from Greenhouse (2010, viewed online 7/17/10). See also Forrer (2010) and www.altagraciaapparel.com.
38. The rest of this section relies on a variety of sources, especially Vogel (2006).
39. Conley (2005).
40. Marwaha et al. (2007, p. 172).
41. "Sustainability," *The World in 2009* (2009, p. 20).
42. Reich (2007, p. 86).
43. "Just Good Business" (2008).
44. Frank (2004, p. 66).
45. Porter and Kramer (2006).
46. Heal (2008).
47. See www.10000women.org. The Blankfein quotation is from Rappeport (2009).

48. http://www.corp.att.com/ehs/annual_reports/ehs_report/triple_bottom_line. html , accessed 4/2/09.

49. Vogel (2006).

50. In practice, though, because carpets are often made in homes and other small workshops, it becomes very difficult to state with 100% certainty that no children are involved in the production process. For a penetrating analysis of this issue, see Tully (2002).

51. More information is available at http://www.globalexchange.org/campaigns/ fairtrade/coffee/background.html. The Ellgass statement is reported in Downie (2007).

52. Roberts and Engardio (2006).

53. See, for example, Vogel (2006, pp. 77–82), Locke et al. (2007a, b), and Heal (2008).

54. Harrison and Scorse (2006).

55. The quotation is from Harrison and Scorse (2006, p. 158). What if Nike had raised its wages and sales had *not* increased? Nike itself makes a profit of about $4 per pair of shoes. The direct labor cost per pair of shoes is estimated at $2.59. Holding other things equal, doubling labor cost would reduce profits by more than half. It is good for Nike and for the workers at Nike that sales increased so much (Heal, 2008, pp. 168–169).

56. Engardio (2007, p. 60).

57. Vogel (2006) and "Just Good Business" (2008, p. 10).

58. Vogel (2006, pp. 2–4).

CHAPTER 9

1. In normal English, "wage" refers to payments made on an hourly or other short-term basis, while "salary" refers to payments on an annual or other longer-term basis. In the United States, salaries are usually quoted in annual terms, but in most other countries, a monthly salary is understood. When translating from the Spanish, "salaried employment" is used to cover both wage employment and salaried employment as those terms are used in American English. In this chapter, the terms "paid employment," "wage employment," and "salaried employment" are used synonymously.

2. Luce (2007) and National Commission for Enterprises in the Unorganised Sector (2009).

3. Kristof (2009a).

4. See Bardhan (2010, pp. 29–30).

5. Economists use the term "market-clearing level" for the compensation level that causes the amount of labor supplied to equal the amount of labor demanded.

6. For evidence from around the world, see Hamermesh (1993).

7. The data presented below come from Fields (2009b) and the references cited there.

8. Apartheid was a vicious, racist system in which the white minority government used all the force in its arsenal to repress the black majority and the mixed-race minority.

9. This phenomenon is by no means limited to developing countries. Hallock (2009) quotes a French business executive who says it is so difficult to fire workers in France that he will never hire any more workers there.

10. Fallon and Lucas (1993).

11. Besley and Burgess (2004, p. 124).

12. Ahsan and Pagés (2009, p. 62).
13. Gupta, Hasan, and Kumar (2009, p. 33).
14. Harriss-White (2003, p. 37).
15. Padhi et al. (2004).
16. See, for example, Anant et al. (2006) and Bhattacharjea (2006).
17. South African author J. M. Coetzee won the Nobel Prize in literature for his novel *Disgrace* (Coetzee, 2000). One theme among the book's many powerful ones is how a dysfunctional employee cannot be let go. *Disgrace* is a highly evocative and deeply disturbing look into the psyche of today's South Africa.
18. Psacharopoulos and Patrinos (2004).
19. See Bennell (1996) and Pritchett (2001).
20. Fox and Gaal (2008).
21. *World Development Report 2007*, p. 70.
22. World Bank (2007).
23. Conditional cash transfers are also found in the health area, whereby pregnant women must go for regular prenatal checkups and babies must go for well visits if they are to receive government-provided benefits.
24. Schultz (2004), Rawlings (2005), Fiszbein and Schady (2009), and Banerjee and Duflo (2011).
25. Miguel and Kremer (2004) and Karlan and Appel (2011).
26. Calderón-Madrid and Trejo (2001).
27. Friedman (2008).
28. Galasso and Ravallion (2005).
29. Osmani and Chowdhury (1983).
30. Fields (2001, p. 219).
31. The material in the following paragraphs is taken from www.nrega.nic.in, Mehrotra (2008), and NCEUS (2009, chapter 9).
32. Happily, during a field visit to Ghambirpur village in Medak district in the state of Andhra Pradesh in 2011, the problems discussed in the following paragraphs were not reported.
33. See, for instance, the collection of papers in Indian Society of Labour Economics (2009).
34. See Niehaus and Sukhtankar (2009).
35. Drèze, Khera, and Siddhartha (2008). On corruption in India more generally, see Luce (2007, chapters 2 and 5).
36. "Special Report: The Landscape of Telecoms" (2009).
37. Ravallion (2009). For an earlier analysis, see Lipton (1998).

CHAPTER 10

1. Good information is available from the World Bank at http://publications.world-bank.org/ecommerce/catalog/product?item_id=6532716 , from the OECD at http://www.oecd.org/document/54/0,3343,en_2649_33935_42024438_1_1_1_1,00.html , from the ILO at http://www.ilo.org/public/english/support/lib/resource/subject/informal.htm , and from WIEGO at www.wiego.org .
2. Others have similar lists. For example, to upgrade self-employment, the Asian Development Bank (2005, p. 71) highlights improvements in access to credit, technical assistance, building management capacity, market assistance, and the facilitation of business linkages with other firms including those in the formal sector.

3. The material in this section is based on Cooper-Hewitt (2007) and Polak (2008).
4. We economists don't have such nice ways of putting things. We talk about "capital market imperfections," but the point remains the same.
5. A particularly powerful film depicting this cycle is Satish Manwar's *The Damned Rain*. A preview is available at http://www.youtube.com/watch?v=tLSzUN_E8Q4, viewed 7/3/11.
6. http://www.ibtimes.com/articles/101313/20110114/the-story-of-mohamed-bouazizi-the-man-who-toppled-tunisia.htm, accessed 3/7/11.
7. Skinner (2008).
8. Valodia (2007).
9. This exchange provoked a discussion during which I learned that the Philippines devised a workable system. There, street traders are issued licenses with photographs and large numbers on them as well as bright-colored vests on which the licenses must be displayed. That way, if anything untoward happens, those who "need protection" will know whom to complain about, much as now happens with licensed taxi-drivers in much of the world.
10. For more on Bulungula, visit www.bulungula.com and http://bulungulaincubator.wordpress.com/.
11. Food and Agricultural Organization of the United Nations, http://faostat.fao.org/default.aspx, accessed 10/28/08.
12. World Bank (2008, p. 26).
13. Source: Davis and others, as reported in World Bank (2008, p. 76).
14. World Bank (2008, p. 73).
15. Sachs (2007).
16. Cord (2007).
17. "How to Feed the World" and "The Miracle of the Cerrado" (2010).
18. International Fund for Agricultural Development (2008a, b).
19. Banerjee and Duflo (2007, p. 148).
20. Nagayets (2005).
21. Anríquez and Bonomi, as reported in World Bank (2008, p. 87).
22. One source is Binswanger, Deininger, and Feder (1995).
23. World Bank (2008).
24. Duflo (2006b) and Duflo, Kremer, and Robinson (2010).
25. For an introduction to SRI, see http://ciifad.cornell.edu/SRI/sripapers.html.
26. World Bank (2008, Chapter 6).
27. Government of Turkey (2006, p. 2).
28. Government of Turkey (2008, p. 5).
29. Author's interview with Gokhan Guder, October 31, 2009.
30. Spielman and Pandya-Lorch (2009).
31. See Lin (2004) and Asian Development Bank (2005, p. 70).
32. Lanjouw and Shariff (2004).
33. Reardon et al. (1998).
34. Banerjee and Duflo (2007, pp. 152–153).
35. Barrett et al. (2001).
36. The data in this paragraph come from Otsuka and Yamano (2006)
37. Dercon and Krishnan (1996, p. 857).
38. Bagachwa and Stewart (1992).
39. Lanjouw and Lanjouw (2001, p. 10).

40. Minot et al. (2006).
41. This story is narrated in DeParle (2007).
42. See McKenzie and Woodruff (2006) and de Mel, McKenzie, and Woodruff (2008).
43. Sachs (2005, pp. 244–245).
44. Paulson and Townsend (2004).
45. DeSoto (2000); Fairbourne, Gibson, and Dyer (2007).
46. The technical name for this phenomenon is diminishing marginal returns to capital.
47. Lucas (1990).
48. The real world of finance for the poor is detailed in Armendáriz and Morduch (2005) and Collins, Morduch, Rutherford, and Ruthven (2009).
49. Karlan and Mullainathan (2011).
50. For penetrating economic analyses of why microcredit works as it does, see Banerjee and Duflo (2011, chapter 7) and Karlan and Appel (2011, chapters 4 and 6). An interesting layperson's account with a focus on women is Kristof and WuDunn (2009, chapter 11).
51. Zeller (2006).
52. As a sign of the globalized world in which we live, I first learned about the New York City program when I was in India and read about it in a front-page article in the *Indian Express*, March, 11, 2008.
53. Chu (2007).
54. Malkin (2008).
55. "Microfight," (2010).
56. Author's interview with B. Rajsekhar, June 24, 2011. Lending in Andhra Pradesh is regulated by a 2010 state microfinance ordinance, available at http://india-microfinance.com/download-andhra-microfinance-ordinance-908172.html and Reserve Bank of India guidelines issued by the Malegam Committee, available at http://www.rbi.org.in/scripts/PublicationReportDetails.aspx?Url Page=&ID=608 . Information about SERP is available at http://www.serp.ap.gov.in/SHG/index.jsp . The stories of successful borrowers are told in Society for the Elimination of Rural Poverty, *How I Became a Lakhier*, . . . n.d.
57. See "The Mountain Man" (2005), "Doing Good by Doing Very Nicely Indeed" (2008), Bruck (2006), Epstein and Smith (2007), and Malkin (2008).
58. Quoted in Bruck (2006, p. 64).
59. Quoted in Malkin (2008).
60. Labarthe and Yunus are quoted in Weiner (2003).
61. Lipton (1998).
62. Armendáriz and Morduch (2005, chapter 8).
63. See Smith (2005), Karlan and Valdivia (2009), Karlan and Zinman (2009), Karlan (2009), and Banerjee, Duflo, Glennerster, and Kinnan (2009).
64. ILO, (2001).
65. ILO (2008a).
66. ILO (2008a).
67. Pfitzer and Krishnaswamy (2007). The Potter quotation is from a personal interview conducted by the author, January 28, 2009.
68. More information is available at www.10000women.org.
69. See www.sewa.org.
70. Verner and Verner (2005).
71. These results are from Karlan and Valdivia (2009).

72. http://www.grameenfoundation.org/where_we_work/sub_saharan_africa/
rwanda/marie_claire_s_story/, 2/17/09.
73. Hundreds of thousands of women have benefited from the Village Phones program in Bangladesh. For information, see http://www.grameen-info.org/index.
php?option=com_content&task=view&id=681&Itemid=676, accessed 1/13/10.
74. Novogratz (2009).
75. The rest of this section and the examples in it draw heavily on Fairbourne,
Gibson, and Dyer (2007).
76. http://www.visionspring.org/home/home.php.
77. www.honeycareafrica.com.

CHAPTER 11
1. See Fields (1980).
2. The quotation is reported in Kristof (2009b).

REFERENCES

Abraham, Vinoj, "Employment Growth in Rural India: Distress-Driven?" *Economic and Political Weekly*, April 18, 2009, pp. 97–104.

Acemoglu, Daron, Simon Johnson, and James A. Robinson, "The Colonial Origins of Comparative Development: An Empirical Investigation," *American Economic Review* 91(5), 2001, pp. 1369–1401.

Ahluwalia, Montek S., "Planning," in Kaushik Basu, ed., *The Oxford Companion to Economics in India* (New Delhi: Oxford University Press, 2007).

Ahmad, Ehtisham, Jean Drèze, John Hills, and Amartya Sen, *Social Security in Developing Countries* (Oxford: Clarendon, 1991).

Ahsan, Ahmad, and Ashish Narain, "Labor Markets in India: Developments and Challenges," in Sadiq Ahmed, ed., *Job Creation and Poverty Reduction in India* (New Delhi: World Bank and Sage, 2007).

Ahsan, Ahmad, and Carmen Pagés, "Are All Labor Regulations Equal? Evidence from Indian Manufacturing," *Journal of Comparative Economics* 37, 2009, pp. 62–75.

Anant, T. C. A., R. Hasan, P. Mohapatra, R. Nagaraj, and S. K. Sasikumar, "Labor Markets in India: Issues and Perspectives," in Jesus Felipe and Rana Hasan, eds., *Labor Markets in Asia: Issues and Perspectives* (Manila: Asian Development Bank, 2006).

Angrist, Joshua D., and Alan B. Krueger, "Does Compulsory School Attendance Affect Schooling and Earnings?" *Quarterly Journal of Economics* 106(4), November 1991, pp. 979–1014.

Angrist, Joshua D., and Victor Lavy, "Using Maimonides' Rule to Estimate the Effect of Class Size on Scholastic Achievement," *Quarterly Journal of Economics* 114(2), May 1999, pp. 533–575.

Anonymous, "Special Report: The Cancun Challenge," *The Economist*, September 6, 2003.

Anonymous, "The Hidden Wealth of the Poor: A Survey of Microfinance," *The Economist,* November 5, 2005 (a) , pp. 3–14.

Anonymous, "The Mountain Man and the Surgeon," *The Economist*, December 20, 2005 (b).

Anonymous, "Hungry Tiger, Dancing Elephant," *The Economist*, April 7, 2007, pp. 67–69.

Anonymous, "It's Not Business' Business," *Business Week,* September 10, 2007, p. 86.

Anonymous, "Doing Good by Doing Very Nicely Indeed: In Support of Profiting from the Poor," *The Economist,* June 28, 2008 (a), p. 18.

Anonymous, "An Elephant, Not a Tiger: A Special Report on India," *The Economist,* December 13, 2008 (b).

Anonymous, "A Bigger World: A Special Report on Globalization," *The Economist,* September 20, 2008 (c), pp. 1–26.

Anonymous, "Just Good Business: A Special Report on Corporate Social Responsibility," *The Economist,* January 19, 2008 (d).

Anonymous, "Roses Are Red," *The Economist,* February 9, 2008 (e), p. 71.

Anonymous, "A Clean Plate," *The Economist,* February 21, 2009 (a).

Anonymous, "Bourgeoning Bourgeoisie: A Special Report on the New Middle Classes in Emerging Markets," *The Economist,* February 14, 2009 (b), pp. 1–24.

Anonymous, "Sustainability," *The World in 2009,* p. 20, 2009 (c).

Anonymous, "Special Report: The Landscape of Telecoms," *The Economist,* September 24, 2009 (d).

Anonymous, "How to Feed the World" and "The Miracle of the Cerrado," *The Economist,* August 26, 2010 (a).

Anonymous, "Microfight," *The Economist,* July 31, 2010 (b).

Anonymous, "The Next China," *The Economist,* July 31, 2010 (c).

Appleton, Simon, Lina Song, and Qingjie Xia, "Has China Crossed the River? The Evolution of Wage Structure in Urban China during Reform and Retrenchment," *Journal of Comparative Economics* 33(4), 2005, pp. 644–663.

Armendáriz, Beatríz, and Jonathan Morduch, *The Economics of Microfinance* (Cambridge, MA: MIT Press, 2005).

Asian Development Bank, "Labor Markets in Asia: Promoting Full, Productive, and Decent Employment," in Asian Development Bank, *Key Indicators 2005* (Manila: Asian Development Bank, 2005).

Azariadis, Costa, and John Stachurski, "Poverty Traps," in Philippe Aghion and Steven N. Durlauf, eds., *Handbook of Economic Growth, Volume IA* (Amsterdam: Elsevier, 2005).

Bagachwa, M. D., and F. Stewart, "Rural Industries and Rural Linkages," in F. Stewart, S. Lall, and S. Wangwe, eds., *Alternative Development Strategies in Sub-Saharan Africa* (London: Macmillan, 1992).

Banerjee, Abhijit, *Making Aid Work* (Cambridge: Boston Review and MIT Press, 2007).

Banerjee, Abhijit, and Esther Duflo, "The Economic Lives of the Poor," *Journal of Economic Perspectives,* 21(1), Winter, 2007, 141–167.

Banerjee, Abhijit, and Esther Duflo, "What Is Middle Class about the Middle Classes around the World?" *Journal of Economic Perspectives* 22(2), Spring 2008, 3–28.

Banerjee, Abhijit, and Esther Duflo, *Poor Economics* (New York: Public Affairs, 2011).

Banerjee, Abhijit, Esther Duflo, Rachel Glennerster, and Cynthia Kinnan, "The Miracle of Microfinance? Evidence from a Randomized Evaluation," Jameel Poverty Action Lab Working Paper, October 2009.

Bardhan, Pranab K., *Awakening Giants, Feet of Clay* (Princeton: Princeton University Press, 2010).

Barney, Jay B., "Firm Resources and Sustained Competitive Advantage," *Journal of Management* 17, 1991, pp. 99–120.

Barney, Jay B., *Gaining and Sustaining Competitive Advantage,* 2nd ed. (Upper Saddle River, NJ: Prentice Hall, 2002).

Barrett, Christopher, Thomas Reardon, and Patrick Webb, "Nonfarm Income Diversification and Household Livelihood Strategies in Rural Africa: Concepts, Dynamics, and Policy Implications," *Food Policy,* 26 (2001), 315–331.

BBC News, "World: Asia-Pacific Global March against Child Labor Begins," January 17, 1998, http://news.bbc.co.uk/2/hi/asia-pacific/48267.stm, accessed 2/2/09.

"Beijing Plays Hedge Ball," *Wall Street Journal*, September 9, 2009.

Bennell, Paul, "Rates of Return to Education: Does the Conventional Pattern Prevail in Sub-Saharan Africa?" *World Development* 24(1), 1996, pp. 183–199.

Bertrand, Marianne, "From the Invisible Handshake to the Invisible Hand? How Import Competition Changes the Employment Relationship," *Journal of Labor Economics* 22(4), October 2004, pp. 723–766.

Bertrand, Marianne, Sendhil Mullainathan, and Eldar Shafir, "A Behavioral Economics View of Poverty," *American Economic Review Papers and Proceedings*, May, 2004, pp. 419–423.

Besley, Timothy J., and Robin Burgess, "Halving Global Poverty," *Journal of Economic Perspectives* 17(3), 2003, 3–22.

Besley, Timothy J., and Robin Burgess, "Can Labor Regulation Hinder Economic Performance? Evidence from India," *Quarterly Journal of Economics* 119(1), 2004, pp. 91–134.

Bhagwati, Jagdish, *In Defense of Globalization* (New York: Oxford University Press, 2005).

Bhagwati, Jagdish N., Arvind Panagariya, and T. N. Srinivasan,, "The Muddles over Outsourcing," *Journal of Economic Perspectives* 18(4), 2004, pp. 93–114.

Bhattacharjea, Aditya, "Labour Market Regulation and Industrial Performance in India—A Critical Review of the Empirical Evidence," Delhi School of Economics Working Paper, 2006.

Binswanger, Hans, Klaus Deininger, and Gershon Feder, "Power, Distortions, Revolt, and Reform in Agricultural Land Relations," in Jere Behrman and T. N. Srinivasan, eds., *Handbook of Development Economics*, Vol. 3 (Amsterdam: Elsevier, 1995).

Birchard, Bill, "Doing Well by Doing Good," *Harvard Management Update*, December 1999, pp. 5–7.

Blanchard, Olivier, "Is There a Viable European Social and Economic Model?" Van Lanschot Lecture, Tilburg University, June 2006.

Blinder, Alan, *Hard Heads, Soft Hearts: Tough-Minded Economics for a Just Society* (Reading, MA: Addison Wesley, 1987).

Blitstein, Ryan, "Which Poverty-Fighting Policies Work? J-PAL Has the Answer," *Fast Company*, December 1, 2009, http://www.fastcompany.com/magazine/141/solve-for-why.html?page=0%2C0, accessed 2/3/10.

Blustein, Paul, "WTO Rules against Cotton Subsidies," *Washington Post*, April 27, 2004, p. E1.

Bourguignon, François, "Development Strategies for More and Better Jobs," presentation at the conference "Help Wanted: More and Better Jobs in a Globalized Economy," Washington, Carnegie Endowment for International Peace, April 2005.

Bowles, Samuel, Steven N. Durlauf, and Karla Hoff, *Poverty Traps* (Princeton: Princeton University Press, 2006).

Brainard, Lael, ed., *Transforming the Development Landscape: The Role of the Private Sector.* (Washington: Brookings Institution Press, 2006).

Bradsher, Keith, "Investors Seek Asian Options to Costly China" *New York Times*, June 18, 2008.

Bruck, Connie, "Millions for Millions," *New Yorker*, October 30, 2006, pp. 62–73.

Burkhauser, Richard V., and Joseph J. Sabia, *Raising the Minimum Wage: Another Empty Promise to the Working Poor* (Washington: Employment Policies Institute, 2005).

Calderón-Madrid, Angel, and Belem Trejo, "The Impact of the Mexican Training Program for Unemployed Workers on Re-employment Dynamics and on Earnings," report prepared for the Inter-American Development Bank, 2001.

Carrillo, Jorge, and Redi Gomis, *La Maquiladora en Datos: Resultados de una encuesta sobre aprendizaje y tecnología* (Tijuana: Colegio de la Frontera Norte, 2004).

Carroll, Lewis, *Alice's Adventures in Wonderland* (London: Macmillan, 1865).

Case, Anne, and Angus Deaton, "School Inputs and Educational Outcomes in South Africa," *Quarterly Journal of Economics* 114, 1999, pp. 1047–1084.

Cassidy, John, "Relatively Deprived," *New Yorker,* April 3, 2006, pp. 42–47.

Chandra, Vandana, and John Pascal Nganou, "Obstacles to Formal Employment Creation in South Africa: Evidence from Recent Firm Surveys," paper presented at the Conference on Labor Markets and Poverty in South Africa, Pretoria, November, 2001.

Chang, Ha-Joon, *Bad Samaritans* (London: Random House Business Books, 2007).

Charmes, Jacques, "Concepts, Measurement and Trends," in Juan R. de Laiglesia and Johannes Jütting, eds., *Is Informal Normal? Towards More and Better Jobs in Developing Countries* (Paris: Organisation for Economic Co-operation and Development, 2009).

Chaudhury, Shubham, and Martin Ravallion, "Partially Awakened Giants: Uneven Growth in China and India," in L. Alan Winters and Shahid Yusuf, eds., *Dancing with Giants: China, India, and the Global Economy* (Washington: World Bank, 2007).

Chen, Martha, Ralf Hussmanns, and Joann Vanek, "Measuring the Informal Economy: Concepts and Definitions," WIEGO (Women in Informal Employment: Globalizing and Organizing) Working Paper, 2007. Chen, Martha, and Joann Vanek, "Informal Employment: Rethinking Workforce Development," in Tony Avirgan, L. Josh Bivens, and Sarah Gammage, eds., *Good Jobs, Bad Jobs, No Jobs* (Washington: Global Policy Network and Economic Policy Institute, 2005).

Chen, Martha, Joann Vanek, Francie Lund, and James Heintz with Renana Jhabvala and Christine Bonner, *Progress of the World's Women 2005* (New York: United Nations Development Fund for Women [UNIFEM], 2005).

Chen, Shaohua, and Martin Ravallion, "The Developing World Is Poorer Than We Thought, but No Less Successful in the Fight against Poverty," *Quarterly Journal of Economics*, November, 2010, pp. 1577–1625.

Chronic Poverty Research Centre, *The Chronic Poverty Report 2008–09: Escaping Poverty Traps* (Northampton: Belmont Press Limited, 2008).

Chu, Michael, "Microfinance: Business, Profitability, and Creation of Social Value," in Rangan V. Kasturi, John A. Quelch, Gustavo Herrero, and Brooke Barton, eds., *Business Solutions for the Global Poor* (San Francisco: Jossey Bass, 2007).

Clemens, Michael, "One Small Way to Fix the World: Welcome Guest Workers," *Global Development: Views from the Center,* June 22, 2009.

Coalition of Service Industries (CSI), "CSI Background Paper—Russian Telecommunications Services," http://www.uscsi.org/publications/papers/telecom.htm, accessed 10/05/09.

Coetzee, J. M., *Disgrace* (New York: Penguin Books, 2000).

Cohen, Jessica L., and William Easterly, "Introduction: Thinking Big versus Thinking Small," in Jessica L. Cohen and William Easterly, *What Works in Development? Thinking Big and Thinking Small* (Washington: Brookings Institution Press, 2009).

Cohen, Joshua, and Charles Sabel, "Flexicurity," *Pathways,* Spring 2009, pp. 10–14.

Collier, Paul, *The Bottom Billion* (Oxford: Oxford University Press, 2007).

Collier, Paul, and Catherine Pattillo, *Investment and Risk in Africa* (New York: St. Martin's Press, 2000).

Collins, Daryl, Jonathan Morduch, Stuart Rutherford, and Orlanda Ruthven, *Portfolios of the Poor* (Princeton: Princeton University Press, 2009).

Commission on Growth and Development, *The Growth Report: Strategies for Sustained Growth and Inclusive Development* (Washington: World Bank, 2008).

Commission on Growth and Development, *Post-Crisis Growth in Developing Countries* (Washington: World Bank. Version presented at the World Bank-IMF joint meetings, Istanbul, Turkey, October 2009), http://www.growthcommission .org/index.php?option=com_content&task=view&id=115&Itemid=213, accessed 10/6/09.

Compa, Lance, "Corporate Social Responsibility and Workers' Rights," *Comparative Labor Law and Policy Journal* 30(1), Fall 2008, pp. 1–10.

Conley, John, "A Responsibility to Talk the Talk," *Guardian Weekly,* May 27, 2005.

Cooper-Hewitt, the National Design Museum of the Smithsonian Institution, *Design for the Other 90%* (New York: Smithsonian Institution, 2007).

Cord, Louise, "Overview," in Timothy Besley and Louise Cord, eds., *Delivering on the Promise of Pro-Poor Growth* (New York: Palgrave-Macmillan, 2007).

Crowell, Jimmy, "C.U. Severs Ties with Russell," *Cornell Daily Sun,* February 23, 2009, p. 1.

Dam, Kenneth W., *The Law-Growth Nexus: The Rule of Law and Economic Development* (Washington: Brookings Institution Press, 2006).

Davis, Donald R., and Prachi Mishra, "Stolper-Samuelson Is Dead and Other Crimes of Theory and Data," in Ann Harrison, ed., *Globalization and Poverty* (Cambridge, MA: National Bureau of Economic Research, 2007).

Davis, Peter, "Poverty in Time," in Tony Addison, David Hulme, and Ravi Kanbur, eds., *Poverty Dynamics* (Oxford: Oxford University Press, 2007).

de Laiglesia, Juan R., and Johannes Jütting, eds., *Is Informal Normal? Towards More and Better Jobs in Developing Countries* (Paris: Organisation for Economic Co-operation and Development, 2009).

de Mel, Suresh, David McKenzie, and Christopher Woodruff, "Returns to Capital in Microenterprises: Evidence from a Field Experiment," *Quarterly Journal of Economics,* 123, November 2008, pp. 1329–1372.

Deaton, Angus, "Instruments, Randomization, and Learning about Development," *Journal of Economic Literature* 47(2), June 2010, pp. 424–455.

DeParle, Jason. "What If Labor Were Allowed to Go Global?" *International Herald Tribune,* June 9–10, 2007, pp. 11–12.

DeParle, Jason, and Robert Gebeloff, "Food Stamp Use Soars, and Stigma Fades," *New York Times,* November 28, 2009.

Dercon, Stefan, and Pramila Krishnan, "Income Portfolios in Rural Ethiopia and Tanzania: Choices and Constraints," *Journal of Development Studies* 32(6), 1996, pp. 850–875.

DeSoto, Hernando. *The Mystery of Capital: Why Capitalism Triumphs in the West and Fails Everywhere Else* (New York: Basic Books, 2000).

Dixit, Avinash, "Evaluating Recipes for Development Success," *World Bank Research Observer* 22(2), 2007, pp. 131–157.

Downie, Andrew, "Fair Trade in Bloom," *New York Times*, October 2, 2007.

Dreier, Peter and Richard Appelbaum, "Campus Breakthrough on Sweatshop Labor," *The Nation*, June 1, 2006.

Drèze, Jean, Reetika Khera, and Siddhartha, "Corruption in NREGA: Myths and Reality," *Hindu*, January 22, 2008.

Duflo, Esther, "Field Experiments in Development Economics," in Richard Blundell, Whitney Newey, and Torsten Persson, eds., *Advances in Economic Theory and Econometrics* (Cambridge: Cambridge University Press, 2006a).

Duflo, Esther, "Poor But Rational?" in Abhijit Vinayak Banerjee, Roland Bénabou, and Dilip Mookherjee, eds., *Understanding Poverty* (Oxford: Oxford University Press, 2006b).

Duflo, Esther, "Review of *How to Spend $50 Billion to Make the World a Better Place* by Bjørn Lomborg," *Journal of Economic Literature* 45(4), December 2007, pp. 1048–1049.

Duflo, Esther, and Rema Hanna, "Monitoring Works: Getting Teachers to Come to School," National Bureau of Economic Research Working Paper No. 11880, 2005.

Duflo, Esther, Michael Kremer, and Jonathan Robinson, "Nudging Farmers to Use Fertilizer: Theory and Experimental Evidence from Kenya," Cambridge, MA: Jameel Poverty Action Lab Working Paper, March 2010.

Easterly, William, *The Elusive Quest for Growth* (Cambridge: MIT Press, 2001).

Easterly, William, "The Big Push Déjà Vu: A Review of Jeffrey Sachs's *The End of Poverty: Economic Possibilities for Our Time*," *Journal of Economic Literature* 44(1), March 2006a, pp. 96–105.

Easterly, William, *The White Man's Burden* (New York: Penguin, 2006b).

Edmonds, Eric, "Child Labor," in T. Paul Schultz and John Strauss, eds., *Handbook of Development Economics,* Vol. 4 (Amsterdam: North Holland, 2008).

Ehrenberg, Ronald G., and Robert S. Smith, *Modern Labor Economics,* 10th ed. (Boston: Pearson/Addison Wesley, 2009).

Eizenstat, Stuart E., and Marney L. Cheek, "Ending the Trade War in Washington: Saving the Trade Agenda by Protecting Workers," *Foreign Affairs,* May/June, 2007.

El-Erian, Mohamed A. and Michael Spence, "Growth Strategies and Dynamics: Insights from Country Experiences," Working Paper No. 6, Commission on Growth and Development (Washington: The World Bank, 2008).

Engardio, Pete, "Special Report: The Future of Outsourcing," *Business Week,* January 30, 2006, pp. 50–58.

Engardio, Pete, "Special Report: Beyond the Green Corporation," *Business Week,* January 29, 2007, pp. 50–64.

Epstein, Keith, and Geri Smith, "The Ugly Side of Micro-Lending," *Business Week,* December 24, 2007.

Ertuna, Ibrahim Özer, *Wealth, Welfare and the Global Free Market* (Farnham, UK: Gower, 2009).

Evans, David, Michael Kremer, and Muthoni Ngatia, "The Impact of Distributing School Uniforms on Children's Education in Kenya," Working paper, Harvard University, 2008.

Faiola, Anthony. "Sustaining the Medellin Miracle," *Washington Post,* July 11, 2008.

Fairbourne, Jason S., Stephen W. Gibson, and W. Gibb Dyer, Jr., eds., *Microfranchising: Creating Wealth at the Bottom of the Pyramid* (Cheltenham, UK: Edward Elgar, 2007).

Fallon, Peter R., and Robert E. B. Lucas, "Job Security Regulations and the Dynamic Demand for Industrial Labor in India and Zimbabwe," *Journal of Development Economics* 40, 1993, pp. 241–273.

Felipe, Jesus, and Rana Hasan, *Labor Markets in Asia* (Manila: Asian Development Bank, 2006).

Fields, Gary S., "The Private Demand for Education in Relation to Labor Market Conditions in Less Developed Countries," *Economic Journal*, December 1974, pp. 906–925.

Fields, Gary S., "Rural-Urban Migration, Urban Unemployment and Underemployment, and Job Search Activity in LDCs," *Journal of Development Economics*, June 1975, pp. 165–188.

Fields, Gary S., *Distribution and Development* (New York: Cambridge University Press, 1980).

Fields, Gary S., "Employment, Income Distribution, and Economic Growth in Seven Small Open Economies," *Economic Journal*, March 1984, pp. 74–83.

Fields, Gary S., "Industrialization and Employment in Hong Kong, Korea, Singapore, and Taiwan," in Walter Galenson, ed., *Foreign Trade and Investment: The Newly-Industrializing Asian Countries* (Madison: University of Wisconsin Press, 1985).

Fields, Gary S., *Distribution and Development: A New Look at the Developing World* (Cambridge, MA: MIT Press and Russell Sage Foundation, 2001).

Fields, Gary S., "Employment in Low-Income Countries: Beyond Labor Market Segmentation" in Pierella Paci and Pieter Serneels, eds., *Employment and Shared Growth* (Washington:World Bank, 2007a).

Fields, Gary S., "How Much Should We Care about Changing Income Inequality in the Course of Economic Growth?" *Journal of Policy Modeling*, July/August 2007(b), pp. 577–586.

Fields, Gary S., *Bottom Line Management* (Heidelberg: Springer Verlag, 2009a).

Fields, Gary S., "Segmented Labor Market Models in Developing Countries," in Harold Kincaid and Don Ross, *The Oxford Handbook of the Philosophy of Economic Science* (Oxford: Oxford University Press, 2009b).

Fields, Gary S., and Walter S. Bagg, "Long-Term Economic Mobility and the Private Sector in Developing Countries," in Gary S. Fields and Guy Pfeffermann, eds., *Pathways Out of Poverty.* (Dordecht, the Netherlands: Kluwer Academic, 2003).

Fields, Gary S., and Ravi Kanbur, "Minimum Wages and Poverty with Income Sharing," *Journal of Economic Inequality*, August 2007, pp. 135–147.

Fields, Gary S., and Henry Y. Wan, Jr., "Wage-Setting Institutions and Economic Growth," *World Development*, September 1989, pp. 1471–1484.

Fisman, Raymond, and Edward Miguel, *Economic Gangsters* (Princeton: Princeton University Press, 2008).

Fiszbein, Ariel, and Norbert Schady, *Conditional Cash Transfers: Reducing Present and Future Poverty* (Washington: World Bank, 2009).

Forrer, Juan, "C.U. Adds Sweatshop-Free Clothes," *Cornell Daily Sun*, September 14, 2010.

Foster, Andrew, and Mark Rosenzweig, "Economic Development and the Decline of Agricultural Employment," in T. Paul Schultz and John Strauss, eds., *Handbook of Development Economics*, Vol. 4 (Amsterdam: North Holland, 2008).

Fox, M. Louise, and Melissa Sekkel Gaal, *Working Out of Poverty: Job Creation and the Quality of Growth in Africa* (Washington: World Bank, 2008).

Frank, Robert, *What Price the Moral High Ground? Ethical Dilemmas in Competitive Environments* (Princeton: Princeton University Press, 2004).

Freeman, Richard, "What Really Ails Europe (and America): The Doubling of the Global Workforce," *Globalist,* June 3, 2005.

Freeman, Richard, "People Flows in Globalization," *Journal of Economic Perspectives,* Spring 2006, pp. 145–170.

Friedman, Milton, "The Social Responsibility of Business Is to Increase Its Profits," *New York Times Magazine,* September 13, 1970.

Friedman, Thomas. *The World Is Flat: A Brief History of the Twenty-First Century* (New York: Farrar, Straus and Giroux, 2005, 2007).

Friedman, Thomas, "China to the Rescue?" *International Herald Tribune,* December 22, 2008, p. 7.

Friedman, Thomas, "A Word from the Wise," *New York Times,* March 3, 2010.

Friedman, Thomas, *Hot, Flat, and Crowded 2.0,* 2010, file:///C:/My%20Documents/Papers/Friedman%27s%20Hot,%20Flat,%20and%20Crowded%20Excerpt.htm, accessed 2/8/10.

Fung, K. C., A. Garcia-Herrero, H. Iizaka, A. Siu, "Hard or Soft? Institutional Reforms and Infrastructure Spending as Determinants of Foreign Direct Investment in China," Madrid, Banco de España Working Paper 0616, 2006.

Galasso, Emanuela, and Martin Ravallion, "Decentralized Targeting of an Antipoverty Program," *Journal of Public Economics* 85, 2005, pp. 705–727.

Galgut, Damon, *The Good Doctor* (New York: Grove Press, 2003).

Gates, Bill, "2010 Annual Letter from Bill Gates," Bill and Melinda Gates Foundation, January 2010.

Gautié, Jérôme, and John Schmitt, eds., *Low-Wage Work in the Wealthy World* (New York: Russell Sage Foundation, 2009).

Gertler, Paul, Manisha Shah, and Stefano Bertozzi, "Sex Sells, but Risky Sex Sells for More," *Journal of Political Economy,* 2005, pp. 518–550.

Ghose, Ajit K., *Jobs and Incomes in a Globalizing World* (Geneva: International Labour Organisation, 2003).

Ghose, Ajit K., Nomaan Majid, and Chistoph Ernst, *The Global Employment Challenge* (Geneva: International Labour Organisation, 2008).

Gifford, Rob, *China Road* (New York: Random House, 2007).

Gladwell, Malcolm, *Blink* (New York: Little, Brown, 2005).

Glewwe, Paul, Michael Kremer, Sylvie Moulin, and Eric Zitzewitz, "Retrospective vs. Prospective Analyses of School Inputs: The Case of Flip Charts in Kenya," *Journal of Development Economics* 74(1), June 2004, pp. 151–268.

Glinskaya, Elena, and Michael Lokshin, "Wage Differentials in the Public and Private Sectors in India," Washington, World Bank Working Paper No. 3574, 2005.

"Globalization of Labor," *Finance and Development,* June 2007, pp. 20–21.

"Google Goes Amharic," *The Big Issue,* Novemeber, 2006, pp. 29–32.

Gosselin, Peter, *High Wire: The Precarious Financial Lives of American Families* (New York: Basic Books, 2008).

Government of Turkey, *Latest Situation on Southeastern Anatolia Project: Activities of the GAP Administration* (Ankara: June 2006).

Government of Turkey, *Southeastern Anatolia Action Plan 2008–2012.* (Ankara: May 2008).

Greenhouse, Steven, *The Big Squeeze: Tough Times for the American Worker* (New York: Knopf, 2008).

Greenhouse, Steven, "Factory Defies Sweatshop Label, but Can It Thrive?" *New York Times*, July 17, 2010.

Günther, Isabel, and Andrey Launov, "Informal Employment in Developing Countries: Opportunity or Last Resort?" *Journal of Development Economics*, forthcoming.

Gupta, Poonam, Rana Hasan, and Utsav Kumar, "Big Reforms but Small Payoffs: Explaining the Weak Record of Growth and Employment in Indian Manufacturing," Munich Personal RePEC Archive Paper No. 13496, February 2009.

Gutierrez, Catalina, Pierella Paci, and Marco Ranzani, *Making Work Pay in Nicaragua* (Washington: World Bank, 2008).

Hallock, Kevin F., "Job Loss and the Fraying of the Implicit Employment Contract," *Journal of Economic Perspectives* 23(4), Fall 2009, pp. 69–94.

Hamermesh, Daniel, *Labor Demand* (Princeton: Princeton University Press, 1993).

Hamlin, Kevin, "Chinese Manufacturers Shun Low-Wage Inland for Vietnam, India," bloomberg.com, May 11, 2008, accessed 5/15/08.

Hamm, Steve, "The Trouble with India," *Business Week*, March 19, 2007.

Hanushek, Eric A., "Interpreting Recent Research on Schooling in Developing Countries," *World Bank Research Observer* 10(2), August 1995, pp. 227–246.

Hanushek, Eric A., "School Policy: Implications of Recent Research for Human Capital Investments in South Asia and Other Developing Countries," *Education Economics* 17(3), November 2009, pp. 291–313.

Harris, John, and Michael Todaro , "Migration, Unemployment, and Development: A Two-Sector Analysis," *American Economic Review* 60, March 1970, pp. 126–142.

Harrison, Ann, ed., *Globalization and Poverty* (Cambridge, MA: National Bureau of Economic Research, 2007).

Harrison, Ann, and Jason Scorse, "Improving the Conditions of Workers? Minimum Wage Legislation and Anti-Sweatshop Activism," *California Management Review* 48(2), Winter 2006, pp. 144–160.

Harriss-White, Barbara, *India Working* (Cambridge: Cambridge University Press, 2003).

Hart, Stuart L., *Capitalism at the Crossroads*, 2nd ed. (Upper Saddle River, NJ: Wharton School Publishing, 2007).

Hasan, R., and R. Magsombol, "Labor Markets in India: Some Findings from NSS Data," Manila, Economics Research Department, Asian Development Bank, 2005.

Hatem, Fabrice, *International Investment* (Geneva: United Nations, 1997).

Heal, Geoffrey, *When Principles Pay* (New York: Columbia Business School, 2008).

Heckman, James J., "Micro Data, Heterogeneity, and the Evaluation of Public Policy: Nobel Lecture," *Journal of Political Economy* 109(4), 2001, pp. 673–748.

Hoftijzer, Margo, and Pierella Paci, *Making Work Pay in Madagascar* (Washington: World Bank, 2008).

Immelt, Jeffrey, "Time to Re-Embrace Globalisation," *The World in 2009*, p. 141.

Indian Society of Labour Economics, *51st Annual Conference: Summaries of the Conference Papers*, New Delhi, Indian Society of Labour Economics, December 2009.

"Indonesia: Suharto Tops List of Embezzling Leaders," *New York Times*, March 26, 2004.

Inter-American Development Bank (IDB), *Good Jobs Wanted* (Washington: IDB, 2003).

International Finance Corporation (IFC), *Paths Out of Poverty* (Washington: IFC, 2000).

International Finance Corporation and theWorld Bank, *Doing Business Report* serial.

International Fund for Agricultural Development, "Promoting Equitable Access to Land and Tenure Security for Rural Poverty Reduction," Rome, January 2008a.

International Fund for Agricultural Development, "Rural Poverty Knowledgebase: Land Statistics," 2008b, http://www.ruralpovertyportal.org/english/topics/land/statistics.htm, accessed 10/28/08.

International Labour Organisation (ILO), *Employment, Incomes, and Equality: A Strategy for Increasing Productive Employment in Kenya* (Geneva: ILO, 1972).

International Labour Organisation (ILO), *Decent Work. Report of the Director-General to the 87th Session of the International Labour Conference* (Geneva: ILO, 1999).

International Labour Organisation (ILO), *Training for Work in the Informal Sector: Evidence from Kenya, Tanzania and Uganda* (Geneva: ILO, 2001).

International Labour Organisation (ILO), *World Employment Report 2004–05* (Geneva: ILO, 2004).

International Labour Organisation (ILO), *The End of Child Labor: Within Reach* (Geneva: ILO, 2006).

International Labour Organisation (ILO), *Labour Shares.* Technical Brief Number 01 (Geneva: ILO, 2007a).

International Labour Organisation (ILO), *World Social Security Forum—Building a "Social Security Floor" Worldwide Where Growth Can Meet Equity* (Geneva: ILO, 2007b).

International Labour Organisation (ILO), *Working Time around the World: Trends in Working Hours, Laws and Policies in a Global Comparative Perspective* (Geneva: ILO, 2007c).

International Labour Organisation (ILO), *From Veil to Camera: Empowering Women through Skills Training*, 2008a, http://www.ilo.org/global/About_the_ILO/Media_and_public_information/Feature_stories/lang--en/WCMS_100390/index.htm, accessed 2/24/09.

International Labour Organisation (ILO), *World of Work Report 2008b* (Geneva: ILO, 2008).

International Labour Organisation (ILO), *Global Employment Trends for Women* (Geneva: ILO, 2009a).

International Labour Organisation (ILO), "Stemming the Crisis: World Leaders Forge a Global Jobs Pact," *World of Work*, August 2009b, pp. 4–9.

International Labour Organisation (ILO), *Global Employment Trends* (Geneva: ILO, January 2011).

International Labour Organisation (ILO), "Facts on Decent Work," July 1, 2006, http://www.ilo.org/global/About_the_ILO/Media_and_public_information/Factsheets/lang--en/docName--WCMS_082654/index.htm, accessed 1/29/09.

"It's Not Business' Business," *Business Week*, September 10, 2007, p. 86.

Jalan, Jyotsna, and Martin Ravallion, "Estimating the Benefit Incidence of an Antipoverty Program by Propensity-Score Matching," *Journal of Business and Economic Statistics* 21(1) , 2003, pp. 19–30.

John Templeton Foundation, *Does the Free Market Corrode Moral Values?* 2008, http://www.templeton.org/market/PDF/BQ%20Market%20Essays.pdf, accessed 2/2/09.

Jütting, Johannes, and Juan R. de Laiglesia, *Is Informal Normal?* (Paris: Organization for Economic Cooperation and Development, 2009).

Kannan, K. P., "Dualism, Informality, and Social Inequality," presidential address to the Indian Society of Labour Economics, *Indian Journal of Labour Economics* 52(1), January–March 2009, pp. 1–32.

Kaplan, David, Presentation at the Conference on Growth, Jobs, and Taxes, Pretoria, South Africa, April 2005.

Karlan, Dean, "Strength in Numbers," *Microfinance Insights*, September–October 2009, pp. 10–11.

Karlan, Dean, and Jacob Appel, *More Than Good Intentions* (New York: Dutton, 2011).

Karlan, Dean, and Sendhil Mullainathan, "Debt Cycles," Yale University and Harvard University, working paper, 2011.

Karlan, Dean, and Martín Valdivia, "Teaching Entrepreneurship. Impact of Business Training on Microfinance Clients and Institutions," New Haven, Innovations for Poverty Action, Working Paper, May 2009.

Karlan, Dean, and Jonathan Zinman, "Expanding Microenterprise Credit Access: Using Randomized Supply Decisions to Estimate the Impact in Manila," Cambridge, MA, Jameel Poverty Action Lab Working Paper, July, 2009.

Kearney, A. T. *Making Offshore Decisions. A.T. Kearney's 2003 Offshore Location Attractiveness Index*, 2004, http://www.atkearney.sk/index.php/Publications/making-offshore-decisions.html, accessed 3/26/09.

Khanna, Tarun, *Billions of Entrepreneurs* (New Delhi: Penguin/Viking, 2007).

Klein, Michael U., and Bita Hadjimichael, *The Private Sector in Development* (Washington: World Bank, 2003).

Kletzer, Lori, "Trade-Related Job Loss and Wage Insurance: A Synthetic Review," *Review of International Economics* 12(5), 2004, pp. 724–748.

Kremer, Michael, "The O-Ring Theory of Economic Development," *Quarterly Journal of Economics* August 1993, pp. 551–576.

Kremer, Michael, and Alaka Holla, "Pricing and Access: Lessons from Randomized Evaluations," in Jessica L. Cohen and William Easterly, eds., *What Works in Development? Thinking Big and Thinking Small* (Washington: Brookings Institution Press, 2009).

Krishna, Anirudh, "Subjective Assessments, Participatory Methods, and Poverty Dynamics: The Stages of Progress Method," in Tony Addison, David Hulme, and Ravi Kanbur, eds., *Poverty Dynamics* (Oxford: Oxford University Press, 2007).

Kristof, Nicholas, "Where Sweatshops Are a Dream," *New York Times*, January 15, 2009a.

Kristof, Nicholas, "Bill Gates's Next Big Thing," *New York Times*, January 25, 2009b.

Kristof, Nicholas, "Moonshine or the Kids?" *New York Times*, May 22, 2010.

Krugman, Paul, "Punishing the Jobless," *New York Times*, July 4, 2010.

Krugman, Paul R., and Maurice Obstfeld, *International Economics*, 6th ed. (Boston: Addison Wesley, 2003).

Kucera, David, and Leanne Roncolato, "Informal Employment: Two Contested Policy Issues," *International Labour Review* 147(4), 2008, pp. 321–348.

Lanjouw, Jean O., and Peter Lanjouw, "The Rural Nonfarm Sector: Issues and Evidence from Developing Countries," *Agricultural Economics* 26, 2001, pp. 1–23.

Lanjouw, Peter, and Abusaleh Shariff, "Rural Non-Farm Employment in India: Access, Incomes and Poverty Impact," *Economic and Political Weekly* October 2, 2004, pp. 4429–4446.

Lee, Joseph, ed., *Labour Market Trends in Taiwan's New Knowledge Economy* (Cheltenham, UK: Edward Elgar, 2006).

Levy, Santiago, *Good Intentions, Bad Outcomes* (Washington: Brookings Institution Press, 2008).

Lin, Justin Y., "Rural Reforms and Agricultural Growth in China," *American Economic Review* 82(1), 1992, pp. 34–51.

Lin, Justin Y., "Development Strategies for Inclusive Growth in Developing Asia," *Asian Development Review* 21(2), 2004, pp. 1–27.

Lipton, Michael, *Successes in Anti-Poverty* (Geneva: International Labour Organisation, 1998).

Locke, Richard M., et al., "Beyond Corporate Codes of Conduct: Work Organization and Labour Standards at Nike's Suppliers," *International Labour Review* 146 (1–2), 2007a, pp. 21–40.

Locke, Richard M., et al., "Does Monitoring Improve Labor Standards? Lessons from Nike," *Industrial and Labor Relations Review* 61(1), October 2007b, pp. 3–31.

Lucas, Robert. "Why Doesn't Capital Flow from Rich to Poor Countries?" *American Economic Review Papers and Proceedings* 80(2), May 1990, pp. 92–96.

Luce, Edward, *In Spite of the Gods* (New York: Doubleday, 2007).

Malkin, Elisabeth, "Microfinance's Success Sets Off a Debate in Mexico," *New York Times*, April 5, 2008.

Maloney, William F. "Informality Revisited." *World Development* 32(7), 2004, pp. 1159–1178.

Marwaha, Kapil, Anil B. Kulkarni, Jipan K. Mukhopadhyay, and S. Sivakumar, "Creating Strong Businesses by Developing and Leveraging the Productive Capacity of the Poor," in Rangan, V. Kasturi, John A. Quelch, Gustavo Herrero, and Brooke Barton, eds., *Business Solutions for the Global Poor* (San Francisco: Jossey Bass, 2007).

McKenzie, David J., and Christopher Woodruff, "Do Entry Costs Provide an Empirical Basis for Poverty Traps? Evidence from Mexican Microenterprises," *Economic Development and Cultural Change* 55(1), October 2006, pp. 3–42.

Mehrotra, Santosh, "NREG Two Years On: Where Do We Go from Here?" *Economic and Political Weekly*, August 2, 2008, pp. 27–35.

Miguel, Edward, and Michael Kremer, "Worms: Identifying Impacts on Education and Health in the Presence of Treatment Externalities," *Econometrica*, 2004, 72(1), pp. 159–217.

Millennium Challenge Corporation, *Private Sector Initiatives Toolkit*, 2008.

Minot, Nicholas, Michael Epprecht, Tran Thi Tram Anh, and Le Quang Trung, "Previous Research on Income Diversification," in International Food Policy Research Institute, *Diversification and Poverty in the Northern Uplands of Vietnam*, Washington, Research Report No. 145, 2006.

Mittal, Lakshmi, "A New Economic Order," *The World in 2009*, p. 130.

"Montek Singh Ahluwalia: 'Inclusive Growth Does Not Mean Everybody Has to Be Protected," *India Knowledge @ Wharton*, November 1, 2007.

Moyo, Dambisa, *Dead Aid: Why Aid Is Not Working and How There Is a Better Way for Africa* (London: Allen Lane, 2009).

Mullainathan, Sendhil, and Eldar Shafir, "Savings Policy and Decisionmaking in Low-Income Households," in Rebecca M. Blank and Michael S. Barr, eds., *Insufficient Funds: Savings, Assets, Credit, and Banking among Low-Income Households* (New York: Russell Sage Foundation, 2009).

Nagayets, Oksana, "Small Farms: Current Status and Key Trends," International Food Policy Research Institute Working Paper, Washington, 2005.

Narayan, Deepa, Robert Chambers, Meera Kaul Shah, and Patti Petesch, *Voices of the Poor: Crying Out for Change* (New York: Oxford University Press, 2000).

Narayan, Deepa, and Patti Petesch, *Moving Out of Poverty* (Washington: World Bank, 2007).

National Commission for Enterprises in the Unorganised Sector (NCEUS), *The Challenge of Employment in India: An Informal Economy Perspective* (Delhi: Academic Foundation, 2009).

Nattrass, Nicoli, and Jeremy Seekings, *Class, Race, and Inequality in South Africa* (New Haven: Yale University Press, 2005).

Naughton, Barry, *The Chinese Economy: Transitions and Growth* (Cambridge, MA: MIT Press, 2007).

Niehaus, Barry, and Sandip Sukhtankar, "Corruption Dynamics: The Golden Goose Effect," Bureau for Research and Economic Analysis of Development Working Paper, April 2009.

Novogratz, Jacqueline, *The Blue Sweater* (New York: Rodale, 2009).

Oh, Cecilia, "Patents and Monopoly Profits." http://www.twnside.org.sg/title/twr131b.htm, accessed 10/5/09.

Organisation for Economic Co-Operation and Development (OECD), *Employment Outlook 2007* (Paris: OECD).

Osmani, S. R., and O. H. Chowdhury, "Short-Run Impacts of Food for Work Programme in Bangladesh," *Bangladesh Development Studies*, 1983.

Otsuka, K., and T. Yamano, "Introduction to the Special Issue on the Role of Nonfarm Income in Poverty Reduction: Evidence from Asia and East Africa," *Agricultural Economics* 35 (supplement), 2006, pp. 393–397.

Oxfam, *Dumping without Borders.* Briefing Paper No. 50, 2003.

Paci, Pierella, and Marcin Sasin, *Making Work Pay in Bangladesh* (Washington: World Bank, 2008).

Padhi, Asutosh, Geert Pauwels, and Charlie Taylor, "Freeing India's Textile Industry," *McKinsey Quarterly*, special edition, 2004, pp. 9–11.

Paes de Barros, Ricardo. "The Recent Decline in Brazilian Income Inequality: Magnitude, Determinants, and Consequences," paper presented at the Workshop on Income Inequality, Santiago, Chile, December 2006.

Pagés, Carmen, Gaëlle Pierre, and Stefano Scarpetta, *Job Creation in Latin America and the Caribbean* (Washington: Inter-American Development Bank and the World Bank, 2009).

Paulson, Anna, and Robert Townsend, "Entrepreneurship and Financial Constraints in Thailand," *Journal of Corporate Finance* 10, 2004, pp. 229–262.

Peek, Peter, "Labor Market Indicators," presentation at the Conference on Labor Markets and Growth, International Development Research Centre (Canada), Ottawa, November 2006.

Pfitzer, Marc, and Ramya Krishnaswamy. "The Role of the Food and Beverage Sector in Expanding Economic Opportunity: Coca-Cola Sabco," Harvard University Working Paper, Cambridge, MA, 2007.

Pincus, Jonathan, and John Sender, "Quantifying Poverty in Viet Nam: Who Counts?" *Journal of Vietnamese Studies* 3(1), 2008, pp. 108–150.

Polak, Paul, *Out of Poverty* (San Francisco: Berrett-Koehler, 2008).

Porter, Michael E., and Mark R. Kramer, "Strategy and Society: The Link between Competitive Advantage and Corporate Social Responsibility," *Harvard Business Review*, December 2006, pp. 78–92.

Prahalad, C. K., *The Fortune at the Bottom of the Pyramid* (Upper Saddle River, NJ: Wharton School Publishing, 2006).

Prahalad, C. K., and Stuart Hart, "The Fortune at the Bottom of the Pyramid," *Strategy+Business* January 2002, pp. 54–67.

Pritchett, Lant, "Where Has All the Education Gone?" *World Bank Economic Review* 15(3), 2001, pp. 367–391.

Psacharopoulos, George, and Harry Patrinos, "Returns to Investment in Education: A Further Update," *Education Economics* 12(2), 2004, pp. 111–134.

Rangan, V. Kasturi, John A. Quelch, Gustavo Herrero, and Brooke Barton, eds., *Business Solutions for the Global Poor* (San Francisco: Jossey Bass, 2007).

Rappeport, Alan, "Goldman Sees High Return on Investing in Women," *FT.com,* September 23, 2009.

Ravallion, Martin, "Evaluating Anti-Poverty Programs," in T. Paul Schultz and John Strauss, eds., *Handbook of Development Economics*, Vol. 4 (Amsterdam: North-Holland, 2008).

Ravallion, Martin, "Bailing Out the World's Poorest," *Challenge,* March 2009, pp. 55–80.

Ravallion, Martin, "Poverty Lines Across the World," in Philip N. Jefferson, ed., *Oxford Handbook of the Economics of Poverty* (New York: Oxford University Press, forthcoming.)

Ravallion, Martin, and Gaurav Datt, "Growth and Poverty in Rural India," World Bank Policy Research Working Paper 1405, Washington, 1995.

Rawlings, Laura, "Evaluating the Impact of Conditional Cash Transfer Programs," *World Bank Research Observer,* 2005, 20(1), pp. 37–61.

Reardon, T., K. Stamoulis, A. Balisacan, M. E. Cruz, J. Berdegué, and B. Banks, "Rural Non-Farm Incomes in Developing Countries," in Food and Agriculture Organization (FAO), *State of Food and Agriculture* (Rome: FAO, 1998).

Reich, Robert, "It's Not Business' Business," *Business Week,* September 10, 2007, p. 86.

Roberts, Dexter, "China's Factory Blues," *Business Week,* April 7, 2008.

Roberts, Dexter, "As Factories Fail, China's Business Law Does, Too," *Business Week,* April 13, 2009.

Roberts, Dexter, and Pete Engardio, "Secrets, Lies, and Sweatshops," *Business Week,* November 27, 2006.

Rodrik, Dani, *Has Globalization Gone Too Far?* (Washington: Institute for International Economics, 1997).

Rodrik, Dani, "Goodbye Washington Consensus, Hello Washington Confusion?" *Journal of Economic Literature* December 2006, pp. 969–983.

Rodrik, Dani, *One Economics, Many Recipes: Globalization, Institutions, and Economic Growth* (Princeton: Princeton University Press, 2007).

Rosenzweig, Mark, "Labor Markets in Low Income Countries: Distortions, Mobility, and Migration," in Hollis Chenery and T. N. Srinivasan, eds., *Handbook of Development Economics* (Amsterdam: Elsevier, 1988).

Sachs, Jeffrey, *The End of Poverty* (New York: Penguin Books, 2005).

Sachs, Jeffrey, "Rapid Victories against Extreme Poverty," *Scientific American* 296(4), April 2007.

Salgado, Sebastião, *Workers* (New York: Aperture, 1993).

Scheve, Kenneth, and Matthew Slaughter, "A New Deal for Globalization," *Foreign Affairs* July–August, 2007, pp. 34–47.

Schultz, T. Paul, "School Subsidies for the Poor: Evaluating the Mexican Progresa Poverty Program," *Journal of Development Economics* 74(1), pp. 199–250.

Schumpeter, Joseph, *Capitalism, Socialism, and Democracy* (New York: Harper, 1950).

Sen, Amartya, *Poverty and Famines* (Oxford: Clarendon Press, 1981).

Sen, Amartya, *Development as Freedom* (New York: Alfred Knopf, 1999).

Sen, Binayak, Mustafa K. Mujeri, and Quazi Shahabuddin, "Explaining Pro-Poor Growth in Bangladesh: Puzzles, Evidence, and Implications," in Timothy Besley and Louise Cord, eds., *Delivering on the Promise of Pro-Poor Growth* (New York: Palgrave Macmillan, 2007).

Sherman, Arloc, *Safety Net Effective at Fighting Poverty but Has Weakened for the Very Poorest* (Washington: Center on Budget and Policy Priorities, 2009) http://www.cbpp.org/cms/index.cfm?fa=view&id=2859, accessed 10/6/09.

Sirkin, Hal, Jim Hemerling, and Arindam Bhattacharya, *Globality: Competing with Everyone from Everywhere for Everything* (New York: Hachette, 2008).

Skinner, Caroline, "The Struggle for the Streets: Processes of Exclusion and Inclusion of Street Vendors in Durban, South Africa," *Development Southern Africa*, June 2008, pp. 247–242.

Smith, Stephen C., *Ending Global Poverty* (New York: Macmillan, 2005).

Solow, Robert, "The Last 50 Years in Growth Theory and the Next 10." *Oxford Review of Economic Policy* 23(1) 2007, pp. 3–14.

Spar, Deborah, "Attracting High Technology Investment: Intel's Costa Rica Plant," World Bank Foreign Investment Advisory Service Occasional Paper #11, Washington, 1998.

Spielman, David J., and Rajul Pandya-Lorch, *Millions Fed: Proven Successes in Agricultural Development* (Washington: International Food Policy Research Institute, 2009).

Squire, Lyn, *Employment Policy in Developing Countries: A Survey of Issues and Evidence* (New York, Oxford University Press, 1981).

Stein, Jeff, "Nike Bows to C.U. Pressure on Labor," *Cornell Daily Sun,* August 27, 2010, p. 1.

Stern, Nicholas, interview with CNN Sunday Morning, September 29, 2002, http://transcripts.cnn.com/TRANSCRIPTS/0209/29/sm.11.html, accessed 1/26/10.

Stiglitz, Joseph, *Globalization and Its Discontents* (New York: Norton, 2002).

Stiglitz, Joseph, *Making Globalization Work* (New York: Norton, 2006).

Stiglitz, Joseph, and Andrew Charlton, *Fair Trade for All* (Oxford: Oxford University Press, 2005).

Stroll, Eric, and Robert Thornton, "Do Large Employers Pay More in Developing Countries? The Case of Five African Countries," Bonn, IZA Working Paper No. 660, 2002.

Styron, William, *Sophie's Choice* (New York: Random House, 1979).

Surowiecki, James, "What Microloans Miss," *The New Yorker,* March 17, 2008.

Taber, George M., "A Question Revisited: Is Capitalism Working?" *Knowledge@Wharton,* March 4, 2009.

Tao, Ran, "The Labor Market in the People's Republic of China: Development and Policy Challenges in Economic Transition," in Jesus Felipe and Rana Hasan, eds., *Labor Markets in Asia: Issues and Perspectives* (Manila: Asian Development Bank, 2006).

Thorbecke, Erik, "The Employment Problem: A Critical Evaluation of Four ILO Comprehensive Country Reports," *International Labor Review* 107(5), 1973, pp. 393–423.

Tully, Mark, *India in Slow Motion* (New Delhi: Viking, 2002).

Turnham, David, *The Employment Problem in Less Developed Countries* (Paris: Organization for Economic Cooperation and Development, 1971).

Turnham, David, *Employment and Development: A New Review of Evidence* (Paris: Organization for Economic Cooperation and Development, 1993).

Uchitelle, Louis, "To Mend the Flaws in Trade: Economist Wants Business and Social Aims to Be in Sync," *New York Times,* January 30, 2007.

United Nations, *Human Development Report* (New York: United Nations Development Program, serial).

United Nations, "Kenya: Bangaisha na Mzungus—Youth, Sex, and Tourism on the Kenyan Coast," 2007, http://www.irinnews.org/InDepthMain.aspx?InDepthI d=28&ReportId=69989&Country=Yes, accessed 2/2/09.

United States Bureau of Labor Statistics, *Hourly Compensation Costs for Production Workers in Manufacturing,* April 30, 2007, ftp://ftp.bls.gov/pub/special. requests/ForeignLabor/indCountryTable.txt, accessed 1/18/10.

United States Census Bureau, *Current Population Projections* (Washington: U.S. Census Bureau).

United States Census Bureau, *Income Poverty, and Health Insurance Coverage in the United States: 2009.* Report P60-238, Washington, September 2010.

United States House of Representatives, Committee on Ways and Means, *Green Book,* 2004, http://waysandmeans.house.gov/Documents.asp?section=813 , accessed 10/07/09.

Valodia, Imraan, ed., "The Informal Economy in South Africa: Issues, Debates, and Policies," Durban, Research Report No. 75, School of Development Studies, University of KwaZulu-Natal, 2007.

Verner, Dorte and Mette Verner. "Economic Impacts of Professional Training in the Informal Sector: The Case of the Labor Force Training Program in Côte d'Ivoire," Washington, World Bank Policy Research Working Paper 2668, July, 2005.

Vogel, David, *The Market for Virtue* (Washington, DC: Brookings Institution Press, 2006).

"What Is Globalization?" *Yale Global Online,* http://yaleglobal.yale.edu/about, accessed 6/26/08.

Weiner, Tim. "With Little Loans, Mexican Women Overcome," *New York Times*, March 19, 2003.

Wittenberg, Martin, "Job Search in South Africa: A Nonparametric Analysis," *South African Journal of Economics* 70(8), December 2002, pp. 1163–1197.

Wolf, Martin, *Why Globalization Works* (New Haven: Yale, 2005).

World Bank, *The East Asian Miracle* (Washington: World Bank, 1993).

World Bank, *Economic Growth in the 1990s: Learning from a Decade of Reform* (Washington: World Bank, 2005).

World Bank, "Promoting Gender Equality and Women's Empowerment," ch. 3 of *Global Monitoring Report 2007* (Washington: World Bank, 2007).

World Bank, *World Development Report*, serial.

Wright, Lawrence, "Slim's Time," *The New Yorker,* June 1, 2009, pp. 52–67.

Zeller, Manfred, "A Comparative Review of Major Types of Rural Microfinance Institutions in Developing Countries," *Agricultural Finance Review,* Fall, 2006, pp. 195–213.

INDEX